Practical Subversion

Second Edition

Daniel Berlin and Garrett Rooney

Apress®

Practical Subversion, Second Edition

Copyright © 2006 by Daniel Berlin and Garrett Rooney

ISBN-13 (pbk): 978-1-59059-753-8

ISBN-10 (pbk): 1-59059-753-2

Printed and bound in the United States of America 9 8 7 6 5 4 3 2 1

Lead Editor: Jason Gilmore
Technical Reviewer: Malcolm Rowe
Editorial Board: Steve Anglin, Ewan Buckingham, Gary Cornell, Jason Gilmore, Jonathan Gennick, Jonathan Hassell, James Huddleston, Chris Mills, Matthew Moodie, Dominic Shakeshaft, Jim Sumser, Keir Thomas, Matt Wade
Project Manager: Tracy Brown Collins
Copy Edit Manager: Nicole Flores
Copy Editor: Jennifer Whipple
Assistant Production Director: Kari Brooks-Copony
Production Editor: Laura Esterman
Compositor/Artist: Kinetic Publishing Services, LLC
Proofreader: April Eddy
Indexer: Julie Grady
Cover Designer: Kurt Krames
Manufacturing Director: Tom Debolski

Distributed to the book trade worldwide by Springer-Verlag New York, Inc., 233 Spring Street, 6th Floor, New York, NY 10013. Phone 1-800-SPRINGER, fax 201-348-4505, e-mail orders-ny@springer-sbm.com, or visit http://www.springeronline.com.

For information on translations, please contact Apress directly at 2560 Ninth Street, Suite 219, Berkeley, CA 94710. Phone 510-549-5930, fax 510-549-5939, e-mail info@apress.com, or visit http://www.apress.com.

The source code for this book is available to readers at http://www.apress.com in the Source Code/Download section.

Contents at a Glance

Contents

About the Authors

 **DANIEL BERLIN** is a software engineer at Google Inc., where he works in the Open Source Program Office. He graduated from the University of Rochester with a degree in computer science, and has a JD from George Washington University Law School. He has contributed to a large number of open source projects, but loves the Subversion developer community the most. Besides contributing to Subversion itself, he is responsible for maintaining the Subversion repositories of several large open source projects, including GCC.

GARRETT ROONEY is a senior software engineer at CollabNet, where he works on Subversion. He graduated from Rensselaer Polytechnic Institute (RPI) with a degree in computer science, after narrowly avoiding ending up as a mechanical engineer. Over the past few years, he has contributed to a variety of open source projects, but lately the vast majority of his recreational programming time has been curtailed by his work on the Subversion project. In addition to contributing to Subversion itself, he has written about using the Subversion client libraries for the O'Reilly Network and has spoken about Subversion best practices at the O'Reilly Open Source Convention (OSCON).

About the Technical Reviewer

MALCOLM ROWE is a senior consultant for a leading independent business intelligence company in the United Kingdom. While his day-to-day work involves the design of data warehouses and multidimensional databases, his real interest lies in assisting the development of open source software. He has made contributions to a variety of open source projects over the years, though the vast majority of his recent time has been taken up specifically with the development of Subversion. His other interests include web standards, cryptography, and usability design.

Acknowledgments

First and foremost, we'd like to thank the Subversion development team. In the time we've spent with the project we've learned more than we could have imagined possible. Each of you has helped to make us better developers, and it has been a privilege to work with you. Without your contributions, this book clearly would not exist.

Daniel Berlin and Garrett Rooney

I'd like to thank my father, who encouraged me to learn programming at a very young age and has always supported me in everything I do. To my wife, thank you for putting up with me during my time working on this book. To Malcolm Rowe, thanks for doing the thankless task of ensuring everything we write actually works and is technically correct. To all the folks at Apress who helped, I cannot thank you guys enough.

Daniel Berlin

I'd like to thank those who encouraged my technical writing. To chromatic, thank you for publishing my first articles about using the Subversion libraries. To Martin Streicher, thanks for reading them and asking me if I was interested in writing this book. To Justin Erenkrantz, thanks for pointing Martin my way and later for serving as my technical reviewer. You have made this book a hundred times more accurate than I could have on my own, and any errors that remain are my fault, not yours.

I cannot express enough thanks to the people at Apress. My writing has improved countless times over due to the suggestions of my various editors, especially Jason Gilmore, who taught me how to avoid the word *simply*, and Nicole Flores and Jennifer Whipple, who turned my writing into something more closely resembling English. Again, any faults that remain are clearly due to my own failings, not theirs.

Finally, I'd like to thank my friends and family. Over the past year, you have all heard me use the "I'm sorry, I have to work on the book" excuse far too many times. Thank you for giving me the time to write when I needed it, and for dragging me out and making me have a good time when I needed that.

Garrett Rooney

Introduction

We are always amazed when we read statistics about the number of software developers who do not use version control tools in their work. When we think about the number of times that we've personally lost work because we carelessly deleted the wrong file or introduced a bug into previously working code, and the number of times we've been saved from such a fate by version control, we truly can't understand how someone would chose not to use the tools that are designed to prevent just such catastrophes.

Similarly, in this day and age, when powerful open source version control tools are free for all to use, we can't understand how people can stand to use systems that can at best be classified as subpar. We hope the answer is that they simply don't know any better, and if that is the case, then this book can help.

Subversion is a powerful open source version control system designed from the ground up to meet the needs of today's software developers. It builds upon the experience gained from previous systems, taking the best parts of the interface provided by the wildly popular CVS and placing it on top of a state-of-the-art, well-engineered core that has been carefully crafted to meet the needs of a new generation of software development.

This book starts right at the beginning, teaching you everything you need to know to make use of Subversion in your day-to-day development work. From there, you'll dive into the details of how to manage your own Subversion repository. Next, you'll learn to leverage Subversion's Apache integration to pick and choose from the capabilities provided by countless Apache modules that can work with Subversion. After that, you'll be ready to step back and learn some best practices, to allow you to take better advantage of the capabilities Subversion provides. You'll be introduced to some of the third-party tools that integrate with Subversion; and finally, you'll learn how to use Subversion libraries themselves to add such support to your own tools.

## CHAPTER 1

Introducing Subversion

So you're holding in your hands a copy of *Practical Subversion*, and that suggests that you're curious about the Subversion version control system. Before diving into the details of how to use Subversion, you'll need to know a little about what *version control* is and why you probably should be using it, and a bit about Subversion itself. This chapter will cover all of that.

What Is Version Control?

Any sufficiently large project eventually hits a point at which communication between the participants becomes a bottleneck. Making sure everyone has the latest version of some crucial bit of information, avoiding duplication of effort, and ensuring that one person doesn't inadvertently overwrite the work of another starts out looking easy, but as the scope of a project grows and the number of people involved grows with it, what once seemed simple becomes more and more complex, and as a result takes more time and effort.

In the software development world, one of the ways to manage this complexity is through the use of version control systems.

Version control provides a way to manage the complexity of working with a team of people on a specific project. It allows you to store the ongoing results of the project (in software development, that would be the source code and documentation for the program being developed) in a central location so that the various members of the team always have access to the latest versions of critical files. It automates the process of updating your local working copy of the project to incorporate the latest changes from your teammates, and it allows you to push your changes upstream into the repository so that other users can have access to them. Finally, and perhaps most importantly, it provides you with historical data regarding the progress of the project, tracking each and every change that was made in the process of its creation. This might not seem important at first glance, but eventually in the life cycle of a project you'll want to go back and see how and why the project evolved into its current form, either to understand the source of a bug, to retrieve some bit of work that was inadvertently removed from the current version, or perhaps to extract a particular change so that it can be applied to another version of the project.

In general, using a version control system as part of your project works as follows: First a space for the project is created in the repository and the initial version is checked in. Then each person working on the project checks out a local copy, and as someone makes changes, he pushes them back into the repository. The repository keeps track of the history of the project, storing each change that's submitted. From time to time each user updates his local copy, and each of the changes other users have made to the repository is applied to the user's local copy. Different systems use different techniques to ensure that changes from one user don't conflict with the work other users have in progress, so you don't have to worry about two people changing the same part of a project and accidentally overwriting each other's work. Because the full history of each change is kept, usually with additional comments from each change's author explaining the change's purpose, it's easy to go back in time and figure out why any given change was made, which becomes quite valuable when debugging problems in the future.

Each of these pieces of functionality is useful, but the combination becomes invaluable, and once you've used a version control system as part of your job, it's unlikely that you'll ever go back to working without one.

The Concurrent Versioning System

Within the open source community, and among a great many other software developers worldwide, the Concurrent Versioning System (CVS) has long been the accepted standard in version control software. Its open access and nonlocking mode of operation has enabled countless developers to collaborate on projects both large and small.

CVS originated as a set of scripts wrapped around an older version control system, the Revision Control System (RCS). While none of the code from the original shell script form of CVS remains in its current incarnation, many of the algorithms used for conflict resolution in CVS originated in RCS.

You see, unlike RCS, and many other version control systems before it, CVS is generally *nonlocking*. This means that when a user is editing a file, there's nothing to prevent another user from also changing that file at the same time. This might seem counterintuitive at first, because there's nothing preventing the two users from making conflicting changes, but in practice it turns out to work quite well. Even when two people make changes to the same file, those changes can usually be merged together automatically. The first user who checks in her change simply goes on without knowing that another user is editing the file, and when the second user tries to check in his change, he's informed that his copy is out-of-date. He updates his local copy, and CVS tries to merge his changes in with the new change that was committed to the repository. Assuming the changes don't conflict, that's all there is to it. The user verifies that his changes are still correct and tries to check it in again; and this time it succeeds. If there's a conflict between the two changes—because the users edited the same part of the file, for example—the second user is presented with all three versions (the original, his modified version, and the new version in the repository), and he can manually resolve the conflict.

This type of workflow seems rather chaotic at first, with nothing to prevent two users from modifying the same file at the same time. In reality, though, it works very well, especially in situations in which a development team is distributed across a country, or even across the world. Because of this, and the fact that it's freely available, CVS has been adopted as the de facto standard in version control for open source software development, and for much commercial software development as well.

Despite its widespread adoption and use, CVS is far from perfect, as anyone who has used it for any length of time will likely be happy to tell you. Its user interface can be idiosyncratic; its implementation is often inefficient; and more often than not, attempts to improve CVS are hamstrung by overwhelming amounts of historical baggage. There's only so much that can be done to improve a system that was built on top of a shaky foundation, and CVS's RCS roots are in many ways rather unstable.

Because CVS was built on top of RCS, it inherited a number of problems. The RCS file format is designed to track changes on a per-file basis; it has no concept of directories; and any change that includes a file has to modify that file's associated RCS file. This means that things such as marking all the files in your project as belonging to a particular version of your software (commonly referred to as *tagging*) or starting a new line of development so that one version of your project can evolve separately from the mainline development version (commonly known as *branching*) take time and space proportional to the number of files they affect, which can become problematic as time goes on. Similarly, because changes are made on a per-file basis, it's possible for half of a commit to succeed but for the remainder to fail, say because the user's network connection died partway through. Worse yet, even if everything goes fine during the commit, it can take a long time; meanwhile, it's possible for another user to update and get only part of the change. The result of both situations is an inconsistent set of files, which can be quite annoying for users.

Yet even with all of CVS's shortcomings, there's never been an acceptable replacement that could really fill its shoes. Until now.

What Is Subversion?

In early 2000, CollabNet Inc. (http://www.collab.net/) decided that its collaborative software suite, SourceCast, required a version control system that could replace CVS. Although CVS had many useful features, it was clear that CollabNet's users were running up against its limitations, and the company's solution was to create a new open source project with the goal of creating a CVS replacement. CollabNet contacted Karl Fogel, the author of a well-known book on CVS, and asked him to work on the project. Fogel and his friend Jim Blandy, an engineer at Red Hat Inc., had been discussing a design for a new version control system, and Blandy had even come up with a name, Subversion. Fogel went to work for CollabNet, and Blandy convinced Red Hat to let him work on the project full time. With the help of the higher-ups at CollabNet, many of whom are well-known open source developers in their own right, Subversion began to attract a community of developers interested in replacing CVS with something similar, but better.

Subversion became *self-hosting* on August 31, 2001, which means that the Subversion developers stopped using CVS to hold Subversion's own code and started using Subversion instead. A series of releases followed, culminating in a beta release on December 19, 2003, and finally version 1.0 on February 23, 2004. It was a long road, but the Subversion developers had created something wonderful. Since that time, Subversion has had three more major version releases, with the current version being 1.3.2, and 1.4 expected soon.

Subversion retains many of the general concepts of CVS and corrects most of the egregious problems. The Subversion developers, many of whom are longtime CVS users and developers, have taken great care to preserve the portions of CVS that are most useful, while simultaneously improving upon it in countless ways. Specifically, Subversion provides the following big-ticket improvements over CVS, described in the next section.

Versioned Directories, Renames, and File Metadata

Whereas CVS works in terms of individual files, Subversion versions entire trees, which allows it to track historical data that CVS simply can't store. Many CVS users will admit to being shocked when they first realized there was no simple way to rename a file or delete a directory, or that they couldn't have an empty directory in their CVS repository.

When we say that files and directories have *metadata*, it means that arbitrary bits of data about each file or directory can be stored by Subversion. This data is used by Subversion itself for keeping track of things such as the line-ending style used by the file, the fact that the file is executable, or the keywords that Subversion should expand within the file. Additionally, you can create your own bits of data to associate with files and directories. Perhaps you want to track the last time the translation of a particular bit of documentation was updated, or who holds the copyright on the file, or any other piece of information you can think of, really. The possibilities are limitless.

To learn how to manage directories, files, and their associated metadata, see Chapter 2.

Atomic Changes to the Repository

With truly atomic changes, all parts of a given change go into the Subversion repository or none of them do. For example, if you run `svn commit foo.c bar.c`, your changes to both `foo.c` and `bar.c` will either make it into the repository together or not at all.

This might not seem important, but imagine a change that affects hundreds of files. The process of checking in the change might take some time, and in systems without atomic changes, it's possible that someone updating her checked-out copy while the change is happening would get part of the changes, but not all of them. It's easy to see how this could result in a set of files that aren't internally consistent, and thus don't work.

In Subversion, there's no way you can update your checked-out copy of the tree at the wrong time and receive half of a large change, as can often happen in systems such as CVS. We discuss this in more detail in Chapter 2.

Branching and Tagging

There's no reason for creating a new branch or tagging a release to take linear time relative to the number of files involved, as happens in CVS. Instead, in Subversion, branching and tagging take a constant (and small) amount of time and disk space, thanks to the software's advanced repository design. For more information on using branches, see Chapters 2 and 6.

Client/Server Application Design

Software developers will appreciate that Subversion has been designed from the start to meet their many requirements, rather than evolving to meet them, as CVS did. Subversion has been carefully designed as a native client/server system, with well-defined boundaries between its constituent libraries, making it much more approachable for a developer looking to add a feature or fix a bug. For more information on Subversion's network support, see Chapter 3.

Saving Bandwidth

If the Subversion client has access to both the original version of a file you checked out from the repository and the new version you're trying to check in, it can get away with only sending the difference between the two files to the server, which takes considerably less bandwidth than sending the entire new file.

Disconnected Operations Support

Network bandwidth is generally cheap, but disk space has become cheaper, so Subversion is optimized to avoid network traffic whenever possible, caching data on the client side and allowing many actions to avoid using the network at all.

We haven't devoted time in any specific part of the book to discuss this in detail, but keep it in mind as you read through these first few chapters. You're likely to see several places where design decisions are made in such a way as to use extra disk space to minimize network traffic.

Well-Supported Binary Files

Experience has proven that CVS handles binary files poorly (at best). Subversion improves on this in two ways. First, the client is designed to make it difficult for a user to make an error that results in the destruction of his file. (In CVS, it's all too easy to have end-of-line conversion or keyword translation performed on a binary file, rendering it useless—or worse, unrecoverable.) Second, the Subversion repository uses an efficient binary diff algorithm, so that storing each revision of a binary file separately (as CVS does) isn't necessary. For information about Subversion's handling of binary files, see Chapter 2 (specifically the "Properties" section).

Sharing a Repository Over a Network

If you're looking for simplicity, a custom TCP has been written, with a simple server process. This protocol can be tunneled over SSH if necessary, leveraging the existing security infrastructure that's evolved to support CVS. If you're looking for even more flexibility, Subversion can use a WebDAV-based protocol, sending HTTP requests over the wire to the most time-tested server process around, Apache. The Apache-based server allows you to make use of a giant pool of existing Apache modules, many of which can provide Subversion with capabilities far in excess of what Subversion's developers could provide on their own. For example, you can use an Apache module to allow your Subversion server to store its list of users and passwords in a MySQL database rather than a file on disk, or to compress the data that's transmitted over the network via the `zlib` library.

For more information on Subversion's networking options, see Chapters 3 and 5.

Workflow Similar to CVS

Perhaps most important for CVS users everywhere, Subversion is similar enough to CVS that you can quickly jump to using Subversion with a minimum amount of difficulty. The similarities between Subversion and CVS, combined with Subversion's consistent command-line user interface, make switching to Subversion considerably more palatable to those who have been dissatisfied with CVS in the past.

Like CVS before it, Subversion is an open source project. While the project is sponsored by CollabNet, a commercial company, the code for Subversion is available under an Apache-like license, free for any and all to use for any purpose.

Since Subversion's beginnings in early 2000, a thriving community of developers has grown up around it, all working to produce a system they can readily use in their day-to-day work. To learn more about participating in the Subversion community, see the README in the Subversion source distribution, and the HACKING file online at http://subversion.tigris.org/hacking.html, or visit the project's web page at http://subversion.tigris.org/.

Key Technologies

Subversion can make use of a number of technologies, such as the Apache web server and Berkeley DB, in order to provide option features. Whether you use them or not, you'll be able to better understand the rest of the book if you know a little bit about the technologies Subversion is built on.

Apache Web Server and WebDAV

The Apache HTTPD server (`http://httpd.apache.org/`) is the Internet's most popular web server. At any given time, between 60% and 70% of the world's web pages are served up by some version of Apache (see `http://www.netcraft.com/` for statistics on HTTPD server use).

WebDAV (`http://www.webdav.org/`) is a set of extensions to HTTP (the underlying protocol used by web browsers and web servers) that allow users to edit and manage files on remote web servers.

If you install a recent version of Apache and configure `mod_dav`, the module that provides Apache's WebDAV support, you can use a WebDAV client to manage the content served up by your server, rather than just reading it in a browser. A number of common operating systems have support for WebDAV built right in. For example, Mac OS X's Finder allows you to mount a WebDAV share right on your desktop as a network drive. Windows XP's Web Folders allow you to do essentially the same thing, as does GNOME's Nautilus file manager.

Subversion's `mod_dav_svn` Apache module and `libsvn_ra_dav` library make use of a subset of WebDAV and an extension to WebDAV known as DeltaV to allow a Subversion client to access a Subversion repository through an Apache web server. See Chapters 3 and 5 for more information on using `mod_dav_svn` and Apache with Subversion.

Berkeley DB

Subversion has two back ends in which it can store data. One of these is a filesystem-based back end, which is now the default, which will work best for the majority of people. However, some people feel safer if the data is stored in a real database, in which case Subversion provides a back end where the data is stored in a database using Berkeley DB.

Berkeley DB is an embedded database. Everything that's required for Subversion to access Berkeley DB, if you choose to use it, is built right in to Subversion itself.

We will cover which back end you should choose for your particular needs in Chapter 3.

Obtaining Subversion

Like many open source projects, Subversion is readily available in source code form. Tarballs of each release are made available from `http://subversion.tigris.org/` in the Documents & Files section of the site. Once you've downloaded the latest release tarball, building a Subversion client is relatively straightforward. On the other hand, if you're not interested in compiling Subversion yourself, precompiled packages and binaries are available for most major platforms.

Obtaining Precompiled Binaries

If you're not comfortable building Subversion from source or you don't have access to the tools required to build it, that's not a problem, as the developer community provides prepackaged releases for a wide variety of operating systems. Simply check http://subversion.tigris.org/ project_packages.html for your operating system of choice and follow your platform's standard procedure for installing third-party software. Then you should be all set.

Building Subversion on Unix Systems

Before we describe the process of building and installing Subversion, it's worth pointing out that the INSTALL file in the top level of the release contains up-to-the-minute information on installing Subversion, which could be more up-to-date than the instructions presented here.

Once you've downloaded a tarball from http://subversion.tigris.org/, getting a basic client compiled is as simple as unpacking the tarball, running the configure script, and running make and make install, as the following shows:

```
$ curl -O http://subversion.tigris.org/tarballs/subversion-1.3.1.tar.gz
  % Total    % Received % Xferd  Average Speed          Time          Curr.
                                 Dload  Upload Total   Current Left   Speed
100 8572k  100 8572k    0     0   251k      0  0:00:28 0:00:28 0:00:00  244k
$ tar zxf subversion-1.3.1.tar.gz
$ cd subversion-1.3.1
$ ./configure --prefix=/opt/packages/subversion
[ ... lots of output ... ]
$ make
[ ... even more output ... ]
# make install
[ ... still more output ... ]
$ /opt/packages/subversion/bin/svn
Type 'svn help' for usage.
$
```

If you just want to access an existing repository hosted on another machine, these are the basic steps you'll need to take. If you want to create your own repository, set up a server so that other people can access your repository, and run through most of the examples in the book yourself, you may need to do a few other things. Specifically, if you want to use mod_dav_svn, the Apache module that allows you to use an Apache HTTPD server as your Subversion server, you'll have to tell configure how to find your HTTPD install.

To create and access a Subversion repository using the database back end, you'll need to install an appropriate version of Berkeley DB (available from http://sleepycat.com/download/ index.shtml) and ensure that Subversion can find it by passing a few options to the configure script.

Subversion will work with any of the earlier 4.x series of Berkeley DB releases. In particular, the absolute newest version, 4.4, is not supported by any Subversion that has been released. That said, developers have encountered various issues when using the 4.1.x versions, so you're almost certainly better off using either a 4.2.x or a 4.3.x version of Berkeley DB. Furthermore, Berkeley DB version 4.2.52 and later support additional features (such as automatic cleanup of old log files) that are nice to have, and the Subversion team has seen the best stability and performance with the 4.3.x series of releases, so if it is at all possible you should probably use a recent version from the 4.3.x series. If that isn't possible for some reason, the next best option is 4.2.x. The 4.1.x releases are best avoided.

Besides Berkeley DB, Subversion makes use of the Apache Portable Runtime (APR) to abstract away the various platform-specific details of the operating systems it runs on, and it additionally makes use of the APR-Util library, a set of useful bits and pieces of code that are built on top of APR, which makes use of Berkeley DB. To lower the odds of shooting yourself in the foot by linking against multiple conflicting versions of Berkeley DB, Subversion simply makes use of whatever version of Berkeley DB that APR-Util uses. If your version of Berkeley DB is installed in a fairly standard place, APR-Util's configure script will most likely be able to find it. To play it safe, though, you should probably ensure that APR-Util links against the correct version of Berkeley DB. There are two options you can pass to APR-Util's configure script to make this happen. First, the --with-dbm=db4 option will keep APR-Util from picking up earlier versions of Berkeley DB. Second, the --with-berkeley-db=/path/to/berkeley/db option will force APR-Util to use a version of Berkeley DB installed in the directory /path/to/berkeley/db.

■**Note** Of course, you should replace /path/to/berkeley/db with the path to your Berkeley DB install, which is probably something like /usr/local or /usr/local/BerkeleyDB.4.2.

If you're using the versions of APR and APR-Util that are bundled with Subversion, you can ensure that these options are passed to APR-Util's configure script by passing them to Subversion's configure script. Similarly, if you're using the versions of APR and APR-Util that are compiled into the Apache HTTPD, you can simply pass those options to the HTTPD configure script. Sadly, one pitfall when building mod_dav_svn is that Subversion *must* be linked with the same versions of APR and APR-Util that Apache is. Subversion's configure script should take care of this for you, assuming you passed it the --with-apxs flag, but you can probably still get yourself into trouble with the --with-apr and --with-apr-util flags; so if you're building mod_dav_svn you should avoid those two flags. If you use the bundled versions, the whole thing looks something like this:

```
$ tar zxvf subversion-1.3.1.tar.gz
$ cd subversion-1.3.1
$ ./configure --with-dbm=db4 --with-berkeley-db=/opt/packages/bdb43
[ ... lots of output ... ]
$ make && make install
[ ... still more output ... ]
$
```

When using Apache with Subversion, there's another case where you may need to tell Subversion's configure script what to do. If Apache isn't installed in a standard place, you'll have to pass the --with-apxs=/path/to/your/apxs flag to Subversion's configure script. This will allow configure to use the apxs script that comes with Apache to figure out how to use your Apache installation when building Subversion.

Here's something else you should know about using Subversion with Apache: You absolutely must use a recent version of Apache 2.x—the older Apache 1.3.x simply will not work. If you have Apache 1.3.x installed, you can still use Subversion, but you'll have to install Apache 2.x to use mod_dav_svn as your server.

Last in the list of pitfalls related to building Subversion with Apache support is that Apache needs to be compiled with a few special flags. First of all, mod_dav_svn depends on mod_dav, so you need to pass --enable-dav to Apache's configure. Second, because mod_dav_svn is normally compiled as a loadable module, you need to compile loadable module support into Apache. To do that, you need to pass --enable-so to Apache's configure, as shown in the following code:

```
$ tar zxvf httpd-2.0.55.tar.gz
$ cd httpd-2.0.55
$ ./configure --prefix=/opt/packages/apache2 \
              --with-dbm=db4 \
              --with-berkeley-db=/opt/packages/bdb43 \
              --enable-dav \
              --enable-so
[ ... lots of output ... ]
$ make && make install
[ ... lots of output ... ]
$ cd ..
$ tar zxvf subversion-1.3.1.tar.gz
$ cd subversion-1.3.1
$ ./configure --with-apxs=/opt/packages/apache2/bin/apxs
[ ... lots of output ... ]
$ make && make install
[ ... a lot more output ... ]
$
```

Table 1-1 summarizes the most commonly used Subversion configure script flags.

Table 1-1. *Useful configure Flags for Subversion*

Flag	Argument	Notes
--prefix	Path you want Subversion installed into	
--with-dbm	Version of Berkeley DB you want to find (e.g., db4)	Also applies to Apache and APR-Util configure scripts
--with-berkeley-db	Path to Berkeley DB install directory	Also applies to Apache and APR-Util configure scripts
--with-apxs	Path to apxs binary for installed Apache	
--with-neon	Path to installed Neon library	Only needed if you don't want to use the bundled version of Neon
--with-apr	Path to installed APR library	Only needed if you don't want to use the bundled version of APR
--with-apr-util	Path to installed APR-Util library	Only needed if you don't want to use the bundled version of APR-Util

So there you have it. When building Subversion from source on Unix you have to be concerned about three things. First, if you want the database back end, you need to be sure you have the correct version of Berkeley DB installed. Second, you need to ensure that your version of APR-Util is linked against that version of Berkeley DB. And third, if you're building mod_dav_svn, you need to ensure that you have the correct version of Apache installed and that Subversion can find it.

Of course if you're only concerned with building a Subversion client and you have no desire to create repositories using the database back end, or to run servers that access repositories using the database back end, you don't need to worry about any of this. Just running configure, make, and make install in the Subversion tarball should be enough.

Installing Subversion on Windows Systems

Building Subversion on Windows systems is both considerably more complex than doing so on Unix machines and considerably less common, due primarily to the fact that most Windows users don't have access to the tools necessary to compile software themselves. As a result, virtually everyone who runs Subversion on Windows uses precompiled binaries.

There are two options available to you when it comes to binary distributions of Subversion for Windows. Precompiled versions of Subversion for Windows come as either a ZIP file or a prepackaged installer. The ZIP file simply contains the binaries, the libraries they depend on, and the Apache modules. The installer wraps the same binaries up and automatically installs them for you. You can use whichever you're more comfortable with, although the installer is the easier of the two to use. Unless you know what you're doing it's probably best to simply use the installer, as it minimizes your chances of making a mistake in the installation process.

If you're interested in making modifications to the Subversion source code yourself, or you're trying to debug a problem in Subversion, you can find instructions on how to build Subversion on Windows using Visual C++ 6.x in the INSTALL file in the top level of the Subversion distribution. You'll have to obtain most of the same libraries that are used with the Unix build (Neon, and so on); you'll have to build your APR-Iconv in addition to APR and APR-Util; and you'll need both Perl and Python installed for various parts of the process. Needless to say, this isn't for inexperienced developers, and if you decide to just download the precompiled binaries, nobody will think less of you.

If you aren't scared yet, the INSTALL file is really the best guide to the process, so we'll just refer you to it from here on.

It's also possible to build Subversion with Visual Studio .NET, but the process is more difficult and not as well documented.

Configuration Files

The client side of the Subversion libraries (and some parts of the server side) make use of a number of configuration files to allow the user to tweak several aspects of the system. Subversion's configuration files make use of an INI-style format, which is compatible with the Python ConfigParser module, found at http://www.python.org/doc/current/lib/module-ConfigParser.html.

Here's an example of a section from the ~/.subversion/config file, so you can see what Subversion configuration files look like:

```
[auth]
store-auth-creds = no
```

In this case, there is a single section, [auth], and within it there is one variable, store-auth-creds, which is set to no. Wherever you see a Boolean option, the value can be any of true, false, yes, no, on, off, 1, or 0.

There are two types of configuration files on a system. The first are the systemwide configuration files, which are by default located in /etc/subversion on Unix and are optional. The second are the per-user configuration files, which on Unix are located in ~/.subversion. The first time you run a Subversion command, the ~/.subversion directory will be created and populated with sample configuration files. Subversion currently makes use of two configuration files: servers, which holds options related to connecting to Subversion servers over the network, and config, which holds more general options.

On Windows systems, the system configuration files are located in C:\Documents and Settings\All Users\Application Data\Subversion,[1] and the per-user configuration files are located in C:\Documents and Settings\rooneg\Application Data\Subversion[2] (well, if your username is rooneg anyway; if it isn't you'll have to replace that part with your own username). Additionally, you can place configuration options in the Windows Registry instead of in the configuration files. The systemwide configuration is stored in HKLM\Software\Tigris.org\Subversion, and the per-user configuration is stored in HKCU\Software\Tigris.org\Subversion.

■**Note** For the rest of the book, we'll be using the Unix-style locations for the configuration files, so if we refer to ~/.subversion/servers, and you're using Windows, just mentally replace ~/.subversion with your Application Data directory.

For more details on the configuration files and their contents, see the README.txt file in the ~/.subversion directory and the sample configuration files themselves.

Summary

In this chapter, we explained a little about version control in general and Subversion in particular. We covered how to install Subversion on your system, and you learned a little about how Subversion's configuration files work. Now you're ready to move on to Chapter 2, which presents an in-depth tutorial on how to use Subversion.

---

1. OK, technically, they're located in %ALLUSERSPROFILE%\Application Data\Subversion, but usually %ALLUSERSPROFILE% is C:\Documents and Settings\All Users.

2. Again, technically that's %APPDATA%\Subversion, but if you're on a typical Windows machine, %APPDATA% is the Application Data directory in your user profile.

CHAPTER 2

■ ■ ■

A Crash Course in Subversion

If you're already familiar with version control, Subversion is reasonably simple to use. The workflow is quite similar to that of several other version control systems (notably CVS), so you shouldn't have too much trouble transitioning to Subversion. This chapter begins with a simple overview of Subversion and then dives into the specifics you need to know to use the software. Along the way, we compare Subversion commands to the equivalent commands in other version control systems, such as CVS and Perforce.

Conceptually, Subversion's design is similar to that of CVS. There is a single central repository that holds all versions of each file that is under Subversion's control. You (and others) can interact with the repository in two different ways: either by checking out a particular revision of the versioned data into a local *working copy*, or by acting directly on the repository itself, without the need for an intermediate working copy. Generally, you'll check out a local working copy, make changes, and then commit those changes back into the central repository. Unlike some other version control systems, and Visual SourceSafe in particular, there is no need to check out again after you've committed.

Locking vs. Nonlocking

An important difference between Subversion and many other version control systems is that like CVS, Subversion's mode of operation is *nonlocking*. That means that if two users have checked out working copies that contain the same file, nothing prohibits both of them from making changes to that file. For users of systems such as Visual SourceSafe, this may seem odd, as there is no way to ensure that the two users' changes to the file don't conflict with each other. In truth, this is by design.

In the vast majority of cases, the two users' changes don't conflict. Even if the two users change the same file, it's likely that they'll change separate parts of the file, and those disparate changes can easily be merged together later. In this kind of situation, allowing one user to lock the file would result in unneeded contention, with one user forced to wait until the other has completed his changes. Even worse is the situation in which the second user changes the file despite the fact that the file is locked. When the first user completes his change and unlocks the file, the second user is stuck merging the changes together manually, introducing an element of human error into something that the computer can handle far better.

Worse yet are the problems of *stale locks*. In a version control system that uses locks, there's always the danger of a user taking out a lock on a file and not returning it by unlocking the file when she's done. Every developer has run into something like this at some point. You begin work on a new bug or feature, and in your first stab at the solution you end up editing a file. Because you're making changes to the file, you take out the lock on it to ensure that nobody else changes it out from under you. At this point you can get into trouble in several ways. Perhaps once you get further into the solution, you realize that you were wrong to change that file, so you return the file to its previous state and move on to another solution, without unlocking the file. Perhaps your focus moves to some other issue and your work on the first problem sits there for a long period of time—and all the while you're holding the lock. Eventually, someone else is going to need to edit that same file, and to do so he'll need to find you and ask you to remove the lock before he can proceed. Even more problematic, he could try to work around the version control system and edit the file anyway, which leads to more complicated merging issues in the future. Or what if you're on vacation or have left the company when this happens? An administrator will have to intercede and break the lock, creating an even greater chance of someone's work getting lost in the shuffle.

So in the typical case in which there are no conflicts, the nonlocking strategy used by Subversion is a clear win. But what about the rare case in which changes really do conflict? Then the first user to complete his change commits that change to the repository. When the second user tries to commit, she'll be told that her working copy is out-of-date and that she must update before she can commit. The act of updating will give Subversion a chance to show that the changes conflict, and the user will be required to resolve the problem.

This may seem similar to what would happen in the locking case, except for a couple of critical differences. First, the conflict forces the second user to stop and deal with the differences, avoiding the chance that the second user might just copy her version over the first version and destroy the first change in the process. Second, Subversion can help with the merging process by placing conflict markers in the file and providing access to the old, new, and local versions so the user can easily compare them with some other tool.

If you've never used a version control system that makes use of conflict markers, the best way to understand them is through an example. Suppose you have a file in your working copy, hello.c, that looks like this:

```
#include <stdio.h>
int
main (int argc, char *argv[])
{
  printf ("hello world\n");
  return 0;
}
```

Then say you change the hello world string to Hello World, and before checking in your changes you update your working copy and find that someone else has already changed that line of the file. The copy of hello.c in your working copy will end up looking something like this:

```
#include <stdio.h>
int
main (int argc, char *argv[])
{
<<<<<<< .mine
```

```
  printf ("Hello World\n");
=======
  printf ("hello world!\n");
>>>>>>> .r5
  return 0;
}
```

The <<<<<<<, =======, and >>>>>>> lines are used to indicate which of your changes con-flict. In this case, it means that your version of the section of hello.c that you changed looks like printf ("Hello World\n");, but in a newer version of the file that has already been checked into the repository, that line was changed to printf ("hello world!\n");.

Of course, all of this only works if the file in question is in a format that Subversion under-stands well enough that it can merge the changes automatically. At the moment, that means the file must be textual in nature. Changes to binary files such as image files, sound files, Word documents, and so forth, can't be merged automatically. Any conflicts with such files will have to be handled manually by the user. To assist in that merging, Subversion provides you with copies of the original version of the file you checked out, your modified version, and the new version from the repository, so you can compare them using some other tool.

■**Note** Historically, most version control systems were designed to handle plain-text content—for example, a computer program's source code. As a result, they developed formats for storing historical data that were designed with plain text in mind. For example, RCS files work in terms of a textual file, adding or removing lines from the file in each new revision. For a binary file, which doesn't have "lines" at all, this breaks down, so systems based on these formats usually end up dealing with binary data by storing each revision sepa-rately, meaning that each time you make a change you use up space in the repository equal to the size of the file you modified. In addition, these systems often include other features, such as keyword replacement or end-of-line conversion, which not only don't make sense in terms of binary files, but also can actually damage them, because a binary file format probably won't survive intact if you replace all instances of Id with a new string, or all the newline bytes with carriage return/linefeed combinations.

In addition to helping you handle the situation in which a conflict does occur, the use of a nonlocking model helps in another way: it removes the false sense of security that a locking model gives you. In the majority of cases, when you make a change to one part of a program, the effect of that change isn't isolated to just that file. For example, if you're changing a header file in a C program, you're really affecting all the files that include that header. Locking access to that one file doesn't buy much safety, because your changes can still quite easily conflict with any number of potential changes in other parts of the program. Locking gives you the illusion that it's safe to make changes, but in reality you need the same amount of communi-cation among developers that you'd need in the nonlocking mode. Locking just makes it easier to forget that.

Now none of this is meant to imply that the only possible solution to the version control problem is a nonlocking system. There are certainly situations in which locking is a valuable tool, perhaps with files that truly shouldn't be modified except by certain key individuals, or perhaps when you're working with binary files that can't be easily merged. For these cases, you can use the svn lock and svn unlock to lock files or directories. You can also mark files with the svn:needs-lock property to inform Subversion that they needed to be locked before modification.

Other Differentiating Features

In addition to Subversion's nonlocking workflow, a couple more things differentiate it from some other version control systems. First, all changes to the repository are atomic; either all parts of a change go in, or none of them do. As a result, there's a single repository-wide revision number, which describes the state of the entire tree. So when you refer to "version 247 of foo.c," it's really more correct to say "foo.c as it exists in revision 247 of the repository." This is similar to the changeset number in Perforce, and although it may seem odd to not have per-file revisions (which exist in Perforce and are the only kind of revision in CVS), thinking in terms of atomic changes that can encompass multiple separate files rather than several different changes to different files is quite easy to adjust to. In fact, it's a good idea to start thinking in those terms anyway because it helps you focus on forming coherent atomic changes, something that helps ensure the source tree is always in a usable state. Second, Subversion doesn't just keep track of changes to files, it actually versions entire directory trees. This means that directories are first-class items to Subversion, and they can be added and removed just like files can be.

Throughout the rest of this chapter, we'll cover what you need to know to be an effective Subversion user. This crash course includes how to use the svn command-line client and the concepts you need to be aware of to make effective use of it. By the end of the chapter, you should be well-prepared to start making use of Subversion in your daily development work.

The Most Important Subversion Commands

Before you get started with Subversion it's important to be aware of a few commands that are going to prove very useful to you. Both of the major Subversion executables (svn, the command-line client, and svnadmin, the repository administration tool) have built-in help for each of their commands. To access the help, just use the help command, like this:

```
$ svn help
```

```
usage: svn <subcommand> [options] [args]
Subversion command-line client, version 1.3.2.
Type 'svn help <subcommand>' for help on a specific subcommand.

Most subcommands take file and/or directory arguments, recursing
on the directories.  If no arguments are supplied to such a
command, it recurses on the current directory (inclusive) by default.

Available subcommands:
   add
   blame (praise, annotate, ann)
   cat
```

```
checkout (co)
cleanup
commit (ci)
copy (cp)
delete (del, remove, rm)
diff (di)
export
help (?, h)
import
info
list (ls)
lock
log
merge
mkdir
move (mv, rename, ren)
propdel (pdel, pd)
propedit (pedit, pe)
propget (pget, pg)
proplist (plist, pl)
propset (pset, ps)
resolved
revert
status (stat, st)
switch (sw)
unlock
update (up)

Subversion is a tool for version control.
For additional information, see http://subversion.tigris.org/
$
```

Many of the subcommands include both a canonical primary name, such as diff, and some shorter aliases that appear in parentheses after the canonical primary name, such as di. In the help output, the aliases for each subcommand are always shown in parentheses.

In everyday use, it's common to use the shorter versions of the commands. For example, if someone mentions running svn up to update his working copy, he's really talking about the svn update command. It's probably a good idea to at least become familiar with the various aliases for just this reason. In this book we use the longer names in our examples, because they tend to more clearly represent what the command actually does. The shorter names generally exist for historical reasons (i.e., if CVS uses the same alias for a similar command and there isn't a compelling reason not to support it, Subversion likely has the same alias) or because the aliases are similar to some common command-line utility. Both types of shortcuts serve to help people remember the name of the command.

The remainder of this chapter introduces the commands you're likely to use on a day-to-day basis as a Subversion user. For more specific information about an svn subcommand, just run svn help subcommand, which gives you output like this:

```
$ svn help add
```

```
add: Put files and directories under version control, scheduling
them for addition to repository.  They will be added in next commit.
usage: add PATH...

Valid options:
  --targets arg            : pass contents of file ARG as additional args
  -N [--non-recursive]     : operate on single directory only
  -q [--quiet]             : print as little as possible
  --config-dir arg         : read user configuration files from directory ARG
  --force                  : force operation to run
  --no-ignore              : disregard default and svn:ignore property ignores
  --auto-props             : enable automatic properties
  --no-auto-props          : disable automatic properties
$
```

---

svn help will quickly become your new best friend, as it provides the quick hints you need as you get used to the new commands.

For more in-depth documentation of each of the commands, please see the glossary of Subversion commands in Appendix A.

Revisions and URLs

The majority of Subversion's commands prefer you to refer to a particular revision of an entity in the repository, where the entity could be a file or a directory. You generally specify this entity by using a URL and possibly a revision. If, for example, your repository is located at /home/repos/projects, then the URL file:///home/repos/projects/trunk/final refers to whatever is located at /trunk/final, in this case most likely a directory, which would likely contain other items. If you're on a Windows system and you need to refer to a repository on a drive different from the one your current working directory is on, the syntax looks like this: file:///C:/path/to/repos or file:///C|/path/to/repos.

In addition to file://-based URLs, Subversion can be built with support for four other URL schemes, each of which refers to repositories that are accessed via a different repository access layer. URLs that start with http:// or https:// refer to repositories that are accessed via ra_dav, which uses a WebDAV-based protocol. svn:// or svn+ssh:// URLs refer to repositories that are accessed via ra_svn, a custom TCP written just for Subversion. In both cases, the URLs used to access repositories via these protocols include the name of the server the repository is located on after the schema, then a path to the location of the repository, followed by the location within the repository you're interested in. When a URL is used alone, without a specific revision, it refers to the newest revision of the item at that path within the repository.

Table 2-1 breaks down the components that make up a number of different Subversion URLs. Note that, in general, it is not possible to determine from a URL which portion refers to the repository and which portion refers to the path inside the repository.

Table 2-1. *URL Breakdown*

URL	RA Layer	Host	Repository	Path
http://example.org/ repos/trunk/README	ra_dav	example.org/	repos/	trunk/README
file:///path/to/ /repos/branches/ 1.0.x/src/main.c	ra_local	N/A	path/ to/repos/	branches/1.0.x/ src/main.c
svn://example.org/ repos/sandbox/tags/ 0.47/HACKING	ra_svn	example.org/	repos/ sandbox/	tags/0.47/HACKING
svn+ssh://example. org/home/repos/ dev/trunk/ include/globals.h	ra_svn over ssh	example.org/	home/repos/ dev/	trunk/include/ globals.h

You can specify a revision in Subversion in several different ways. First off, you can always specify the literal revision number, which is a monotonically increasing integer. Zero is the initial revision of the repository, before any data is added to it, and for each change that is made the revision increases by one. In addition to using literal revision numbers, you can use shortcuts, such as the HEAD keyword, which refers to the most recent revision in the repository. There's also BASE, which refers to the version of an item that you have in your working copy; COMMITTED, which is the revision in which the item was last changed; and PREV, which is the revision before the item was last changed. If you're looking to specify the revision the repository was at on a particular date, you can just use the date enclosed in curly braces. For example, {1978-02-05} indicates the revision the item was at on February 5, 1978, at midnight. Table 2-2 shows the various ways you can specify revisions to Subversion.

Note Any mix of these formats is allowed in a range, so that {1978-02-05}:HEAD is a valid range.

Table 2-2. *Revision Specifications*

Revision Specification	Meaning
10	Literal revision 10
10:20	A range of revisions from 10 to 20
HEAD	Youngest revision in the repository
BASE	Current revision of the working copy
COMMITTED	Revision in which an entry was last changed in the working copy (working copy only)
PREV	Revision before COMMITTED
{2003-03-25}	Revision the item was at on March 25, 2003, at midnight
{2003-02-27 10:00}	Revision the item was at on February 27, 2003, at 10:00

In most cases you specify revisions by using the `--revision` keyword, which can be abbreviated with -r, followed by the revision (e.g., `svn update --revision 10`). If the command refers to a range of revisions, the revisions are separated by colons, as in `svn diff --revision 9:10`, where you're indicating that the `svn diff` command should start at revision 9 and end at revision 10.

Creating and Populating the Repository

Before you can really do anything with Subversion, you need to have access to a Subversion repository.

Because you'll need to have the ability to commit changes to a repository to do anything interesting (which is pretty much required if you want to learn more than just the basics), you'll want to create your own repository. The `svnadmin` program is used for this purpose (among other things, of course, which we'll discuss further in Chapter 3). Run the `svnadmin create` command, and you're ready to go. It looks something like this:

```
$ svnadmin create myrepos
$ ls -l myrepos/
```

```
-rw-r--r--   1 rooneg  staff  376 May 31 17:32 README.txt
drwxr-xr-x   2 rooneg  staff   68 May 31 17:32 conf/
drwxr-xr-x   2 rooneg  staff   68 May 31 17:32 dav/
drwxr-sr-x  17 rooneg  staff  578 May 31 17:32 db/
-rw-r--r--   1 rooneg  staff    2 May 31 17:32 format
drwxr-xr-x   7 rooneg  staff  238 May 31 17:32 hooks/
drwxr-xr-x   3 rooneg  staff  102 May 31 17:32 locks/
$
```

Inside the repository you just created are a number of files and directories, each of which has a specific purpose. You'll find out more about them later, so for the moment don't touch them. With a few exceptions, you shouldn't modify anything inside the repository by hand. Instead, you should always use the `svnadmin` and `svn` programs to access the repository (that is unless you really know what you're doing—but in that case, why are you reading this chapter?).

Now that you've created a repository, you'll need to put something in it before it's much use to anyone. The first step is to create an initial repository layout. Unlike other version control systems, Subversion uses directories (and copies of directories) as tags and branches. This means that creating a new tag or branch is exactly the same as copying a directory. The only difference is a social one. The developers agree to treat certain copies of a directory in a specific way, either by confining some kind of development to them (as in a branch) or by leaving them completely read-only (as in a tag). We'll go into greater depth on how to work with tags and branches later, but for the moment you just need to know that if you want to make use of branches or tags in the future you'll want to create some subdirectories in your repository to hold them. Traditionally, most people create three top-level directories in their repository: one named /trunk to hold the main copy of the project where most development occurs, one named /branches to hold separate lines of development (remember, those will just be copies of /trunk), and one named /tags to hold copies of the project as it exists at significant points of time, such as a release. The only difference between the copies of /trunk that end up in

/tags and the ones that end up in /branches is that everyone agrees not to modify the ones in /tags—they're only there because they're of historical interest.

You might be wondering why Subversion doesn't just create these top-level directories for you. The reason is quite simple: Subversion doesn't have any idea what you're going to put in your repository or what kinds of conventions you're going to use for repository layout. If you have a single project in your repository, the traditional top-level layout makes sense, but if you want your repository to hold multiple projects, you'll probably want each project to have its own /trunk, /tags, and /branches directories contained within a top-level directory named after the project. Chapter 3 details the issues involved in selecting a repository layout.

Before you create your top-level directories, we should mention something about how to use the svn command-line client program. All of svn's subcommands take a target as one (or more) of their arguments. In many cases, this target can be either a local path or a URL that refers to something inside a repository. For many of these commands, if you don't provide a target, the command will assume you want to use your current working directory as the target. If the command targets something in your local working copy, no change you make will be reflected in the repository until you commit it in a separate command. Conversely, any change you make that targets the repository directly will cause an immediate commit, requiring you to specify a log message as with any other commit and creating a new revision in the repository.

Now let's move on to actually create your initial repository layout. You'll need to create each top-level directory via an svn mkdir that targets the repository directly.

Tip On Unix systems, it is usually a great time-saver to use shell variables to store repo URLS, rather than retyping them everywhere.

The process looks like this:

```
$ svnadmin create repos
$ svn mkdir file:///absolute/path/to/repos/trunk \
            file:///absolute/path/to/repos/branches \
            file:///absolute/path/to/repos/tags \
            -m "creating initial repository layout"
```

```
Committed revision 1.
$
```

Let's examine that command for a second and see what else you can learn from it. First of all, you see the syntax for accessing a repository via a file:// URL. Whenever a Subversion command uses the file:// schema for a URL, it means it's directly accessing the repository via a path in your filesystem. This path may lead to some network share (i.e., an SMB/CIFS server, or an NFS server), or be local to our machine. For paths that lead to Berkeley DB repositories, you need read-write access to the database files to perform an operation. For FSFS repositories, you only need read access for read-only operations, and write access to perform modifications of the repositories (such as commits). Chapter 3 has more details about the internals of the repository.

Look closely at the URLs you used to specify the directories you created. First, there are three slashes after `file:`, which might seem a bit odd; but if you think about it, it makes sense. It's just like accessing a web page over HTTP, except the part of the URL that would contain the domain name is empty, thus it skips directly to the third slash. Second, you used the -m flag to pass a log message for the commit on the command line. Because you're committing this change directly to the repository, a log message is required. If you don't pass one on the command line (either via -m or in a file specified with the --file argument), the client will run your editor of choice to give you an opportunity to enter one.[1]

Now that the directories in question exist in the repository, let's confirm that fact via svn list (most people probably know this command better as svn ls):

```
$ svn list file:///absolute/path/to/repos
```

```
branches/
tags/
trunk/
$
```

Here you can see that the top level of the repository contains the three directories you just created. Of course, empty directories aren't all that useful, so let's put some data in them. Assuming that you already have some kind of project you want to bring into Subversion, you can import it via the svn import command. This command's command-line arguments are an optional path to a directory of files you want to import (if you don't specify a path, your current working directory is imported) and a URL to indicate where in the repository to place the data you're importing. Any directories at the end of the URL that don't yet exist in the repository will be automatically created. Take a look at this example to see what we mean:

```
$ ls my-project/
```

```
foo.c bar.c main.c
```

```
$ svn import my-project file:///path/to/repository/trunk \
            -m "importing my project"
```

---

1. Here, the "editor of choice" is determined by checking the -editor-cmd command-line option, then the SVN_EDITOR environment variable, then the editor-cmd option from the helpers section of ~/subversion/config, then the VISUAL environment variable, then the EDITOR environment variable, and finally, a possible hard-coded default specified in the source code. As you might guess, it took a long time to get the developers to agree on that sequence of places to try to find a text editor.

```
Adding          my-project/bar.c
Adding          my-project/foo.c
Adding          my-project/main.c

Committed revision 2.
```

```
$ svn list file:///path/to/repository/trunk
```

```
foo.c
bar.c
main.c
$
```

This is a basic example that imports a directory of files directly into the trunk of the repository. Note that once again you have to specify a log message because you're committing a change to the repository. If you want to import the files into a subdirectory of /trunk, the process looks like this:

```
$ ls my-project/
```

```
foo.c
bar.c
main.c
```

```
$ svn import my-project file:///path/to/repository/trunk/new-directory \
        -m "importing my project into new-directory"
```

```
Adding          my-project/bar.c
Adding          my-project/foo.c
Adding          my-project/main.c

Committed revision 3.
```

```
$ svn list file:///path/to/repository/trunk/
```

```
foo.c
bar.c
main.c
new-directory/
```

```
$ svn list file:///path/to/repository/trunk/new-directory/
```

```
foo.c
bar.c
main.c
```

```
$ svn delete file:///path/to/repository/trunk/new-directory \
      -m "get rid of extra directory because it's not very useful"
```

```
Committed revision 4.
$
```

Finally, you can verify that the content of the files you just imported is actually in the repository by using the svn cat command. svn cat prints the contents of a file in the repository to the screen, and it can be a quick and dirty way to see what a given revision of a file looks like:

```
$ svn cat file:///path/to/repository/trunk/main.c
```

```
#include <stdio.h>
int
main (int argc, char *argv[])
{
  printf ("hello world\n");
  return 0;
}
```

```
$ cat my-project/main.c
```

```
#include <stdio.h>
int
main (int argc, char *argv[])
{
  printf ("hello world\n");
  return 0;
}
$
```

As you can see, there's no difference between the contents of main.c in your original directory and the contents of main.c in the trunk directory of the repository. The import has worked as you'd expect, loading the contents of your directory tree directly into the repository.

Basic Workflow

Now that you have data in your Subversion repository, it's time to do something with it. The first step is to check out a working copy. A Subversion working copy is an ordinary directory in your filesystem. It contains any number of files and subdirectories, almost all of which correspond to files and directories in your Subversion repository. In addition to your files and directories, each working copy directory contains a special subdirectory named .svn/. This is known as an *administrative directory*, and Subversion uses it to store some bookkeeping information about the files and directories in your working copy. Note that the administrative directory's contents are under Subversion's control, and you shouldn't edit them in any way. If you do change them manually, you're likely to render your working copy unusable.

Once you have a working copy, you can edit the files, make changes to the files, and eventually commit those changes back to the repository so others can see them. In the process of making your changes, you can ask Subversion to tell you about the status of your changes, view the difference between your current version and the version you checked out (or any other revision, for that matter), or update your working copy to take into account other users' changes. These actions comprise the majority of the Subversion workflow, so let's examine exactly how they work.

Checking Out a Working Copy

To check out a working copy you use the command svn checkout. There's only one required argument: a URL that indicates what directory in the repository you're checking out. Other than that, the most interesting options are an optional path, which specifies the name of the directory you want to check out into, with the default being the name of the directory in the repository, and the -r or --revision argument, which allows you to indicate what revision you want to check out. If you don't indicate what revision you want, the HEAD revision of the repository will be used. (Note that this may change in the future to default to the peg revision, then HEAD if a peg revision is not specified. Peg revisions will be explained later in the "Working with Branches and Tags" section.) Let's take a look at an example of checking out the most recent version of a directory in the repository and inspecting the resulting working copy:

```
$ svn checkout file:///path/to/repository/trunk myproject
```

```
A my-project/foo.c
A my-project/bar.c
A my-project/main.c
Checked out revision 2.
```

```
$ ls myproject/
```

```
foo.c  bar.c  main.c
```

```
$ cd myproject
$ svn status
$ svn status -v
```

```
                    2       2      rooneg   .
                    2       2      rooneg   bar.c
                    2       2      rooneg   foo.c
                    2       2      rooneg   main.c
```

$ svn info

```
Path: .
URL: file:///path/to/repository/trunk
Repository Root: file:///path/to/repository
Repository UUID: 18dffd47-64c3-0310-bd18-cbeae88b449f
Revision: 2
Node Kind: directory
Schedule: normal
Last Changed Author: rooneg
Last Changed Rev: 2
Last Changed Date: 2003-07-26 19:03:29 -0400 (Sat, 26 Jul 2003)
```

$ svn info main.c

```
Path: main.c
Name: main.c
URL: file:///path/to/repos/trunk/main.c
Repository Root: file:///path/to/repos
Repository UUID: 18dffd47-64c3-0310-bd18-cbeae88b449f
Revision: 2
Node Kind: file
Schedule: normal
Last Changed Author: rooneg
Last Changed Rev: 2
Last Changed Date: 2003-07-26 19:03:29 -0400 (Sat, 26 Jul 2003)
Text Last Updated: 2003-07-26 19:03:37 -0400 (Sat, 26 Jul 2003)
Properties Last Updated: 2003-07-26 19:03:37 -0400 (Sat, 26 Jul 2003)
Checksum: 0c1ea17162fcd46023bf6712a35dba03
$
```

Getting Information About Your Working Copy

In addition to svn checkout, you've seen two other new commands, svn status and svn info, so let's take a look at them before moving on. svn status is the command you'll probably run most often while using Subversion. It prints out the current status of your working copy.

■**Note** In Perforce, the closest analogous command to `svn status` is `p4 opened`, but `svn status` shows a lot more information because a Subversion working copy is considerably more complex (at least from the client's perspective) than a Perforce client. In CVS, there really isn't a useful status command, so most people just end up running either `cvs diff` or `cvs update` to determine what local changes they've made. The first case isn't all that bad, although `cvs diff` produces quite a bit more information than just the status of the working copy. The second case is particularly bad because the act of updating your working copy and the act of determining what you've changed are two completely different things. When Subversion's command-line client was designed, great care was taken to make the output of `svn status` useful and easy to understand, so that you aren't tempted to resort to running other commands to discover information you should be getting from `svn status`.

When you run just `svn status`, with no arguments, it will tell you only about files and directories in your working copy that you've modified. In this case when you run it the first time, there is no output because you haven't yet modified any of the files in the working copy. Later on in this section, you'll see some examples of the output from `svn status` when the working copy has some modifications. When you add the `-v` flag, `svn status` runs in verbose mode, and you can see some more information. The first eight columns of data are blank because you haven't modified any of the files, but the next ones are the current working copy revision, followed by the revision the file last changed in (i.e., COMMITTED) and the author of the previous commit. Everything after the author is the path to the file.

`svn info`, as you might expect, enables you to find information about items in your working copy. For CVS users, `svn info` is somewhat similar to the `cvs status` command. Some of the more useful bits of information here that aren't available elsewhere are the URL of the item in the repository, the universally unique identifier (UUID) of the repository the item came from, the MD5 checksum of the file's contents, and the dates on which the file's text and properties were last modified. `svn info` isn't used especially often, but at times you'll need information about a working copy that you can't obtain in any other way, so keep it in mind.

In this example, you can see that `svn info` tells you that, among other things, `main.c` has a URL of `file:///path/to/repos/trunk/main.c`; it comes from a repository with a UUID of `18dffd47-64c3-0310-bd18-cbeae88b449f`; it's at revision 2; it was last changed by user `rooneg` on Saturday, July 26, 2003; and it has an MD5 checksum of `0c1ea17162fcd46023bf6712a35dba03`.

Modifying Your Working Copy

Now that you have a working copy checked out, it's time to start making changes to it. Suppose you've made some changes to some files, and you want to see what you've done. Subversion provides two commands for that purpose. First, there's `svn status`, which you've already seen. Second, once you know that your working copy has actually been modified, you can run `svn diff` to see exactly what has been changed. Let's take a look at how these commands work:

```
$ svn status
```

```
M      bar.c
```

```
$ svn status -v
```

	2	2	rooneg	.
M	2	2	rooneg	bar.c
	2	2	rooneg	foo.c
	2	2	rooneg	main.c

```
$ svn diff
```

```
Index: bar.c
===================================================================
--- bar.c        (revision 2)
+++ bar.c        (working copy)
@@ -1,5 +1,5 @@
 void
 bar (int a, int b)
 {
-  printf ("b = %d, a = %d\n", a, b);
+  printf ("b = %d, a = %d\n", b, a);
 }
$
```

svn status shows that bar.c has had its text modified, because the first column in the output is an M, and svn diff shows that you changed a single line in the file.

Assuming that you're sure that this is what you want, it's time to publish the changes for everyone else to see with the svn commit command. Running svn commit is similar to using svn mkdir to create directories directly in the repository, in that both modify the repository. This means that the commit will require a log message, which again can be either specified on the command line via the -m or --file flag, or entered into a text editor before the commit will proceed. Here's an example:

```
$ svn commit
```

```
Sending        bar.c
svn: Commit failed (details follow):
svn: Out of date: '/trunk/bar.c' in txn '8'
svn: Your commit message was left in a temporary file:
svn:     '/home/rooneg/work/myproject/svn-commit.tmp'
$
```

OK, that's definitely not what you would expect to see. It appears that someone has made a change to bar.c since you checked it out from the repository. Let's take a look at some commands that will tell you a bit more about what has happened. You've already learned that you can use svn status to see what you've changed in your local working copy, but it's also possible to pass it the -u flag, which tells svn status to contact the repository and figure out what files have been changed in more recent revisions. You can also use svn diff -rBASE:HEAD to see the difference between your BASE revision (the version you've checked out) and HEAD (the current version in the repository), and you can use svn log -r BASE:HEAD to read the log messages for the commits that may have caused the error. Let's see how this works:

```
$ svn status -u
```

```
M       *       2    bar.c
        *       2    foo.c
?                    svn-commit.tmp
Status against revision:       3
```

```
$ svn diff -r BASE:HEAD
```

```
Index: foo.c
===================================================================
--- foo.c        (working copy)
+++ foo.c        (revision 3)
@@ -1,5 +1,5 @@
 void
 foo(int a, int b)
 {
-  printf ("a = %d, b = %d\n", a, b);
+  printf ("arguments: a = %d, b = %d\n", a, b);
 }
Index: bar.c
===================================================================
--- bar.c        (working copy)
+++ bar.c        (revision 3)
@@ -1,5 +1,5 @@
 void
 bar (int a, int b)
 {
-  printf ("b = %d, a = %d\n", a, b);
+  printf (""arguments: b = %d, a = %d\n", a, b);
 }
```

```
$ svn log -r BASE:HEAD
```

```
------------------------------------------------------------------------
r2 | rooneg | 2003-06-08 09:56:24 -0400 (Sun, 08 Jun 2003) | 1 line
importing my project
------------------------------------------------------------------------
r3 | colonr | 2003-06-08 10:00:42 -0400 (Sun, 08 Jun 2003) | 4 lines
* foo.c
  (foo): changed output.
* bar.c
  (bar): ditto.
------------------------------------------------------------------------
$
```

svn status -u shows you that both foo.c and bar.c have been changed since you checked them out (they have an * in column 8 of the status output), and svn-commit.tmp (which holds the log message from your failed commit) isn't under Subversion's control. Diffing the BASE and HEAD revisions shows you that the line in bar.c that you changed had already changed in HEAD. svn log -r BASE:HEAD shows you that in revision 3 the user colonr changed the output in both foo.c and bar.c, causing the conflict.

Well, now you know why you can't commit the change in its current state, but that doesn't change the fact that you still need to get that bug fix into the repository. To do this, you'll need to run svn update, which will result in a conflict because your changes and those committed in revision 3 by the user colonr both changed the same line of bar.c. Then you'll have to manually fix the conflict and run svn resolved to tell Subversion that you're satisfied with it. Finally, you'll be able to run svn commit to get your fix into the repository.

```
$ svn update
```

```
U  foo.c
C  bar.c
Updated to revision 3.
```

```
$ ls
```

```
bar.c           bar.c.r2        foo.c           svn-commit.tmp
bar.c.mine      bar.c.r3        main.c
```

```
$ cat bar.c
```

```
cat bar.c
void
bar (int a, int b)
{
<<<<<< .mine
  printf ("b = %d, a = %d\n", b, a);
=======
  printf ("arguments: b = %d, a = %d\n", a, b);
>>>>>> .r3
}
$
```

So here you've run svn update, and it merged the change to foo.c into the version in your working copy (which isn't all that difficult, considering that you hadn't changed foo.c locally). Subversion also noticed that revision 3's change to bar.c conflicted with your local change, so it placed bar.c in a conflicted state (note the C in the output from svn update).

When a file is in conflict, several things happen. First, several copies of the file are left in your working copy, one ending with .mine, which is your original modified version; one with .rOLDVERSION (.r2 in this case), which holds the original version you started modifying (the BASE revision); and one ending in .rNEWVERSION (.r3 in this case), which holds the new version (HEAD from the repository). These are present so that you can easily run third-party diff and merge programs on the files, and so you can refer to the various versions of the file easily while performing a merge. Second, assuming that the file in question is a textual file and not a raw binary format, it's modified to show both your modified version of the change and the version from the repository. Third, some bookkeeping information about the conflict is recorded in the administrative directory. The next steps are to resolve the conflict manually and to run svn resolved to tell Subversion that you're satisfied with the changes:

```
$ vi bar.c
```

```
[ ... resolve conflict manually ... ]
```

```
$ cat bar.c
```

```
void
bar (int a, int b)
{
  printf ("arguments: b = %d, a = %d\n", b, a);
}
```

```
$ svn resolved bar.c
```

```
Resolved conflicted state of "bar.c"
```

```
$ svn commit --file svn-commit.tmp
```

```
Sending        bar.c
Transmitting file data .
Committed revision 5.
$
```

Now your change has been committed to the repository. This general sequence of events—edit, update, status, diff, possibly resolve, and commit—will make up the majority of your time spent with Subversion, so be sure to become familiar with it.

Adding, Copying, Renaming, and Removing Files

Well, you've learned the basics, the Subversion commands that fill 90% of your day-to-day routine, but sooner or later you'll need to hit that last 10%, so let's get on with it. So far we've mainly seen commands associated with making changes to the contents of files and committing them to the repository. But if you recall, Subversion doesn't just version file contents, it versions tree structures. This next section covers the commands that let you make changes to those tree structures by adding, copying, renaming, and deleting files and directories.

Adding Files and Directories

At some point you're almost certainly going to want to add some new files or directories to your Subversion repository, so you'll have to become familiar with the svn add command. It works just as you would expect: You check out a working copy, create the file (or directory), and run svn add FILENAME. This schedules the file for addition, and later you can run svn commit to complete the process. The whole procedure looks like this:

```
$ ls
```

```
Makefile bar.c    foo.c    main.c
```

```
$ svn status
```

```
?      Makefile
```

```
$ svn add Makefile
```

```
A        Makefile
```

```
$ svn status
```

```
A      Makefile
```

```
$ svn commit -m "Added Makefile"
```

```
Adding        Makefile
Transmitting file data .
Committed revision 6.
```

```
$ svn status -v
```

```
        3        3     rooneg    .
        6        6     rooneg    Makefile
        5        5     rooneg    bar.c
        4        4     colonr    foo.c
        2        2     rooneg    main.c
$
```

So again, you have some new output to interpret. The first svn status has a ? in the first column of the line about Makefile, which means that Makefile isn't currently under Subversion's control. Next, you run svn add Makefile, and Makefile is scheduled for addition, which you can see from the output of the second svn status, where the first column is an A. You then commit the change, adding Makefile to the repository, and the final svn status -v shows it as any other versioned file.

If you're adding a new directory, there's no need to create and add it in two steps, because you can use Subversion's svn mkdir command, which you used earlier to create directories in the repository, in the working copy as well. Simply run svn mkdir DIRNAME, and it will create the new directory and schedule it for addition when you next commit, all in one step. If you created the directory before you decided to add it, a regular svn add will schedule it, and all of its contents, for addition. If you don't want to add all of the directory's contents, you can pass the --non-recursive flag to svn add, and only the top-level directory will be scheduled for addition.

Copying and Moving Versioned Items

Adding a file or directory to your version control system isn't all that interesting, but where Subversion really shines is in its ability to copy and rename files and directories while still retaining their revision history. Many other version control systems, specifically RCS, and the systems built on top of them, such as Perforce and CVS, don't make it easy to do this. In Perforce, you can work around the lack of a copy or move command by integrating from one file to another, and then possibly deleting the original. In CVS you can fake things by poking around in the repository by hand and copying the RCS files around. But neither gives you a true copy or move command. In Subversion, the operation is as simple as svn copy FROM TO or svn move FROM TO. For simple copying or moving of a file or directory within your project, you generally do this within a working copy, and FROM and TO are the path to the source and destination. For some other operations, it's more convenient to perform the copy or move in the repository directly, but we'll hold off on covering that until we discuss branches and tags later in the "Working with Branches and Tags" section. For now, let's take a look at an example of how to use svn copy and svn move.

```
$ ls
```

```
Makefile  bar.c     foo.c     main.c
```

```
$ svn status
$ svn copy bar.c baz.c
```

```
A         baz.c
```

```
$ svn status
```

```
A  +   baz.c
```

```
$ svn commit -m "copied bar.c to baz.c"
```

```
Adding         baz.c
Committed revision 7.
```

```
$ svn status -v
```

```
                3       3       rooneg   .
                6       6       rooneg   Makefile
                5       5       rooneg   bar.c
                7       7       rooneg   baz.c
                4       4       colonr   foo.c
                2       2       rooneg   main.c
```

```
$ svn move bar.c zot.c
```

```
A         zot.c
D         bar.c
```

```
$ svn status
```

```
D      bar.c
A  +   zot.c
```

```
$ svn commit -m "renamed bar.c to zot.c"
```

```
Deleting        bar.c
Adding          zot.c
Committed revision 8.
```

```
$ svn status -v
```

```
           3         3     rooneg    .
           6         6     rooneg    Makefile
           7         7     rooneg    baz.c
           4         4     colonr    foo.c
           2         2     rooneg    main.c
           8         8     rooneg    zot.c
$
```

You've seen most of this output already, but the second svn status has something new. The fourth column of output for baz.c is a +, which means that the file has been added with history. When the change is committed to the repository, the fact that baz.c is a copy of foo.c is recorded, so the revision history of the file remains intact. Similarly, when you move bar.c to zot.c, the output of svn status shows that foo.c has been deleted (and thus has a D in the first column of its line of status output), and zot.c has been added with history. Again, this fact is recorded in the repository at commit time.

Deleting Versioned Items

Now that you've mastered adding, moving, and copying files, the last of the basic tasks you're likely to perform in the working copy is removing files and directories. As you might expect, the command to do this is svn delete, and it works much as you would expect. svn delete PATH removes the file or directory at PATH and schedules it for removal from the repository. When you next use svn commit, the file or directory is removed from the repository itself. Let's take a look at the process:

```
$ ls
```

```
Makefile  baz.c     foo.c     main.c    zot.c
```

```
$ svn status
$ svn delete baz.c
```

```
D         baz.c
```

```
$ svn status
```

```
D     baz.c
```

```
$ svn commit -m "removing baz.c"
```

```
Deleting        baz.c
Committed revision 9.
```

```
$ svn status -v
```

```
            3       3     rooneg   .
            6       6     rooneg   Makefile
            4       4     colonr   foo.c
            2       2     rooneg   main.c
            8       8     rooneg   zot.c
$
```

This output is quite similar to what you saw when you moved a file. When you've deleted something it shows up in the output of svn status with a D in the first column.

Note that although the file has been removed from the HEAD revision of the repository, it still exists in the previous revisions, and you can easily get the file back either by using svn copy to copy the file from the previous revision into your working copy or by using svn merge to reverse the entire commit that removed it. We discuss the svn merge technique later in the "Working with Branches and Tags" section, but let's now look at how you use svn copy to "undelete" a file:

```
$ ls
```

```
Makefile  foo.c     main.c    zot.c
```

```
$ svn copy --revision 8 file:///path/to/repos/trunk/baz.c baz.c
```

```
A     baz.c
```

```
$ svn commit -m "resurrect baz.c from the repository"
```

```
Adding         baz.c
Committed revision 10.
$
```

OK, so what happened here? You just copied baz.c as it existed in revision 8 (the last revision before you deleted it) directly from the repository into your working copy. Then you committed the change, and the process of restoring the deleted file completed. No matter what kind of change you make to your project in HEAD, all previous versions always exist in the repository, so you can always revert to the previous state if you make a mistake. You can even do this in a single command, without a working copy at all, by performing the copy within the repository itself, something you'll explore in the next section when you learn about using svn copy to work with branches and tags.

Working with Branches and Tags

Another of Subversion's improvements over CVS is its ability to create branches and tags in constant time and space, as opposed to in time and space proportional to the number of files involved, as in CVS. Subversion accomplishes this by leveraging the design of its versioning repository filesystem. Branches and tags are copies of existing directories, usually placed in specific directories so that users know they're "special."

There are a variety of reasons you might want to create a branch or tag. Generally, you use tags to mark a particular version of your project so you can easily refer back to it later. You might want to make a tag when you release a new version of your project, so that later on you don't have to remember what revision of the repository corresponds to that particular release. Instead of remembering what revision of the trunk corresponds to the release, you can just look at the copy you placed under the tags directory.

Branches are a little more complex. Rather than just making a copy and leaving it there so you can look at it later, as with a tag, you create a branch so that it can be modified. Sometimes you might want to make some changes to your project and check them in to the repository so that other people can see them, but you don't want to make them in the main development version. Perhaps they're experimental and might never be committed to the mainline version, or maybe this is a branch you want to make a release from and only want to allow bug fixes. In cases like these you might want to create a new development branch by making a separate copy of the trunk and then commit your changes to the branch. If you later decide that the changes are ready, they can be merged into the version of the project in the trunk and committed so that everyone can see them.

Creating Branches and Tags

Although you could create a branch or tag by checking out the top level of the repository and doing a standard svn copy in your working copy, that would be quite inefficient. You would use up a huge amount of disk space and possibly network bandwidth in creating the initial working copy, because you would be checking out every branch and tag in the repository simultaneously, and then svn copy would have to do a lot of extra disk I/O copying files around, only to end up wasting a lot of bandwidth again committing your branch or tag to the repository. Fortunately the Subversion developers anticipated this problem and designed the svn copy command to run against the repository directly, as well as within the working copy. Creating a tag is as simple as this:

```
$ svn copy file:///path/to/repos/trunk file:///path/to/repos/tags/0.9-release \
    -m "tagging 0.9 release"
```

```
Committed revision 11.
```

```
$ svn diff file:///path/to/repos/trunk file:///path/to/repos/tags/0.9-release
```

```
$
```

As you can see from the output of svn diff, the tag is identical to the HEAD revision of /trunk. Creating a new branch is done in exactly the same way. The only difference is that a tag is intended to never be modified again (this may be enforced by various means; see Chapter 5 for how to do it with Subversion authentication modules), whereas a branch will be used for further development.

■**Note** mod_authz_svn is an Apache module that works with Subversion's Apache-based server to allow you to control which users have access to various parts of your repository. mod_authz_svn might be used to control who can create new branches or tags, or who can write to a particular branch.

Merging Changes Between Branches

For a branch to be of much use, the version control system needs to provide a way to manage the process of merging changes between related branches. Generally a branch is created for some kind of development, and at some point in the future either changes from the branch will have to be merged back into the trunk (or wherever the branch originated) or changes from the trunk will have to be merged into the branch (this is common in the case of long-lived branches to support released versions of software). In Subversion, the process of merging changes is handled by the svn merge command. The merge command has three modes of operation. In the first, you give the command two source URLs (with optional revisions specified with @REVNUM at the end of the URL), and it will merge the differences between the two sources into your current working directory (or another directory if it's specified on the command line). The process looks like this:

```
$ svn copy file:///path/to/repos/tags/0.9-release \
          file:///path/to/repos/branches/my-development-branch \
          -m "create development branch from version 0.9 tag"
```

```
Committed revision 12.
```

```
$ svn checkout file:///path/to/repos/branches/my-development-branch wc
```

```
A  wc/Makefile
A  wc/foo.c
A  wc/baz.c
A  wc/zot.c
A  wc/main.c
Checked out revision 12.
```

```
$ cd wc
```

```
[ ... do some work, make some changes, commit them to the branch ... ]
```

```
$
```

```
[ ... time passes, changes are made in the trunk, version 1.0 is released,
      and now you want to merge changes between 0.9 and 1.0 into your branch ... ]
```

```
$ svn merge file:///path/to/repos/tags/0.9-release \
           file:///path/to/repos/tags/1.0-release \
           .
```

```
A  bar.c
A  README
A  baz.c
D  foo.c
```

```
$ svn status
```

```
A  +    README
A  +    bar.c
A  +    baz.c
D       foo.c
```

```
$ svn commit -m "merge changes from trunk up to 1.0 release into dev branch"
```

```
Adding          README
Adding          bar.c
Adding          baz.c
Deleting        foo.c
Transmitting file data ...
Committed revision 20.
$
```

First, you make a development branch by copying the 0.9-release tag. Then you use the branch for some private development, committing changes into it as desired. In the meantime, more changes are made to the version in /trunk and the 1.0 version is tagged as tags/1.0-release. At this point you merge the changes that occurred between the point you created your branch and the time 1.0 was tagged into your local working copy (which was checked out from the branch) and commit them. Now your branch is up-to-date with regard to all the changes that were made to the trunk. Note that just like when you run svn update, when you merge changes into your working copy there's always the chance of a conflict, and any that occur will have to be resolved before you can continue. Likewise, as with any other change to a working copy, you'll have to svn commit the results of the merge for them to be propagated back into the repository.

More often, you'll need to merge a particular change or set of changes from one branch into another. For example, say you have a branch that's being used to manage the "stable" release of your software, separate from the main development trunk, where more complex, destabilizing changes are being made. When a bug fix is made to the main version of the code in the trunk, you might want to merge that particular change into the stable branch, so it will be in the next release. In this case, when the change you're merging is a particular revision, you can use a slightly simpler version of the svn merge, where there's a single source (which can be a URL or a working copy path), the revisions of which are specified via the standard -r START:END syntax. The changes to that source path over that range of revisions will be merged into your current working directory (or another working copy directory if one is given on the command line). The process looks like this:

```
$ svn merge -r 12:13 file:///path/to/repos/branches/my-development-branch
```

```
U  main.c
U  zot.c
```

```
$ svn status
```

```
M     main.c
M     zot.c
```

```
$ svn commit -m "merged changes from development branch into trunk"
```

```
Sending        main.c
Sending        zot.c
Transmitting file data ..
Committed revision 30.
$
```

Here the change to /branches/my-development-branch from revision 13 has been merged into a checked-out version of the trunk. Once the user verifies that the change is correct, it can be committed and the process will be complete.

USING SVN MERGE TO REVERT A CHANGE

A less common use of svn merge is to revert the change committed in a particular revision. To do this, you simply reverse the order of the revision arguments. For example, to revert the change to main.c that occurred in revision 5, you run svn merge -r 5:4 main.c. This means, literally, to apply the change needed to go from revision 5 of main.c to revision 4 of main.c to the version of main.c in your current working directory. In practice, you can use this to revert a particular change that shouldn't have been committed.

Switching to Another Branch

Because creating branches in Subversion is cheap (in terms of time and disk space at least), some thought has gone into how to make them easier to work with. One feature that makes working with branches considerably simpler is the svn switch command. svn switch lets you move your checked-out working copy (and any changes you made to it, assuming they don't conflict) to another branch in the repository. Standard use is either to migrate an entire working copy from one branch to another or, more commonly, to move specific parts of your working copy to another branch.

The best way to understand this concept is probably through an example. Say that you're adding a new feature to Subversion itself but the work is going to take some time to complete. Subversion uses an *unstable* /trunk policy, which means that most development is done right in the main /trunk branch. However, for changes that are likely to be either disruptive to other developers (by breaking existing functionality for a time, for example) or that are highly experimental and might never be destined to be merged into the trunk, a branch will be created.

The Subversion code base is split into several libraries, each of which lives in its own subdirectory. Because most changes of this sort will be limited to one of those libraries, you might make the branch via an svn copy command targeting the repository directly, and then switch the affected subdirectory over to that branch. As you continue to make modifications to that subdirectory, you can safely commit them to the repository, and none of the other developers will have to see them unless they specifically check out (or switch to) that branch. You can safely svn update all the other directories in your working copy to track the latest changes other developers are making to the trunk.

This ensures that your modifications to one library will continue to work with the latest version of the software (making the eventual merging of the changes into the trunk easier), while avoiding the need to inconvenience other developers by making disruptive changes in the trunk. The only thing you need to remember is that other developers could be making changes to the same library you're working on in the trunk, so as those changes occur, you need to merge them into your development branch to ensure that your final merge doesn't obliterate the other developers' changes. Let's see a quick example of how this can work:

```
$ svn list file:///path/to/repos/trunk
```

```
library_one/
library_two/
library_three/
main.c
```

```
$ svn copy -m "create branch for development of library one" \
      file:///path/to/repos/trunk \
      file:///path/to/repos/branches/library-one-dev
```

```
Committed revision 10.
```

```
$ svn checkout file:///path/to/repos/trunk wc
```

```
[ ... lots of output ... ]
```

```
$ cd wc
$ svn info library_one | grep ^URL
```

```
URL: file:///path/to/repos/trunk/library_one
```

```
$ svn switch file:///path/to/repos/branches/library-one-dev/library_one \
            library_one
```

```
At revision 10.
```

```
$ svn info library_one | grep ^URL
```

```
URL: file:///path/to/repos/branches/library-one-dev/library_one
```

```
$ svn status
```

```
    S  library_one
$
```

In this example, you start out by making a new branch by copying the trunk, which contains a single C file, main.c, and several subdirectories, each of which contains an independent library of code that's used by main.c.

You then check out the trunk, so your copy of the library_one directory has a URL of file:///path/to/repos/trunk/library_one. Next, you use svn switch to switch your copy of library_one over to the development branch. Its URL now points to the version of library_one on the development branch you created, and when you run svn status you can see that it's switched because of the S in the fifth column of the status output.

Going forward, each time you run any command that involves library_one or any of its contents, it will refer to the versions of those files that live on the branch. Updates will pull down changes that occur on the branch, commits of changes you make to it will be committed to the branch, and so forth. This allows you to track the changes that are being made on the branch in the context of the changes to the rest of the project that are going on in the trunk, which can be quite useful for a couple of reasons. First off, it allows the developers not working on changes to the library_one directory to avoid having to deal with your changes, which could be experimental or large enough that they introduce temporary breakage. Second, it allows you to make sure your new changes work with what others are doing in the trunk, without having to explicitly merge those changes over to the trunk, which simplifies the process of working on your branch.

Changing a Repository URL with svn switch --relocate

There's one other time you might need to use svn switch, and that's when the URL you use to access your Subversion repository has changed. This could happen if the URL has moved to another machine, the path it's located at changes, or if you switch from one repository access layer to another (say you want to stop accessing the repository directly via a file:// URL and start accessing over a network with an http:// or an svn:// URL). In these situations you use the --relocate flag with svn switch and give it the portions of the URL you're changing. For example, if the repository was accessed via ra_local on your local machine at the path /home/repos, and you need to change to accessing it over ra_svn, because this working copy has been moved to a different machine, you do something like this:

```
$ svn info | grep ^URL
```

```
URL: file:///home/repos/trunk
```

```
$ svn switch --relocate file:/// svn://servername/
$ svn info | grep ^URL
```

```
URL: svn://servername/home/repos/trunk
$
```

Note that `svn switch --relocate` will work only if the new URL points to the exact same repository. Each Subversion repository has its own UUID, and the client will compare the UUID for the new repository to the one from the old repository and ensure that they're the same before allowing the switch to complete.

Removing Old Branches

One more advantage of Subversion's "everything is a copy" design is that there's no need to keep old development branches around in the HEAD version of the repository. Once a branch's useful life has ended, a simple `svn delete` will remove it from HEAD, and users will no longer be bothered by its presence in the output of `svn list` commands. Of course, the branch will still exist in the history of the repository, so you can easily retrieve any of its contents later by just specifying the correct revision of the repository.

Working with Locks

There are some files that just can't be merged contextually, and as a result don't work well in a nonlocking model. Most of these files are binary files, usually containing drawings or some other unmergable data. Subversion's locking and unlocking features can be used to deal with these files.

Locking a file is a simple matter: you just call `svn lock` on the file, and for kindness to other people trying to figure out why the file is locked, specify a message:

```
$ svn lock unmergable.bin –message "Working on drawing for the next hour"
```

```
'unmergable.bin' locked by user 'dannyb'
```

```
$ svn status unmergable.bin
```

```
    K unmergable.bin
```

The K status means that the file is locked. If someone else attempts to commit changes to this file, they will not be able to and will receive a message that the file is locked.

The user who locked the file can unlock it by committing or by an explicit `svn unlock` command:

```
$ svn unlock unmergable.bin
```

```
'unmergable.bin' unlocked
```

Committing a change will also remove all of your locks in the directories touched by the commit, unless you specifically request otherwise (using the `--no-unlock` option to commit). This is done in order to discourage people from locking files for a long period of time.

Locking should not be treated as a security mechanism of any sort. While, in general, only the person who locked the file can unlock it, it is possible for someone else to break and steal locks. To break a lock, the URL to the file must be provided:

```
$ svn unlock –force http://example/repos/trunk/unmergable.bin
```

```
'unmergable.bin' unlocked
```

Stealing locks can be performed using this command line, with `svn lock` instead of `svn unlock`.

If you want to know whether someone else has a file locked, you can run `svn status -u` on the file (which will display locked files as having O status if they are locked by other people), or `svn info` on the URL. `svn info` will also display the lock comment for a locked file.

Besides the standard commands to work with locks, it is possible to set the policies for locking, stealing, and unlocking, using hook scripts.

Properties

Subversion allows you to associate arbitrary metadata with files, directories, and even revisions in the repository. Each bit of metadata, or *property*, consists of a name, which can be a string consisting of letters, numbers, and colons (with no spaces), and an arbitrary value, which can be anything at all. Internally, this functionality is used to implement a variety of different features of Subversion (log entries are properties associated with each revision, for example), but it's also exposed to users for their own use. You could, for example, choose to mark files with a *maintainer* property to indicate which developer is responsible for it. In addition to your own properties, Subversion reserves all properties starting with the prefix `svn:` for itself, and you can manipulate several properties in that namespace to control Subversion's behavior in useful ways. Before diving into those, though, let's look at the commands you need to use to work with properties.

First, you'll need a way to tell what, if any, properties have been set on a particular versioned resource. The `svn proplist` command, as you might expect, does that for you. Let's take a look at how it works:

```
$ ls -a
```

```
.svn
index.html
button.png
```

```
$ svn proplist index.html
```

```
Properties on 'index.html':
  svn:mime-type
```

```
$ svn proplist button.png
```

```
Properties on 'button.png':
  svn:mime-type
$
```

Here you can see a working copy that holds the contents of a web site. The files index.html and button.png both have the svn:mime-type property, which is a special property Subversion uses internally to track the MIME type of a file.

Well, now you've seen what properties have been set on a particular file, but that's not very useful unless you can determine what value they've been set to. The svn propget command prints out the value of a given property for you. The syntax for the command is simple. It takes as its first argument the name of the property you're printing out, and subsequent arguments are the files it should use as targets:

```
$ svn propget svn:mime-type index.html
```

```
text/html
```

```
$ svn propget svn:mime-type button.png
```

```
image/png
$
```

As you might have guessed, index.html has the svn:mime-type of text/html, and button.png has image/png.

To make use of properties, you'll need to be able to set and change them. To do that, you'll need to use the svn propset and svn propedit commands. svn propset sets the value of a specific property on a versioned entity. You specify the property as its first argument, and then the second argument can be the value or, if you're dealing with a value that would be inconvenient to deal with on the command line, you can specify a file that holds the contents of the property via the -F filename argument. Subsequent arguments are the targets on which the property will be set:

```
$ svn add logo.png
```

```
A  (bin)  logo.png
```

```
$ svn commit -m "added logo.png"
```

```
Adding  (bin)  logo.png
Transmitting file data .
Committed revision 35.
```

```
$ svn propget svn:mime-type logo.png
```

```
application/octet-stream
```

```
$ svn propset svn:mime-type image/png logo.png
```

```
property 'svn:mime-type' set on 'logo.png'
```

```
$ svn status
```

```
M     logo.png
```

```
$ svn propget svn:mime-type logo.png
```

```
image/png
```

```
$ svn commit -m "set mime-type on logo.png to image/png"
```

```
Sending        logo.png
Committed revision 36.
$
```

Note that the MIME type of logo.png was set to application/octet-stream when you first added it. This is the default behavior when Subversion determines that the file isn't plain text, and it will prevent Subversion from doing things like end-of-line conversion or keyword substitution, which would be destructive when applied to a binary file. It also keeps Subversion from attempting to display textual diffs in the output of svn diff or from automatically merging in changes during svn update, both of which aren't possible with binary files. Later, when you set the svn:mime-type to image/png, you'll see yet another new kind of output from svn status. The M in the second column of the output indicates that the file's properties have been modified. Also note that you had to commit the change back to the repository, because like most other things in Subversion, properties that are set on files and directories are versioned.

Similar to svn propset is svn propedit, which allows you to edit the contents of a property in your default text editor. Let's take a look at how this works:

```
$ svn proplist .
```

```
Properties on '':
  svn:ignore
```

```
$ svn propget svn:ignore .
```

```
*~
.*~
```

```
$ svn propedit svn:ignore .
```

```
[
  editor pops up with contents of svn:ignore in it.
  we edit it, save, and exit
]
```

```
$ svn status
```

```
  M     .
```

```
$ svn diff
```

```
Property changes on:
```

```
Name: svn:ignore
   - *~
.*~
   + *~
.*~
.DS_Store
```

```
$ svn commit -m "added .DS_store to svn:ignore"
```

```
Sending        .
Committed revision 50.
$
```

This example shows how you can use svn propedit to edit the svn:ignore property. Also note that the svn diff command shows you the changes you make to properties as well as to the contents of files. Don't focus too much on the specifics of the value of the svn:ignore property (we'll discuss that in a minute)—just remember that the svn propedit command allows you to modify a property with an editor and that svn diff will show you the difference once you do.

As you can see by the long help message for svn propset, Subversion has several special properties, some of which you've already seen. You can set these special properties on your files and directories to control Subversion's behavior in certain ways, as shown in Table 2-3.

Table 2-3. *Special Properties*

Name	Purpose
svn:ignore	Indicates which files in a directory should be ignored by svn status and svn add commands.
svn:keywords	Indicates which RCS style keywords should be expanded in a given file.
svn:executable	Indicates that a given file should be made executable, if such a thing is possible on the operating system in question.
svn:eol-style	Indicates what style line endings should be used for a given textual file.
svn:mime-type	Indicates what MIME type should be used when a given file is served from a mod_dav_svn-enabled Apache server. It is also used to determine whether a file is binary or text for purposes of merging and diffing.
svn:needs-lock	Indicates whether the file should be locked before editing.
svn:externals	Lists directories within a given directory that should be retrieved from alternate URLs.

svn:mime-type

The simplest of Subversion's special properties is svn:mime-type, which tells Subversion what MIME type a particular file is. This is used in two ways. First, if a file has some other MIME type that doesn't start with text, it won't try to automatically merge changes into the file or do end-of-line translation or keyword expansion, which rely on a file being textual in nature. This keeps Subversion from accidentally mangling binary files, something that can be a constant problem in other version control systems (specifically CVS, and to a lesser degree Perforce). When you run svn add on a file, Subversion will attempt to determine if the file you're adding is textual, and if it isn't, it will set the MIME type to application/octet-stream, which just means that the file is some kind of binary format. If you want a more specific MIME type, you'll have to set it manually with svn propset or svn propedit. The second reason for setting an svn:mime-type property is so that Subversion's mod_dav_svn Apache module can serve the file as the correct MIME type. This allows you to browse the repository in a web browser and have things generally work as you expect (e.g., HTML pages are rendered as HTML instead of plain text, images can be viewed as the appropriate image type, etc.). You'll explore mod_dav_svn further in the next chapter.

svn:ignore

The other special property you've already seen is svn:ignore, which is Subversion's equivalent of CVS's .cvsignore feature. Often files will show up in your working copy that don't want to be checked in to Subversion—for example, object files that are generated as part of a program's build process, or backup files that are generated by text editors. To keep these files from constantly showing up in the output of svn status and generally being annoying, you can simply add an entry to the directory's svn:ignore property that matches their filenames, and svn status will ignore them, unless you pass it the --no-ignore option. This can probably be best shown with an example:

```
$ ls -a
```

```
./          Makefile    main.c      foo.c
../          .svn/       main.c~     foo.c~
```

```
$ svn status
```

```
?       main.c~
?       foo.c~
```

```
$ svn propset svn:ignore "*~" .
```

```
property 'svn:ignore' set on "."
```

```
$ svn status
```

```
M       .
```

```
$ svn commit -m "added *~ to svn:ignore"
```

```
Sending         .
Committed revision 70.
```

```
$ svn status
$ svn status --no-ignore
```

```
I       main.c~
I       foo.c~
$
```

As usual, you can find some more information about the output of svn status in this example. At first, the main.c~ and foo.c~ files show up as unversioned files.[2] This is somewhat irritating and clutters up the output of svn status, because you normally don't care about the backup files generated by your editor. To get rid of that output, you set the svn:ignore property on the directory to *~, and you can see that the next svn status shows you the property modification on the directory but doesn't say anything about the files that end in a tilde (~). You then commit, and the third svn status shows you nothing at all. Finally, you see that it's possible to run svn status --no-ignore, and you're informed by the I in the first column that the main.c~ and foo.c~ files are indeed being ignored. To add more patterns to the list of things to be ignored, just place them on separate lines in the property.

svn:needs-lock

One of the nicer features of the locking system is that you can specify which files should be locked before editing them. When this property is set on a file it will be read-only until svn lock is called on the file. This is useful in order to ensure that locking of unmergable files occurs before they are edited. Once svn unlock is used on the file (or the change is committed), the file will become read-only again. It is a recommended practice to set this property on any file that cannot be merged contextually. The reasoning behind this is that if you have an unmergable file, svn lock protects you from wasting time because of commits made by other people, and svn:needs-lock protects other people from making changes while you've got the lock.

svn:keywords

One feature of the RCS-based version control systems that you haven't yet seen in Subversion is the ability to embed special keywords in files and have Subversion expand them into something when the file is checked out. You'll generally use this to embed the revision in which the file was last changed or the URL of the file in the repository (or something like that) in the file so that the information will be easy to access without having to use Subversion. This can be important if you're rolling a release of some software and you want people to be able to accurately report what version of a particular file they have when sending in bug reports. In some other version control systems, keywords turn out to be a mixed blessing, because it's quite possible for there to be a file that contains the keyword, but it would be a bad idea for Subversion to expand it (binary files come to mind). For this reason, Subversion defaults to not expanding any keywords. If you want Subversion to do so, you need only set the svn:keywords property on the file to a string containing the names of the keywords you would like expanded, separated by spaces, and it will expand them for you.

Subversion supports the following keywords: HeadURL (abbreviated as URL), which expands to the URL of the file in the repository; LastChangedBy (abbreviated as Author), which expands to the username of the last person who modified the file; LastChangedDate (abbreviated as Date), which stores the date on which the file was last modified; LastChangedRevision (abbreviated as Rev or Revision), which stores the revision in which the file last changed; and Id, which stores a compressed version of the other four keywords. Let's take a look at how these keywords work in an example:

---

2. Technically, if you run this command in a working copy directory that's full of files ending in a tilde (~), you won't see anything, because the default list of global-ignores used by Subversion includes *~. To modify this list, you can edit the ~/.subversion/config file.

```
$ cat main.c
```

```
#include <stdio.h>
int
main (int argc, char *argv[])
{
  printf ("hello world\n");
  return 0;
}
```

```
$ vi main.c
```

```
[ ... add keywords ... ]
```

```
$ cat main.c
```

```
/* $URL$
 * $Rev$
 * $Author$
 * $Date$
 * $Id$
 */
#include <stdio.h>
int
main (int argc, char *argv[])
{
  printf ("hello world\n");
  return 0;
}
```

```
$ svn propset svn:keywords "Url Rev Author Date Id" main.c
```

```
property 'svn:keywords' set on 'main.c'
```

```
$ svn commit -m "Set svn:keywords on main.c"
```

```
Sending        main.c
Committed revision 75.
```

```
$ cat main.c
```

```
/* $URL: file:///path/to/repos/trunk/main.c $
 * $Rev: 3 $
 * $Author: rooneg $
 * $Date: 2003-06-30 18:37:06 -0400 (Mon, 30 Jun 2003) $
 * $Id: main.c 3 2003-06-30 22:37:06Z rooneg $
 */
#include <stdio.h>
int
main (int argc, char *argv[])
{
  printf ("hello world\n");
  return 0;
}
$
```

In this example, a comment is added to the top of main.c, which contains the URL, $Rev, $Author$, $Date$, and Id keywords. Then the svn:keywords property is set to Url Rev Author Date Id, and the change is committed. After the commit, the keywords in main.c expand to hold information about the current version of main.c.

svn:eol-style

A constant issue for developers of cross-platform software is the fact that different operating systems use different characters to indicate the end of a line in a text file. Worse yet, some tools are extremely picky about the line endings of the files they consume. svn:eol-style makes it a bit easier to deal with such tools. By setting it to native, you can ensure that the file in question is always in the native end-of-line style, making it easy to interoperate with tools on the system. Unix operating systems (including Mac OS X) use LF line endings when native is specified; Windows-based systems use CRLF; and, hypothetically, Classic Mac OS systems would use CR, but that's academic because Subversion doesn't run on Classic Mac OS. For cases in which a specific line-ending style is always required (for example, the .dsp files Microsoft Visual Studio uses must use a carriage return and linefeed at the end of each line), you can set it to LF to indicate only linefeeds should be used, CR to indicate only carriage returns should be used, or CRLF to indicate carriage return/linefeed–style endings. As mentioned in the svn:mime-type discussion, these line-ending conversions can be applied only to files with a textual MIME type.

svn:executable

Another common need for software development is to specify that certain files are *executable*, meaning that the operating system can run them as full-fledged programs. This is a somewhat platform-specific thing to do, as some operating systems, such as Microsoft Windows, don't have a way to indicate that a particular file is executable. In any case, if the svn:executable property is set to any value, Subversion will use whatever platform-specific means it can to make the file executable when it's checked out into a working copy.

svn:externals

To provide something roughly analogous to CVS's modules, Subversion offers the svn:externals property. This property is set on a directory and contains a newline-separated list of module specifications. Each module specification contains a relative path to the directory the module should be checked out into, an optional revision (which is specified as -r REVNUM), and a URL pointing to a location in a Subversion repository. When the directory with the svn:externals property is checked out, the modules will also be checked out into the same working copy. This allows you to pull directories from other parts of the repository, or even completely different repositories, into your working copy, which can be useful if you're sharing code between multiple projects, or if you need to modify the directory layout of your working copy in certain situations:

```
$ svn list file:///path/to/repos
```

```
application/
libedit/
libnetwork/
```

```
$ svn propget file:///path/to/repos/application/trunk/libs svn:externals
```

```
libedit file:///path/to/repos/libedit/trunk
libnetwork file:///path/to/repos/libnetwork/trunk
```

```
$ svn checkout file:///path/to/repos/application/trunk application
```

```
A  application/README
A  application/main.c
A  application/libs
Checked out revision 47.
Fetching external item into libedit
A  application/libs/libedit/Makefile
A  application/libs/libedit/README
A  application/libs/libedit/edit.c
A  application/libs/libedit/history.c
A  application/libs/libedit/prompt.c
Checked out revision 47.
Fetching external item into libnetwork
A  application/libs/libnetwork/Makefile
A  application/libs/libnetwork/README
A  application/libs/libnetwork/socket.c
A  application/libs/libnetwork/marshal.c
Checked out revision 47.
```

```
$ svn info application/libs | grep ^URL
```

```
URL: file:///path/to/repos/application/trunk/libs
```

```
$ svn info application/libs/libedit | grep ^URL
```

```
URl: file:///path/to/repos/libedit/trunk
```

```
$ svn info application/libs/libnetwork | grep ^URL
```

```
URL: file:///path/to/repos/libnetwork/trunk
$
```

Here you can see an example of using svn:externals to allow everyone who checks out the source for an application, which lives in file:///path/to/repos/application/trunk, to also get the source for several libraries that the application depends on. In this case, the libraries are stored in the same repository as the application, but there's nothing that says they have to be. The URLs in the svn:externals property could just as easily point to a completely different repository, and it would work just the same.

Revision Properties

In addition to the standard versioned properties Subversion can store for each file or directory in your repository, there are properties stored for each revision in the repository. These *revprops* are used to record information such as the author of each revision (svn:author), the date and time the revision was created (svn:date), and the log entry for the revision (svn:log). Most of the time, you don't need to care about these properties. They're created automatically, and Subversion is perfectly capable of using them for the commands that require the information they store without any intervention from you.

The exception to this rule, of course, is when you need to go back and edit them. Most of the time you find people doing this when they want to adjust a log entry on an old revision. Because these properties are stored on a per-revision basis, they aren't themselves versioned. That means that if you change them, the previous version is lost for good (unless you resort to looking in your repository backups or something like that). Because of this, Subversion won't allow you to change revision properties unless you explicitly turn this capability on. To do this, you need to enable the pre-revprop-change hook script. The procedure for doing so is documented in the next chapter, so for now, all you need to know is that you should look inside the repository in the hooks directory. There, you'll see a file named pre-revprop-change.tmpl. This is the sample pre-revprop-change hook script. Assuming you're on a Unix machine, you should be able to just copy pre-revprop-change.tmpl to pre-revprop-change, make it executable with a quick chmod +x pre-revprop-change, and you're all set. The default script in pre-revprop-change.tmpl will let you change only the svn:log revprop, so let's take a look at how you can do that:

```
$ ls /path/to/repos/hooks
```

```
post-commit.tmpl              post-unlock.tmpl    pre-revprop-change.tmpl
post-lock.tmpl                pre-commit.tmpl     pre-unlock.tmpl
post-revprop-change.tmpl      pre-lock.tmpl       start-commit.tmpl
```

```
$ cp /path/to/repos/hooks/pre-revprop-change.tmpl \
     /path/to/repos/hooks/pre-revprop-change
$ chmod +x /path/to/repos/hooks/pre-revprop-change
$ svn log --revision 10 file:///path/to/repos
```

```
------------------------------------------------------------------------
r10 |   rooneg | 2003-06-30 18:12:07 -0400 (Mon, 30 Jun 2003) | 1 line
This is revision 10's log entry
------------------------------------------------------------------------
```

```
$ svn propget --revprop svn:log --revision 10 file:///path/to/repos
```

```
This is revision 10's log entry.
```

```
$ svn propset --revprop svn:log --revision 10 \
     "This is revision 10's new log entry" file:///path/to/repos
```

```
property 'svn:log' set on repository revision '10'
```

```
$ svn propget --revprop svn:log --revision 10 file:///path/to/repos
```

```
This is revision 10's new log entry.
```

```
$ svn log --revision 10 file:///path/to/repos
```

```
------------------------------------------------------------------------
r10 |   rooneg | 2003-06-30 18:12:07 -0400 (Mon, 30 Jun 2003) | 1 line
This is revision 10's new log entry
------------------------------------------------------------------------
$
```

There you have it—changing an incorrect log entry is that easy. All you have to do is enable the pre-revprop-change script, use the standard commands you normally use to access Subversion properties, add a --revprop argument and a --revision, and you're done.

Miscellaneous Commands

And now you're down to it, those last few client-side commands that just don't fit into any other specific section of the chapter. Not that svn blame and svn cleanup and svn export aren't important, it's just that they don't fit in with any of the groups of commands we've already talked about. They're still useful though, and you'll most likely find yourself needing them at least every now and then.

svn blame

When you're working on a file that has changed many times over the course of its history it's often nice to be able to ask the question "What revision introduced this particular line?" Although it's possible to manually go back through the revision history diffing files until you find the responsible revision, it's much more convenient to use the svn blame command.[3] svn blame takes a working copy path or URL and optionally a range of revisions, and outputs a formatted version of the file in which each line is prefixed with the revision that line originates from and the username of the author of that revision. The output looks like this:

```
$ svn blame svn://svn.example.org/repos/project/trunk/hello.c
```

```
   12      steve #include <stdio.h>
   10        greg
   10        greg int
   10        greg main (int argc, char *argv)
   10        greg {
   11      robert   printf ("hello world\n");
   10        greg   return 0;
   10        greg }
$
```

From this output, you can see that most of the file originated in revision 10, which was committed by greg, with line 6 being changed by robert in revision 11, and line 1 being changed by steve in revision 12.

---

3. There was a fair amount of controversy when this command was named. Most Subversion developers felt that the name was accurate, determining exactly who wrote the line of code that caused the bug they're tracking down; thus, the canonical name is svn blame. However, a significant number felt that retaining compatibility with the name of the CVS equivalent, annotate, was a more important consideration, and a small but vocal minority felt that "blame" had a negative connotation. Thus, svn blame can also be spelled svn annotate by those whose fingers are accustomed to the CVS command, and svn praise by those who feel that "blame" is too negative.

It's worth noting that although the output from `svn blame` can be exceptionally useful, Subversion's repository design doesn't make it particularly efficient to implement. Because Subversion stores differences using a binary diffing algorithm that doesn't track changes on a line-by-line basis, the current implementation involves downloading each individual revision of the file in question and manually diffing them on the client machine to determine the origin of each line. Thus the command may take quite a while to execute when the file in question has many revisions or when it's quite large. Also keep in mind that `svn blame` is meaningless when applied to a directory or to a binary file.

svn cleanup

The Subversion working copy library is designed to operate like a journaled filesystem, in that as you run commands and your client modifies the working copy, it first locks that portion of the working copy and writes out the changes to disk in the form of a log file. This means that in the event of a problem such as a power outage, an operating system crash, or the client process being interrupted somehow, the working copy will always be returned to a useful state. Should one of these problems occur, you must use the `svn cleanup` command to return everything to working order. `svn cleanup` just takes the path to your working copy as an argument (or uses the current working directory if you don't give it one) and runs through the working copy, finishing up all unfinished work and removing stray locks. Note that you should run `svn cleanup` only on a working copy that isn't being accessed by another Subversion client, as the cleanup code will assume that it's perfectly fine to break locks that the running client has made, which will almost certainly result in significant problems, because the locks are there precisely to keep two processes from changing that part of the working copy at the same time:

```
$ svn update
```

```
svn: Working copy 'docs' locked
svn: run 'svn cleanup' to remove locks (type 'svn help cleanup' for details)
```

```
$ svn status
```

```
   L    docs
M       docs/design.xml
```

```
$ svn cleanup
$ svn status
```

```
M       docs/design.xml
```

```
$ svn update
```

```
At revision 100.
```

Here you can see that something has happened to the docs directory of this working copy to leave it in a locked state, as the third column of its line in the svn status output is an L. Running an svn cleanup completed whatever unfinished work needed to be done for that directory, and the second svn status shows only the modified file in that subdirectory, as it should.

svn export

You've already seen svn import, but there's also a command for the reverse procedure, svn export. The export command is useful when you need to release a version of your software and you don't want to include all the administrative directories from a working copy. svn export will write out a complete directory tree containing all versioned files from either a URL in the repository (with an optional revision) or a working copy path. You can think of it as an svn checkout that doesn't write out the administrative directories:

```
$ svn export file:///path/to/repository/tags/release-1.0 release-1.0
```

```
A   release-1.0
A   release-1.0/foo.c
A   release-1.0/main.c
A   release-1.0/Makefile
A   release-1.0/zot.c
```

```
$ ls -al release-1.0
```

```
total 24
-rw-r--r--  1 rooneg  staff   0 Jul 26 20:53 .
-rw-r--r--  1 rooneg  staff   0 Jul 26 20:53 ..
-rw-r--r--  1 rooneg  staff   0 Jul 26 20:53 Makefile
-rw-r--r--  1 rooneg  staff  76 Jul 26 20:53 foo.c
-rw-r--r--  1 rooneg  staff  99 Jul 26 20:53 main.c
-rw-r--r--  1 rooneg  staff  76 Jul 26 20:53 zot.c
$
```

There isn't a whole lot to say about the output of svn export, as it's substantially similar to that of svn checkout. Just note that the directory you export to isn't a working copy—it has no administrative .svn directory, so you can't use any Subversion commands that require a working copy to function on its contents.

Summary

In this chapter you encountered the majority of the commands you're likely to use in your day-to-day work with Subversion. You created a repository, imported your data, checked out working copies, committed changes, merged conflicts, added and removed files and directories, worked with branches, and covered the lesser-known but still useful Subversion features such as properties. In the process, you gained a general understanding of how to interact with Subversion and what it can do for you. In the next chapter, you'll move beyond everyday use of Subversion, into the realm of the repository administrator, which you've only glimpsed so far.

CHAPTER 3

■■■

Repository Administration

So what exactly is a *repository administrator*? The repository administrator is the person responsible for making sure the repository runs smoothly. This might involve tasks ranging from providing regularly scheduled backups, to configuring the server processes you use to connect to the repository over the network, to setting up access control mechanisms that ensure only the people who are supposed to have access to the repository are using it. In general, it requires a slightly more in-depth knowledge of the inner workings of Subversion than you would need if you were only a user of the software—but don't worry too much. Managing a single-user repository is a fairly trivial affair, and configuring a larger repository intended to be used by many people is only a bit more involved.

Choosing a Repository Type

The first thing a repository administrator should do is choose which back end to use for the repository: FSFS or Berkeley DB. FSFS is the filesystem-based back end, where each revision is stored as a single file. As you might imagine, the Berkeley DB option uses a Berkeley DB database. This really isn't as much of a choice as it seems to be. FSFS is the default, and unless you have a very good reason to not use it, it is what you should stick with.

FSFS is quite fast and will work with the repository stored on a network filesystem (such as NFS or Windows shares). Berkeley DB only works if that which is directly accessing the repository has BDB[1] support compiled in, and FSFS is generally easier to maintain than Berkeley DB. Large open source projects such as KDE, GCC, and Apache use FSFS and are very happy with its performance and maintainability.

After reading this chapter, and noticing all the BDB-specific parts related to backups, log files, repository permissions, and other matters, you will probably have a better understanding of why it is highly recommended you go with the FSFS default. In our opinion, the only real reason to use BDB is if it somehow makes you feel more comfortable to have your data stored in a "real" database. If even after all this you still want to use a Berkeley DB–based repository, you can always convert from one back end to the other using a dump/load cycle, which will be introduced later in this chapter in the section "Dumping and Loading Repository Contents."

---

1. It is common practice in Subversion to abbreviate Berkeley DB to BDB when talking about the filesystem back end that uses Berkeley DB. The terms are entirely interchangeable.

Repository Layout

The second thing you should probably do if you're thinking of serving as a repository administrator is to learn a little more about the layout of the repository. There are two aspects to repository layout that you'll need to be aware of. First, there's the physical *on-disk layout*—the actual files and directories that make up your repository. Second, there's the *in-repository layout*, meaning the versioned files and directories that exist inside the repository, which your users will regularly be interacting with.

The first part is important because you will, in many cases, need to be able to make small changes to the repository's files on disk (the most common example of this is when you're setting up hook scripts, which is described in the "Hooks" section later in this chapter). And even if you aren't actually changing things, you will certainly want to know what files are what, if only so you can know what parts you need to back up. The second part is important because the layout of your repository will influence how your users are able to interact with it, and you need to be able to make informed decisions about how to organize separate projects, branches, tags, vendor branches, and other such things. There are some general guidelines on how to do this, but in the end only you can decide what the best choice is for you, because you're the one who knows how your users are going to use the repository.

The Repository on Disk

Let's take a closer look at the files inside a freshly installed Subversion on-disk repository layout:

```
$ svnadmin create /tmp/repos
$ ls -l /tmp/repos
```

```
-rw-r--r--   1 rooneg  wheel  376 Jul  5 16:08 README.txt
drwxr-xr-x   2 rooneg  wheel  102 Jul  5 16:08 conf/
drwxr-xr-x   2 rooneg  wheel   68 Jul  5 16:08 dav/
drwxr-sr-x  17 rooneg  wheel  578 Jul  5 16:08 db/
-rw-r--r--   1 rooneg  wheel    2 Jul  5 16:08 format
drwxr-xr-x   7 rooneg  wheel  238 Jul  5 16:08 hooks/
drwxr-xr-x   3 rooneg  wheel  102 Jul  5 16:08 locks/
$
```

You can see two files and a number of directories. The files are the simplest part, so let's start there. README.txt is just what you'd expect it to be: a README file. It just says that this is a Subversion repository, gives a few warnings about not messing around with files in here unless you know what you're doing, and points to the places where you really might want to modify things.

The format file contains just the format number of this Subversion repository (currently the repository uses version 3 of the filesystem database schema, but this may have changed by the time you read this). When Subversion tries to access a repository it verifies that it understands the repository version, to avoid trying to access a version of the repository it doesn't understand. Under no circumstances should you edit this file manually. If Subversion is complaining about not understanding the format, it's doing so for a good reason; and trying to outsmart it by editing the file can only result in further problems.

The subdirectories in the repository are a bit more interesting, so let's take a closer look at them. First is the conf directory, which holds Subversion configuration files specific to this repository. Currently the only files within conf are authz (a sample authorization file), passwd (a sample svnserve password file), and svnserve.conf (the configuration file that controls svnserve's behavior when accessing this repository).

Next is the dav directory. This holds mod_dav_svn's bookkeeping data, and unless you're trying to modify mod_dav_svn source code for some reason, you won't need to worry about it.

The next part of the on-disk layout of the repository is the hooks directory. *Hooks* are processes that are run when a particular event occurs, such as a user performing a commit, or a revision property being changed. Generally, these are used to enforce policy, such as limiting access to certain parts of the repository to certain users who can create and steal locks, and in addition to policy, to send e-mail when a commit has occurred. We discuss hooks in detail in the "Hooks" section later in this chapter.

When using the FSFS back end, the db directory contains the FSFS filesystem revisions that hold the data you put in the repository. In a brand new repository, it will look like this:

```
$ ls -l repos/db
```

```
total 28
-rw-r--r-- 1 root root   6 2006-05-27 18:11 current
-r--r--r-- 1 root root   2 2006-05-27 18:11 format
-rw-r--r-- 1 root root   5 2006-05-27 18:11 fs-type
drwxr-sr-x 2 root root  72 2006-05-27 18:11 revprops
drwxr-sr-x 2 root root  72 2006-05-27 18:11 revs
drwxr-sr-x 2 root root  48 2006-05-27 18:11 transactions
-rw-r--r-- 1 root root  37 2006-05-27 18:11 uuid
-rw-r--r-- 1 root root   0 2006-05-27 18:11 write-lock
```

```
$ ls -l repos/db/revs
```

```
total 4
-rw-r--r-- 1 root root 115 2006-05-27 18:11 0
```

The files in the revs dir are the data representation for each revision. There will be one file for each revision stored in the repository. The first revision in any new subversion repository is 0. Maintenancewise, there is nothing you need to worry about in the FSFS repository. It can be copied and backed up like any other bunch of files. The only requirement for backups is that if there are going to be changes made to the repository while the backup is going on, the file named current, which stores the current revision number, needs to be backed up first. As we are about to see, the BDB back end is significantly more complex.

BDB-Specific Files

When the BDB back end is used, the db directory instead contains the Berkeley DB database environment that actually holds the data you put in your repository. In a new BDB-driven repository, that directory will look something like this:

```
$ ls -l /tmp/repos/db
```

```
-rw-r--r--  1 rooneg  wheel     1282 Jul  5 16:08 DB_CONFIG
-rw-r--r--  1 rooneg  wheel     8192 Jul  5 16:08 __db.001
-rw-r--r--  1 rooneg  wheel   270336 Jul  5 16:08 __db.002
-rw-r--r--  1 rooneg  wheel   327680 Jul  5 16:08 __db.003
-rw-r--r--  1 rooneg  wheel   737280 Jul  5 16:08 __db.004
-rw-r--r--  1 rooneg  wheel    16384 Jul  5 16:08 __db.005
-rw-r--r--  1 rooneg  wheel     8192 Jul  5 16:08 changes
-rw-r--r--  1 rooneg  wheel     8192 Jul  5 16:08 copies
-r--r--r--  1 rooneg  wheel        2 Jul  5 16:08 format
-r--r--r--  1 rooneg  wheel        2 Jul  5 16:08 fs-type
rw-r--r--  1 rooneg  wheel     8192 Jul  5 16:08 locks
-rw-r--r--  1 rooneg  wheel     8192 Jul  5 16:08 lock-tokens
-rw-r--r--  1 rooneg  wheel    71948 Jul  5 16:08 log.0000000001
-rw-r--r--  1 rooneg  wheel     8192 Jul  5 16:08 nodes
-rw-r--r--  1 rooneg  wheel     8192 Jul  5 16:08 representations
-rw-r--r--  1 rooneg  wheel     8192 Jul  5 16:08 revisions
-rw-r--r--  1 rooneg  wheel     8192 Jul  5 16:08 strings
-rw-r--r--  1 rooneg  wheel     8192 Jul  5 16:08 transactions
-rw-r--r--  1 rooneg  wheel     8192 Jul  5 16:08 uuids
$
```

Let's look at each of these files in turn. Starting at the top you'll see the DB_CONFIG file. This is the configuration file for the repository's Berkeley DB environment. You might need to edit this file to change some of the parameters used by Berkeley DB (e.g., large repositories might need to increase the number of locks available to Berkeley DB). We discuss this file and how you can make changes to it later in the section "Berkeley DB Tuning."

Next, there are five files named __db.001 through __db.005. These are internal Berkeley DB bookkeeping databases, and you shouldn't need to concern yourself with them. They're managed entirely by Berkeley DB itself.

Now you'll see a number of Berkeley DB database files that are used by Subversion directly. Currently, these include changes, copies, locks, lock-tokens, nodes, representations, revisions, strings, transactions, and uuids. Each of these files holds a different Berkeley DB table that is used as part of the Subversion repository. The files format and fs-type contain information about what type of filesystem it is (in this case BDB) and the format number of this filesystem (so when changes are made to the internal format of the repository, you know which internal format is in use).

Finally, we present the Berkeley DB log file log.0000000001. Whenever a change is made to the Berkeley DB database (and this happens more often than you might think; it isn't just when you commit a change to the repository), that change is first written to the log file. After it has safely been written to the log file, it will then be changed in the actual database. This ensures that if some kind of catastrophic event occurs—be it a power outage, a hardware problem, or even a crash of the Subversion software—the database will always be left in a consistent state, or at the very least you'll be able to return it to a consistent state with a minimum amount of trouble. Note that in a repository that has been in use for a little while, there may be a number of log files holding a rather large amount of data. Depending on how paranoid you are, you might want to preserve all of these log files, because if you have them, you can (if you know enough about Berkeley DB, anyway) return the repository to its exact state at any point in time.

If you're using Berkeley DB version 4.2.52 or newer and you decide you don't want to keep old log files around (and honestly, unless you know a lot about Subversion and Berkeley DB, you probably don't want to keep the old log files around), you can use automatic log file cleanup, which will prompt Berkeley DB to remove each log file once all the changes recorded in it have been safely written to the repository, and thus the log is no longer required. Automatic log file removal is enabled when you create a new repository if your version of Berkeley DB supports it. If you don't want to use it for some reason, you can either use the `--bdb-log-keep` flag to `svnadmin` when creating the repository or remove the `DB_LOG_AUTOREMOVE` flag from the `DB_CONFIG` file, which is discussed later in this chapter in the "Berkeley DB Tuning" section.

If you don't want log files to be deleted automatically, or you're using a version of Berkeley DB that doesn't support automatically deleting log files, you can use the `svnadmin list-unused-dblogs` command, which lists the log files that are no longer being actively used by the repository. The output will look something like this:

```
$ ls /tmp/repos/db/log.*
```

```
/tmp/repos/db/log.0000000001
/tmp/repos/db/log.0000000002
```

```
$ svnadmin list-unused-dblogs /tmp/repos
```

```
/tmp/repos/db/log.0000000001
$
```

This indicates that `log.0000000001` is no longer in use; so after you've backed it up (if you plan to do so), you can safely delete it and recover some much needed disk space.

The final directory in the BDB repository on disk is the `locks` directory, which holds the lock files Subversion uses to coordinate access to the repository. Note that in almost all situations you'll have multiple client processes, each taking out read-write locks on the repository. The only time the locking is used to limit access to a single process is when you're using `svnadmin recover` to perform catastrophic recovery on the repository.

Another vitally important issue for a BDB repository is the kind of filesystem you store it on. A lot of people seem to want to place their repository on a shared network drive (perhaps because it's the only place in their environment where they have access to a lot of disk space). This configuration is only supported when using the FSFS back end. Berkeley DB, and therefore the BDB back end, doesn't interact well with network filesystems, and accessing a repository directly (i.e., via `svnlook`, `svnadmin`, the `svn` program using `file://` URLs, or any other program that makes direct calls into `libsvn_repos` or `libsvn_fs`) is a surefire way to corrupt the repository. All currently available network filesystems just don't have sufficient cache coherency semantics to make it safe to place the Berkeley DB database on them, and doing so is asking for trouble. For more details on the issues involved, see the documentation at `http://www.sleepycat.com/docs/ref/env/remote.html`.

Inside the Repository

More interesting to your users will be the repository layout. Because Subversion uses simple copies for tags and branches, you're given essentially complete freedom to determine how your project is laid out within the repository. In addition to the question of how to handle tags and branches, there are some limitations on how Subversion currently works that might also influence what parts of your project are placed where.

The first decision you need to make is simple. Should you use a single large repository holding multiple projects, or should you use multiple repositories with one or more projects contained within each one? As is often the case in software development, the answer largely depends on one's willingness to make certain trade-offs. Having a single large repository means that in some sense you are "placing all your eggs in one basket," so to speak. If there is some problem with the repository—because of a machine crashing, a disk failing, or any number of other issues that could quite possibly make it impossible for your users to access the repository— all of your users will be unable to make full use of Subversion until the problem is rectified. You probably want to split repositories across administrative or project boundaries.

With multiple repositories, possibly spread across multiple disks or even machines, you can gain some level of protection from such an incident. That said, splitting your code base across multiple repositories has a number of drawbacks, any of which might be good reason to stick to a single repository setup. However, when you split things up into multiple independent systems, you increase the maintenance cost associated with the system as a whole. More repositories means more effort spent backing them up and more effort maintaining the machines they live on. In addition, by using multiple repositories, you increase the system complexity for the user. With one repository, it becomes second nature to refer to commits by their revision number. Users begin to use the revision numbers in technical discussions and in bug reports, both of which become more complex when you need to say "revision 13 in the webfe repository" instead of just "revision 13" (since you now possibly have a revision 13 in webfe, and a revision 13 in whatever other repositories exist). Last, and probably most important for you, if you ever intend to move code from one project to another, and you want to retain the revision history associated with the files, you'll need to place the projects within the same repository. Subversion doesn't currently allow you to copy between repositories, so if your projects are located in different repositories, and you wish to copy between them, you'll need to export them from the source repository and import or add them to the destination repository, losing the associated history in the process.

Once you've determined how many repositories you'll use to hold your source code, you'll need to decide on the layout for each project within the repository. In general, it's a good idea to reserve a few separate directories for each project: one to hold the mainline development branch (often called /trunk), one for other branches, and one for holding tags. If you have a single project in the repository, this kind of layout would look like this:

```
$ svn list file:///path/to/repos
```

```
branches/
tags/
trunk/
```

```
$ svn list file:///path/to/repos/branches
```

```
issue-37-dev/
issue-15-dev/
```

```
$ svn list file:///path/to/repos/tags
```

```
release-1.0/
```

```
$ svn list file:///path/to/repos/trunk
```

```
README
Makefile.in
autogen.sh
configure.in
docs/
include/
src/
$
```

As you can see, there's a single top-level directory, which holds subdirectories named /trunk, /branches, and /tags. Most development will be done in the /trunk directory, with extended work of some kind (either maintenance or development) being done in copies of the /trunk, which are placed in the /branches directory. For convenience, copies of significant versions of the software, such as releases, will be placed in /tags. Note that all of this is only a convention, and nothing is keeping you from using any of these directories (or any others, for that matter) in any way you wish. If you want to enforce some kind of policy for specific directories, you'll want to use a script known as a *hook*, described later in the "Hooks" section.

For repositories that contain multiple projects, the general idea is pretty much the same. You just create a directory for each project, either in the top-level directory or in whatever system of subdirectories makes sense to you, and then you create the /trunk, /branches, and /tags directories in each project's subdirectory. Such a configuration would look like this:

```
$ svn list file:///path/to/repos
```

```
libedit/
client/
```

```
$ svn list file:///path/to/repos/libedit
```

```
branches/
tags/
trunk/
```

```
$ svn list file:///path/to/repos/client
```

```
branches/
tags/
trunk/
$
```

As before, this is just a set of conventions. There's nothing that says you have to set up your repository this way, so if you have an idea for another way that makes more sense to you, feel free to try it out. One of the nice things about Subversion is that you aren't tied to a single layout for your repository; so if you decide at some point after you've started that your repository layout doesn't make sense, you can rearrange it via svn move and svn mkdir. This will be somewhat inconvenient to your users, but in all likelihood they'll be able to recover from the disruption with svn switch, and it will certainly be considerably easier than the kind of gymnastics you would have to go through when rearranging the layout of a CVS repository.

Tools for Working with the Repository

Because Subversion repositories are composed of opaque database files, and it's necessary to use special tools to get a closer look at what's going on inside a repository, it goes without saying that Subversion provides those tools for you. You've already seen the svnadmin command, which provides the primary administrative interface to the repository, but in addition to that there's also the svnlook tool, which provides an easy way to inspect the contents of the repository. Let's take a closer look at each of these tools.

svnadmin

The first tool a repository administrator needs to become familiar with is svnadmin, primarily because it's used to create a repository, and it's rather difficult to administer a repository if you don't have one. Once the repository has been created, the svnadmin command will still be one of the most useful tools available to the administrator, because it provides low-level read-write access to the repository. With svnadmin, you can dump the repository to a neutral backup format and restore it; you can examine old transactions that may have been left in the repository by accident and, if necessary, remove them; and you can return the repository to a stable state after a catastrophic event such as a system crash or a power outage—all of which you'll learn to do in the course of reading this chapter.

Before going into the specifics of how you can use the svnadmin tool, a word of caution: svnadmin gives you read-write access to the underlying repository at a much lower level than the user level svn client. With svn, it's almost impossible to actually lose data. At worst, any change that svn can make to the repository will just create a bogus revision, which can easily be reverted if necessary, because the previous version is still there (the one exception to this is the editing of revision properties, but as discussed in the previous chapter, if you want to do that, you need to explicitly enable it by setting up a hook script, as described in the "Revision Properties" section of Chapter 2). With svnadmin this isn't the case. It's quite easy to do serious, irreversible damage to your repository if you aren't careful; so before you run any svnadmin command, you must be sure you know what you're doing. This gun is always loaded, so point it only at something you intend to shoot.

Now that the warning is out of the way, let's take a look at the most useful of the svnadmin commands. This isn't a definitive list, but it covers everything you're likely to need to use in routine repository administration.

svnadmin create

The first command you are likely to perform with svnadmin is svnadmin create. It takes a single argument: the path to the repository it should create. This command also takes a few optional arguments. First, there is --fs-type, which specifies which back end to use. The only two available types are bdb, which creates a Berkeley DB–based repository, and fsfs, which is the default and uses the filesystem back end. For Berkeley DB repositories, there are two additional options. The first of these options is --bdb-txn-nosync, which causes the repository's Berkeley DB environment to be configured to not use fsync to ensure that data has been flushed to disk by the operating system when transactions are committed. This argument can speed up actions that make changes to the repository, but it removes the guarantee that changes will be committed to disk in an atomic way. Because this is obviously unsafe for use in any real-world setting, this flag should be used only for creation of repositories that are to be used in some kind of nonstandard way, such as for loading a dumpfile or testing of some sort. To re-enable fsync and its associated safety guarantees, remove the set_flags DB_TXN_NOSYNC line from the repository's db/DB_CONFIG file and run svnadmin recover to reinitialize the Berkeley DB environment with its new settings.

Next there is the --bdb-log-keep flag, which was mentioned earlier when discussing automatic log file removal. If your version of Berkeley DB supports automatic log file removal, the default setting will be to enable it. This flag disables that support for the new repository. After the repository is created, you can control the behavior with regard to log files by adding or removing the set_flags DB_LOG_AUTOREMOVE directive in the repository's db/DB_CONFIG file and running svnadmin recover to cause Berkeley DB to reread that file.

BDB Repositories: svnadmin recover

svnadmin recover provides a convenient front end to Berkeley DB's underlying recovery functions. This command does nothing on FSFS repositories.

Occasionally, the Berkeley DB environment that makes up the core of every Subversion repository can be placed in a state where it requires maintenance. To do this, you must first ensure that no other process is accessing the repository (by shutting off any servers that provide access, killing any existing processes that are attached to the collection, and so forth), and then run svnadmin recover /path/to/repos. This will obtain an exclusive lock on the repository and reinitialize the Berkeley DB environment, running any commands in the Berkeley DB log files that have been completed but haven't yet been committed to the repository. This will return the repository to a consistent state, making it possible for clients to use the repository again.

Note that running svnadmin recover on the repository involves taking out an exclusive lock, which means that if any other processes are still accessing the repository, the recovery won't be able to even start, let alone finish.

The obvious question now is, when should you run `svnadmin recover`? The answer is, unfortunately, when you have to. In many cases, Berkeley DB will be able to determine when the recovery is needed and will return an error like this:

```
$ svn list file:///path/to/repos
```

```
svn: Couldn't open a repository.
svn: Unable to open an ra_local session to URL
svn: Unable to open repository 'file:///path/to/repos'
svn: Berkeley DB error while opening environment for filesystem /path/to/repos/db:
DB_RUNRECOVERY: Fatal error, run database recovery
$
```

In a situation like this, it's rather obvious that recovery is needed. Unfortunately, in some situations it isn't possible to make this determination. It's possible for stale locks to be left in the repository by processes that die while they're attached to it. This situation can be caused by a bug in a process accessing the repository, a power failure, a system crash, or any one of a number of other problems. In such a case, the only manifestation of the problem that's visible to the user might well be the fact that processes trying to access the repository hang.

So the question of when recovery is needed is somewhat tricky. If an error message you receive from Subversion indicates that a recovery is needed, it's a good bet that you should run it, but the absence of such an error doesn't mean recovery isn't needed. In general, if your repository is acting strangely, and you have any suspicion that a process might have had some kind of problem accessing it, then trying recovery would be a good idea. If the machine hosting your repository crashes or is powered down unexpectedly, it's certainly prudent to run a recovery before anyone begins to use the repository. Future versions of Subversion, starting with 1.4, will support BDB 4.4, which contains autorecovery and should remove the need to ever run `svnadmin recover`.

■Note Another useful set of `svnadmin` commands are `svnadmin dump` and `svnadmin load`, which are used to dump the history of the repository into a neutral format for transfer between repositories, for archival purposes, or to pass to or from some other tool. These functions are discussed later in this chapter in the section "Dumping and Loading Repository Contents."

Using svnadmin to Manipulate Transactions

The final set of `svnadmin` commands that a repository administrator is likely to need are those that deal with transactions. When applied to Subversion, the word *transaction* has at least two meanings. First, there is the transaction that the underlying repository back-end layer provides to Subversion, which is used to ensure atomicity of any change to the repository. Second, there is the higher-level type of transaction that occurs when you make a change to the repository, happening not all at once but rather in steps. Generally, the process begins by making a transaction by copying an existing revision of the repository. You then alter that transaction to make it match the final state of the tree you're looking for. If you're performing a commit, for example, you build a transaction that matches the current repository revision, and Subversion uses that to compute the differences between the tree you're committing to and your working copy, so it sends only the differences between the two trees to the repository instead of the entire contents of each file.

Unfortunately, because the transaction is built in the repository, it can be left there forever if the client fails to complete whatever it is doing. Because you don't want these transactions sticking around forever, every now and then you should use svnadmin lstxns to find old, abandoned transactions, and use svnadmin rmtxns to remove them. The process looks like this:

```
$ svnadmin lstxns /path/to/repository
```

```
2
3
4
```

```
$ svnadmin rmtxns /path/to/repository 2
Transaction '2' removed
$ svnadmin lstxns /path/to/repository
```

```
3
4
$
```

Of course, you should be careful to remove only those transactions that are no longer being used by client programs, and there's no really good way to determine that a transaction has been "orphaned" except to turn off access to the repository and look to see what transactions are still hanging around. If a transaction is removed while it's still in use, at best it will greatly inconvenience your users, and at worst it could be the cause of some difficult-to-track-down bug reports.

svnlook

Because svnadmin can be such a dangerous tool, you'll often find yourself wishing for a safer way to work with the repository for those times when you don't need all the power that svnadmin gives you. For those occasions there's the svnlook command. As you might surmise from its name, this tool lets you examine the repository in a read-only manner, making it quite safe to use without worrying about breaking things. svnlook is most often used when writing hook scripts, which often need to examine what's going on in the repository to determine how they should act.

The svnlook subcommands fall into two general categories. The first are those that find information about the repository in general, such as svnlook uuid, which prints the UUID of a repository, or svnlook youngest, which prints the current HEAD revision number of the repository. These commands take as their argument the path to the repository.

The remaining svnlook subcommands can each refer to a specific revision or transaction in the repository. In the case in which a revision is given, they can be used to explore the history of the repository, and in the case of a transaction, they can be used to determine what kind of changes a user is making to the repository—something that can be quite useful for a hook script. The specifics of the various subcommands are self-explanatory. Table 3-1 provides a brief summary. All of these commands, except `lock`, accept `–revision` as an argument and almost all accept `--transaction` as an argument.

Table 3-1. *Reading from Transactions and Revisions with svnlook*

Command Name	Extra Arguments	Description
cat	Path to file in the repository	Prints the file's contents to the screen
changed	None	Prints paths that changed in a given revision or transaction
date	None	Prints the datestamp for a transaction or revision
diff	None	Prints the GNU-style diff for the changed files in a transaction or revision
dirs-changed	None	Prints the directories that have changed or whose children have changed in a given transaction or revision
info	None	Prints the author, datestamp, log message size, and log message for a revision or transaction
lock	Path in repository	Prints information about any locks that exist at the specified path in the repository
log	None	Prints the log message for a revision or transaction
propget	Property name and a path in the repository or a revision	Prints the value of a specified property set on a specified path or revision in the repository
proplist	Path in the repository or a revision	Prints the properties set on a path or revision in the repository
tree	Optional path in the repository	Prints the tree (starting at the path in the repository, if one is given) associated with a transaction or revision

Backups

Among the most important activities of a Subversion repository administrator is making repository backups, so that in case of some kind of catastrophe, all is not lost. It might be tempting to just take the easy way out and only make periodic copies of the repository, with something like `cp -r` or even rsync to send a copy to another machine. For the FSFS back end, a tool like rsync is sufficient, and the only requirement is that the `db/current` file be transferred first. Given that restriction, a simple copy of the entire repository suffices. For BDB repositories, things are a little more complicated.

If you copy a repository that's being accessed by any clients via `cp -r` or xcopy, or whatever similar command your operating system provides to recursively copy a directory, you're quite likely to end up with a corrupted repository. The various files that make up the Berkeley DB environment need to be copied in a particular order to ensure that they remain consistent.

Fortunately, there's a simple solution to this problem. `svnadmin` has a special `svnadmin hotcopy` command that copies the repository in such a way that it will remain internally consistent. This function works on both BDB and FSFS repositories. You give it the location of your repository and the location you wish to place the backup, and it will do all the dirty work of copying tables, recopying log files, and running the database recovery routines to ensure that everything is nice and consistent. There is even a `--clean-logs` flag that will automatically delete any unused log files from the source repository after they've been copied into the destination repository. This simplifies the process of periodically backing up your repository and helps avoid most of the common mistakes that can occur when you try to implement the backup procedure correctly.

Note that while this backup procedure might seem complex compared to what you're used to, it buys you a few things. First of all, because of Subversion's atomic commit feature, you're ensured that your backup is consistent. Second, you don't need to stop clients from accessing the repository at any point. For many version control systems, providing both of these features wouldn't be possible, and if you wanted to allow clients access to the repository, you would need to accept the fact that your backup could quite possibly be inconsistent, containing only part of some changes.

Dumping and Loading Repository Contents

It's occasionally useful to convert the contents of a Subversion repository into a back-end neutral format. Perhaps you want to migrate an older Subversion repository to a newer release of the Subversion software; or maybe you want to back up your repository in a more durable way; or, perhaps most interesting, you want to write a tool that converts some other kind of data into a format that Subversion can understand. Subversion provides a simple dumpfile format, consisting of easy-to-parse RFC 822 headers (just like the headers found in e-mail) and the raw contents of the files in the repository, which can be used for all of these purposes.

The original use case for Subversion's dumpfile format was to allow upgrading to new versions of the Subversion software as they were released. Generally, doing this didn't require any special action regarding the actual repository, but occasionally there was a change in the underlying database schema that required some attention from the administrator. Subversion has committed to not requiring a dump/load cycle before version 2.0. This is not to say that it may not occasionally be useful in order to take advantage of some new feature. It just will not be *required* in order to have a functioning repository. The current use case of dumpfiles, besides backups and the occasional upgrade, is to migrate between incompatible BDB versions in an easy fashion. New BDB releases generally do not do this for you and can't access the old formats, which means you will get BDB errors if you upgrade the BDB libraries to a new version without dumping and loading your repository. This is done with the `svnadmin dump` and `svnadmin load` commands. These commands will write out each revision of your repository into a file and then read them back in, replaying each of them in the new repository. The procedure generally looks something like this:

```
$ svn list file:///home/repos
```

```
branches/
tags/
trunk/
```

```
$ svnadmin dump /home/repos > repos.dump
```

```
* Dumped revision 0.
* Dumped revision 1.
* Dumped revision 2.
* Dumped revision 3.
* Dumped revision 4.
```

```
$ pkg_delete subversion-0.35.0
$ pkg_add -r subversion
```

```
Fetching ftp://ftp.freebsd.org/pub/FreeBSD/ports/i386/packages-5.1-release
/Latest/subversion.tbz... Done.
```

```
$ svnadmin create /home/new-repos
$ svnadmin load /home/new-repos < repos.dump
```

```
<<< Started new transaction, based on original revision 1
     * adding path : branches ... done.
     * adding path : tags ... done.
     * adding path : trunk ... done.
------- Committed revision 1 >>>
<<< Started new transaction, based on original revision 2
     * adding path : trunk/bar.c ... done.
     * adding path : trunk/baz.c ... done.
     * adding path : trunk/foo.c ... done.
------- Committed revision 2 >>>
<<< Started new transaction, based on original revision 3
     * editing path : trunk/foo.c ... done.
------- Committed revision 3 >>>
<<< Started new transaction, based on original revision 4
     * adding path : branches/issue-103-dev ...COPIED... done.
------- Committed revision 4 >>>
```

```
$ svn list file:///home/new-repos
```

```
branches/
tags/
trunk/
$
```

Note the version of svnadmin from the older Subversion was used to dump the repository (because it knows how to read the old database format). Then svnadmin was uninstalled (using FreeBSD's pkg_delete tool), and the new version of svnadmin was installed (via pkg_add) and used to load the dumpfile (because it knows how to read the new dumpfile format). Don't worry if the pkg_delete and pkg_add commands aren't familiar to you—the important part is just that the svnadmin that came with the version of Subversion you're upgrading from must be used for the svnadmin dump command, and the svnadmin that came with the version of Subversion you're upgrading to must be used for the svnadmin load command. The actual upgrade process should be done using whatever means you use to install Subversion on your own system.

Another thing to be aware of when dumping and loading repositories is that disk space can quickly become an issue. The dumpfile you're writing out will by default store fulltext for each revision instead of storing the differences between each version. This makes it as simple as possible and reduces the chance of a bug in the dump/restore code (because nobody wants there to be a bug that renders your backups useless). This means that the dumpfile itself can be quite large. Similarly, the process of dumping and loading causes a large number of transactions to occur, and with a Berkeley DB–based repository, it can cause a large number of log files to be written out if you aren't using automatic log file removal. Because of this space usage, if you are not running automatic log file removal, you need to be careful to remove out-of-date log files while the process is running, so you don't run out of disk space. To reduce space, you can use deltas in your dumpfile, by including the --deltas option during a dump. This will reduce space at the expense of processing time necessary to create the deltas.

Besides backup, there are other uses for svnadmin dump and svnadmin load. One use case is to convert between the two repository back ends. Because the dumpfiles are back-end neutral, all it takes to convert between Berkeley DB and FSFS is to create a new repository with the appropriate --fs-type option, create a dump file from the old repository, and svnadmin load it into the new repository. On systems supporting pipes, it is usually more efficient to just pipe the output of the svnadmin dump command directly into an svnadmin load command to avoid having to create an intermediate dumpfile. When finished, you should also remember to copy over the conf and hooks directories.

The dump format used by Subversion is quite simple (see fs_dumprestore.txt in the notes directory of the Subversion distribution for details). It's relatively simple to write a program to parse it, meaning you can translate from dump output into whatever other format you want your data to be in. Similarly, programs can generate data in the dump format, and then you can use svnadmin load to load it into a repository. cvs2svn and p42svn, both of which we discuss in Chapter 4, use just this technique, enabling them to convert CVS and Perforce repositories to Subversion repositories without having to jump through hoops to call into the Subversion C libraries.

In addition to providing a reasonably simple way to get data into and out of a Subversion repository, svnadmin dump can be used in conjunction with the svndumpfilter tool to migrate portions of a repository from one repository to another or to remove specific portions of a repository if data that can't be allowed to exist in the repository at all has been accidentally committed, as in the following example, where you want to filter out the trunk:

```
$ svn list file:///path/to/original/repos
```

```
branches/
tags/
trunk/
```

```
$ svnadmin dump /path/to/original/repos | \
  svndumpfilter include trunk | \
  svnadmin load /path/to/new/repos
```

```
Including prefixes:
  '/trunk'
Dumped revision 0.
* Dumped revision 1.
Revision 0 committed as 0.
Revision 1 committed as 1.
Dropped 2 nodes:
  branches
  tags
<<< Started new transaction, based on original revision 1
     * adding path : trunk ... done.
------- Committed revision 1 >>>
```

```
$ svn list file:///path/to/new/repos
```

```
trunk/
$
```

Here you can see a somewhat contrived example of how to use svndumpfilter. The source repository is empty, except for three empty directories, /trunk, /tags, and /branches. The repository is dumped and the output is passed through svndumpfilter include trunk, which means that /trunk and all its contents will be passed through intact, but all the other directories will be removed. Sure enough, the resulting repository has only a /trunk subdirectory.

When you dump a repository, the resulting dumpfile will be large, mostly because the files in each revision default to being stored as fulltext, as mentioned previously. Because the dumpfiles can get so big, you might be tempted to split them up, dumping a few hundred or thousand revisions at a time and then moving them around individually. This sounds good, but there's a small problem. To ensure that any given dump can be loaded into a repository to produce a useful repository, the first revision of the dump includes all the files and directories; otherwise, you could start a dump somewhere after the repository is created, load it up, and end up with a repository that only includes those files that were modified in each revision. All older files would be missing. If you intend to store several dumpfiles, you don't want that behavior, because you'll always have the previous revisions in the repository before you load the later ones, and storing extra fulltexts in the initial revision of each dump would just be a waste. To make sure the first revision dumped will store only the files and directories that are changed, just use the --incremental flag. With this flag, you can do something like this:

```
$ svnadmin dump --incremental -r 0:5 /path/to/repos > dump-0-5
```

```
* Dumped revision 0.
* Dumped revision 1.
* Dumped revision 2.
* Dumped revision 3.
* Dumped revision 4.
* Dumped revision 5.
```

```
$ svnadmin dump --incremental -r 6:10 /path/to/repos > dump-6-10
```

```
WARNING: Referencing data in revision 5, which is older than the oldest
WARNING: dumped revision (6).  Loading this dump into an empty repository
WARNING: will fail.
* Dumped revision 6.
* Dumped revision 7.
* Dumped revision 8.
* Dumped revision 9.
* Dumped revision 10.
```

```
$ svnadmin create /path/to/new/repos
$ svnadmin load /path/to/new/repos < dump-0-5
```

```
<<< Started new transaction, based on original revision 1
     * adding path : branches ... done.
     * adding path : tags ... done.
     * adding path : trunk ... done.
------- Committed revision 1 >>>
[ ... a great deal more output ... ]
<<< Started new transaction, based on original revision 5
     * editing path : trunk/foo.c ... done.
------- Committed revision 5 >>>
```

```
$ svnadmin load /path/to/new/repos < dump-6-10
```

```
<<< Started new transaction, based on original revision 6
     * editing path : trunk/Makefile ... done.
     * editing path : trunk/README ... done.
------- Committed revision 6 >>>
[ ... a great deal more output ... ]
<<< Started new transaction, based on original revision 10
     * editing path : trunk/bar.c ... done.
------- Committed revision 10 >>>
$
```

So that's kind of cool, but the --incremental flag is really useful for backing up repositories. All you need to do is keep track of the last revision your backup contains a dump for, and you can easily use svnadmin dump --incremental to dump only the newer revisions, which can save you a considerable amount of time for a large repository. A script to do that might look like this:

```
#!/bin/sh
repository="/path/to/repository"
dumpfile="/path/to/dumpfile"
last_dumped="/path/to/last-dumped-record"
if [ -e $last_dumped ]; then
```

```
 last_rev=`cat $last_dumped`
else
 last_rev=0
fi
youngest=`svnlook youngest $repository`
svnadmin dump --incremental -r $last_rev:$youngest $repository > $dumpfile
echo $youngest > $last_dumped
```

So the question becomes, which do you want to use for your backups: rsync (in the FSFS case), a hot backup of your entire repository, or a dump, possibly incremental? Again, the answer depends on which trade-offs you wish to make. If you use rsync, it is fast, but you do have to remember to make sure the db/current file copies first. If you use a hot backup, you have a complete repository ready to use at a moment's notice, so the process of restoring your repository to production use after a catastrophe can be quite simple. Unfortunately, that repository's usefulness is tied to several different things if you use the Berkeley DB back end. It's tied to a particular version of Subversion and a particular version of Berkeley DB; and because Berkeley DB databases (at least as used by Subversion) aren't necessarily portable between different platforms, it can even be tied to a particular operating system. Of course, with a production version of Subversion, you're at least given the promise that the repository version won't change within major number revisions, but if you're running a development version of Subversion, that might still be an issue, and Berkeley DB versioning issues are completely different from Subversion's own. So if you need to set up a new repository in which one or more of these things is different, you may run into problems. On the other hand, a dumpfile is quite portable—it was designed that way—so you can safely move it between systems and versions of Subversion and Berkeley DB without issue.

Unfortunately, loading a large dumpfile into a new repository can take some time. You're essentially running through every change that was ever made to your repository, and that takes a non-negligible amount of time, no matter how it's implemented. So as usual with repository administration, there is no clear answer, and you'll need to decide what's more valuable to you when determining how you'll run your backups.

Berkeley DB Tuning

As mentioned earlier, within the db directory of a Berkeley DB–backed repository is a DB_CONFIG file that contains Berkeley DB–specific configuration options. This file is created when you run svnadmin create, and normally you shouldn't have to change it after that. But what about when you do? Let's take a look at what options you can tweak in this file, and how and why you would want to change them.

First, the *how*. To make a change to the DB_CONFIG file, you need to shut down all access to the repository in question. This means (depending on how you serve your repositories), shutting down Apache, disabling svnserve, and executing chmod -x `which svn`—whatever it takes to ensure your users can't access the repository. Then make your change to the file, save it, and run svnadmin recover /path/to/repos. This will run the Berkeley DB recovery functions on the repository, which has the side effect of reinitializing the database environment, which causes the DB_CONFIG file to be read. So keep in mind that whenever you change this file, you have to be sure to run svnadmin recover on the repository, or it won't have any effect.

There are two main kinds of things you can tweak in the DB_CONFIG file. First are the settings related to Berkeley DB locks, and second are the settings related to Berkeley DB log files.

For locks, there are three variables you can configure: set_lk_max_locks, set_lk_max_lockers, and set_lk_max_objects. These variables are documented at http://www.sleepycat.com/docs/ref/lock/max.html, and if you're really interested you should read up on them there. Roughly speaking, however, these variables control the number of locks you can have active in the database at any given time. The set_lk_max_objects variable controls the number of levels of the internal Berkeley DB database B-tree you can lock at a time; the set_lk_max_lockers variable controls the number of outstanding Berkeley DB–level transactions you can have at a time; and the set_lk_max_locks variable controls the actual number of locks you can have. Subversion ships with these values preset to 2000, but if you're using a very large repository and you're seeing errors related to Berkeley DB locking when someone is performing a large transaction (say, a commit that's touching a lot of files), you might need to bump these numbers up.

For log files, there are three variables you can control. First, the set_lg_bsize variable controls the in-memory log buffer. Subversion sets this to 262144 (256KB for those of you playing along at home); the Subversion developers have found that decreasing this value below 256KB will hurt commit performance. Second is the set_lg_max variable, which controls the size of each log file. This is set to 1048576 (1MB) by default to ensure that a hot backup requires the minimum possible amount of disk space. Berkeley DB actually defaults to a 10MB log file size, but that causes repositories to use up an inordinately large amount of disk space, most of which is just log files. Reducing the log size to 1MB means that you can more quickly remove old log files as they stop being used, saving that disk space for other things, and reducing the amount of data you need to copy around when making hot backups. You shouldn't have to tweak either of these variables, but if you're motivated to do so for some reason, keep these things in mind.

Besides tweaking locks and log file settings, there are two other settings that may affect your repository. First is the DB_TXN_NOSYNC flag, which turns off forced flushing to disk at the end of a transaction, resulting in a large performance increase. This flag is off by default. The other flag is the DB_LOG_AUTOREMOVE flag, which we've already discussed. Adding a set_flags DB_LOG_AUTOREMOVE line to the file will cause Berkeley DB to automatically remove old, unused log files instead of leaving them for you to clean up. This flag is available only in versions of Berkeley DB newer than 4.2.52.

For more details about things that can be configured in the DB_CONFIG file, refer to the documentation at http://www.sleepycat.com/docs/ref/env/db_config.html.

Hooks

It's often convenient to associate some kind of arbitrary action with various parts of the Subversion life cycle. For example, most open source projects have an e-mail list that receives an e-mail whenever someone commits a change to the repository. In CVS this is accomplished through a set of scripts in the CVSROOT directory. In Perforce you use a review daemon, and in Subversion this (and many other things) can be accomplished via a hook script.

As you saw when you first looked at the internals of the repository, there are a number of different hook scripts supported by Subversion. Specifically, you can associate hooks with several points in the commit cycle and a few places in the revision property change cycle.

Each of the nine hooks are run at different times, passed different arguments, and given different data via standard input. Also, each return value is interpreted differently. Table 3-2 summarizes all of this.

Table 3-2. *Hook Script Behavior*

Script Name	When It's Called	Arguments	What's Sent to Standard Input	Significance of Return Value
start-commit	Before the commit's transaction is created	Repository path and the username of the user	Not used	0 indicates the commit should continue; nonzero indicates it should be stopped
pre-commit	After the commit's transaction is created, but before it's committed	Repository path and transaction name	Not used	0 indicates the commit should continue; nonzero indicates it should be stopped
post-commit	After a commit completes	Repository path and revision that the commit created	Not used	Ignored
pre-lock	Before an exclusive lock is created	Repository path, path about to be locked, and user trying to create the lock	Not used	0 indicates the lock should be allowed; nonzero indicates the lock is not allowed
post-lock	After a locking operation completes	Repository path and username that created the lock	The paths that were locked	Ignored
post-unlock	After an unlocking operation completes	Repository path and username that destroyed the lock	The paths that were unlocked	Ignored
pre-unlock	Before an exclusive lock is destroyed	Repository path, path about to be unlocked, and user trying to unlock	Not used	0 indicates the unlock should be allowed; nonzero indicates the unlock is not allowed
pre-revprop-change	Before a revision property is changed	The path to the repository, the revision whose revision property is being modified, the username of the user performing the change, the name of the revision property being changed, and a value indicating whether the property was added, deleted, or modified	The new value of the revision property	0 indicates the change should continue; nonzero indicates it should be stopped
post-revprop-change	After a revision property is changed	The path to the repository, the revision whose revision property is being modified, the user-name of the user performing the change,the name of the revision property being modified, and a value indicating whether the property was added, deleted, or modified	The old value of the revprop	Ignored

Commit Hooks

For commits, you can have a `start-commit` hook, which is called before a commit begins to create its transaction inside the repository and is given the path to the repository and the username of the user making the commit as arguments. This hook is useful for doing some extra user-based authorization checks (since it does not know what paths the user wants to modify, it is not useful for per-path policy). There is also a `pre-commit` hook, which is run right before the user's transaction is committed and is given the path to the repository and the name of the transaction as arguments. This hook is useful to do extra per-path and per-file authorization checks, as well as checks on the log message. Finally, there is a `post-commit` hook, which runs immediately after a commit occurs and is given the path to the repository and the revision that was just committed as arguments. This hook is useful for mailing out notifications of changes, or anything else that you want to do with a finished commit (some people use it to perform per-revision incremental backups, triggering an automatic test suite, and so on). Note that if the `pre-commit` or `start-commit` hooks exit with a 0 exit code, the commit process will continue; otherwise, it will halt.

Locking Hooks

Similar to commits, there are pre- and post- hooks for locking and unlocking. The `pre-lock` hook is called before an exclusive lock is created. The hook is given the repository path and the name of the user attempting to create a lock. The paths the user is trying to lock are passed to standard input. The `pre-lock` hook is used to set policy about who can perform locks and where. If the hook returns nonzero, the lock is disallowed. The `pre-unlock` hook is exactly like the `pre-lock` hook, except it is called for unlock operations. In addition to these pre- hooks, there are post- hooks that can be used to e-mail or otherwise process notifications of locks. The `post-lock` hook is called after a lock succeeds and has the same arguments as the `pre-lock` hook. The `post-unlock` hook is called after the unlock succeeds and has the same arguments as the `pre-unlock` hook.

Revprop Change Hooks

Similar to the commit hooks are the revprop change hooks. As you learned in Chapter 2, revprops are pretty much the only data in a Subversion repository that isn't versioned. As a result, you actually have to specifically set up a `pre-revprop-change` hook script to allow revprops to be changed. If you don't, any attempt to change them will always fail. As with commits, there are both `pre-revprop-change` and `post-revprop-change` hooks, and they're run before and after the change occurs, respectively. The path to the repository, the revision, the user who is trying to modify it, and the name of the property are passed as arguments to the `pre-revprop-change` hook. The property value is passed in as the script's standard input. If the hook exits with anything other than a 0 exit value, the prop change won't go through. The `post-revprop-change` hook receives the same arguments, just without the property value, as the value is now available inside the repository, so if the hook needs it, it can use `svnlook` or some other equivalent utility to get it.

Access Control Hook Scripts

Subversion doesn't currently offer much in the way of built-in access control. Although you can set up various kinds of authentication for each of the repository access methods, the module-based access controls mostly do not allow for more fine-grained control other than specifying whether a person does or does not have read (and/or write) access to a given path. To allow more fine-grained access control limitations to be placed on the repository, several people have written hook scripts that can be installed as `pre-commit` hooks.

In general, the `svnlook` tool is used to examine the transaction the commit has created and figure out what paths are being modified by the commit. Some kind of configuration file holds a description of what paths each user is allowed to modify, and if the commit is trying to modify something the user shouldn't have access to, it will return a nonzero exit code; otherwise, it returns 0 and the commit continues. For some concrete examples of how this is done, see the `commit-access-control.pl` and `svnperms.py` scripts in the `tools/hook-scripts` and `contrib/hook-scripts` subdirectories of the Subversion distribution.

Commit Notification Hook Scripts

Another common need is to send a message out to a mailing list when a commit occurs, so developers can keep track of what's happening in a project. This is a perfect job for a `post-commit` hook script. Again, `svnlook` is used to extract data about the commit that has occurred (normally the log message and the diff), which is then e-mailed off to the mailing list. For a simple example of how to do this, see `commit-email.pl` in the `tools/hook-scripts` directory of the Subversion distribution. We'll discuss a more advanced commit e-mail program, `mailer.py`, when we cover the use of the Subversion Python bindings in Chapter 8.

Writing and Installing Hook Scripts

To install a hook script, you need to place an executable file of the appropriate name (`start-commit`, `pre-commit`, `post-commit`, `pre-revprop-change`, or `post-revprop-change`) in the repository's `hooks` directory. On Unix, this means a file of this name with its executable bit set; on Windows this means a file of that name with an `.exe`, `.bat`, or `.cmd` extension. There are fully documented sample scripts named after each hook (with a `.tmpl` extension) in the `hooks` directory of a newly created repository.

A hook script is really just an executable program with a certain name placed in the repository's `hooks` directory and made executable. Hook scripts on Windows must be executable programs, batch files, or command files, but because a batch file can call out to any other language you have installed, in practice the limitation on what can be executed isn't a problem. In fact, in practice, hook scripts on Unix are usually written much the same way as Windows, by writing a simple shell script and placing it in the `hooks` directory with the proper name and having it call any number of other programs that need to be executed for this particular phase of the commit or revprop change cycle.

Writing hook scripts is very similar to writing CGI scripts. The script is executed by Subversion, not by you, so it's often difficult to tell what's happening. A good way to debug your hook script is often just to write to a log file. The very first thing you should do when trying to figure out why your script isn't working is to have it write to a file somewhere as soon as it is run. If you discover that nothing is being written to the file, you can be relatively certain that your problem is just that the script isn't being executed. If this is the case, you should proceed to check that the file is executable (if your platform supports such a thing) and that it's named correctly.

The next most common issues turn out to be related to the fact that the environment the server runs the hook script in is different from the one you work in at the command line. You can minimize these kinds of errors by ensuring that your script doesn't depend on any environment variables, which includes using absolute paths to any executables you run, avoiding dependence on having particular directories in your PATH. Once you've determined that the script is being executed and that you aren't depending on anything in your environment that won't be there when it's run, any other issues can most likely be resolved by writing debugging information to a file until you've determined what's wrong with the script. The process may seem difficult at first, but with practice, writing hook scripts becomes as simple as developing any other kind of program that must be executed by a process not completely under your control.

Networking with ra_dav

Eventually, you're going to want to access your Subversion repository from more than one machine. To do that you'll need to set up a Subversion server, and the primary way of doing so is through mod_dav_svn, an Apache module that allows the Subversion client to speak to a Subversion repository via a WebDAV-based protocol.

You install and configure mod_dav_svn in much the same as you do any other Apache module. First you need to install Apache 2.x When doing so, be sure that you install the mod_dav module, as mod_dav_svn requires it.

Subversion's install process will add the necessary LoadModule line to httpd.conf that will cause Apache to load mod_dav_svn at startup, but if you're not installing Subversion from source it's possible that you might have to add it yourself. If you're doing so, it's important to ensure that mod_dav_svn is loaded after mod_dav or you'll be unable to start Apache due to unresolved symbols. The appropriate section of your httpd.conf should look like this:

```
LoadModule dav_module       modules/mod_dav.so
LoadModule dav_svn_module   modules/mod_dav_svn.so
```

If mod_dav wasn't compiled as a shared object, you won't need to worry about this. The important thing to keep in mind is that if there's a LoadModule line for mod_dav.so, it must come before the line for mod_dav_svn.so.

To make use of mod_dav_svn, you just need to set up a Location block like this:

```
<Location /svn>
  DAV svn
  SVNPathAuthz off
  SVNPath /path/to/repository
</Location>
```

The DAV line tells mod_dav to use mod_dav_svn as its underlying provider, and the SVNPath line indicates which repository should be made available at /repository. Now all you need to do is ensure that the user Apache runs as can read and write to the repository, and you should be able to access it over ra_dav, like this:

```
$ svn checkout http://server/svn/trunk wc
```

```
A foo.c
A bar.c
Checked out revision 10.
$ cd wc
$ svn info | grep ^URL

URL: http://server/svn/trunk
$
```

■**Note** If you've used Apache modules such as mod_php before, you might be tempted to try to put your repository's Location block in an .htaccess file. You might assume this would let your users configure repositories without needing to change Apache's configuration file directly. Unfortunately, due to the way Location blocks are processed, they don't work in .htaccess, so you'll have to put your repository configuration in your server's httpd.conf file.

If you're like most developers, you won't want everyone who has access to your web server to be able to commit changes to your repository, so you'll want to set up some access controls. With mod_dav_svn, this is just like setting up any other kind of HTTP authentication. You add a few more directives to your Location block in httpd.conf, restart Apache, and you're on your way. Let's first look at the configuration and then cover what each part of it does:

```
<Location /svn>
  DAV svn
  SVNPath /path/to/repository
  SVNPathAuthz off
  AuthType basic
  AuthName "My Subversion Repository"
  AuthUserFile /path/to/users/file
  <LimitExcept GET PROPFIND OPTIONS REPORT>
    Require valid-user
  </LimitExcept>
</Location>
```

Here you can see that you add an AuthType basic line to tell Apache that you want basic HTTP authentication, an AuthName "My Subversion Repository" line to give clients some idea why they're giving a username and password, and an AuthUserFile /path/to/users/file line to tell Apache what file to use to store usernames and passwords. If you want, you could just add a Require valid-user line and that would make Apache require a valid username and password for all access. In this case, though, you go a bit further and wrap the Require valid-user in a LimitExcept block, so that read-only access (which uses the GET, PROPFIND, OPTIONS, and REPORT HTTP methods) won't require any authentication, but all other access (i.e., anything that tries to write to the repository) will need to be authenticated. The file referred to in the AuthUserFile line is a standard Apache password file, created by the htpasswd command.

Accessing a repository that uses authentication is simple. You just access it as normal, and when you try to do something that requires authentication, you'll be prompted for a password. For the first attempt, Subversion will use your login name as your username, but if your first attempt at authentication fails, you'll be prompted again, this time for both a username and a password. Once you've successfully authenticated, Subversion will store your username and password combination in the auth subdirectory of your ~/.subversion directory. In the future you won't be prompted for a username and password on this particular repository. If you don't want your username and password to be cached (perhaps you're using someone else's account, or are on a public machine), you can pass svn the --no-auth-cache flag, and it won't cache any authentication data. If you never want Subversion to cache passwords, you can set store-passwords = no in the [auth] section of ~/.subversion/config.

Here's an example of the authentication handshake from the user's perspective:

```
$ svn list http://servername/svn/repos/
```

```
Authentication realm: <http://servername:80> servername
Password for 'rooneg':
Authentication realm: <http://servername:80> servername
username: garrett
Password for 'garret'
branches/
trunk/
$
```

The first challenge uses the user's local username (in this example, rooneg). When the password doesn't match, the user is given an opportunity to provide a different username. The username and password can be overridden by using the --username and --password flags, so that commands can be run in situations in which it would be impossible for the user to enter a username and password, such as when the command is automated with a shell script of some sort.

Note that there's no reason to use AuthUserFile to control access to your repository. In fact, you can't use Apache access controls to control access to pieces of your repository. However, mod_dav_svn can plug into any of Apache's authentication modules, something you'll explore in greater detail in Chapter 5.

The last of the basic mod_dav_svn configuration options that you might find useful is SVNParentPath. This lets you indicate that a single parent directory contains several Subversion repositories, so you don't have to list them each in their own individual Location block. For example, in the previous Location example, you could replace the SVNPath /path/to/repository line with SVNParentPath /home/svn. Now if you place repositories named foo and bar within the /home/svn directory, you could access them via http://server/svn/foo/ and http://server/svn/bar/. There is also an SVNListParentPath option that enables a web browser accessing SVNParentPath to display a list of repositories. Please note that SVNPath and SVNParentPath are mutually exclusive.

Networking with ra_svn

If you're not comfortable with running an Apache server, or if you want to reuse your existing ssh infrastructure for securing your Subversion connections, you can use ra_svn for your repository access layer. The ra_svn library implements a custom protocol designed specifically for Subversion and provides a lightweight server process that speaks to it. The server, svnserve, can be run stand-alone or via inetd to provide anonymous access to the repository, or for those who need something a bit more secure, it can be used in a tunneled mode, with all access happening via ssh or some other tunnel agent if you so choose. For a stand-alone server, you access the repository with an svn:// URL; and for access via a tunnel agent, you use svn+agent:// syntax, where agent is the name associated with this particular way of creating a tunnel (support for ssh is built in, and later on in this section you'll see how to define your own).

■**Note** A *tunnel agent* is an external program Subversion uses to run svnserve, usually on another machine. The tunnel agent logs into the machine where the repository resides, runs the svnserve -t program there, and uses its standard input and output for the connection between the client and server. Most of the time, people use ssh as their tunnel agent, but it's certainly possible to use other programs, as long as they're capable of running svnserve -t and managing the connection between it and the client.

Setting up svnserve is considerably simpler than setting up Apache. The basic server can be started by passing it the --daemon flag. This will start the server up as a daemon process, listening on port 3690 (this is the official IANA-assigned port number for Subversion's custom protocol). Just using the --daemon flag makes the server provide access to the entire filesystem of the machine it's running on, meaning that every repository the server has access to will be accessible to anyone who can connect to the server. A more common way to run svnserve is to restrict access to everything under a particular root directory on the server via the --root flag. To run svnserve in daemon mode with access restricted to repositories under the /home/repos directory, you would use svnserve --daemon --root /home/repos.

Each Subversion repository contains a configuration file (conf/svnserve.conf) that controls what people are allowed to do with it when they access it via ra_svn. Here's an example of what such a configuration file looks like:

```
[general]
anon-access = read
auth-access = write
password-db = passwd
authz-db = authz
realm = My First Repository
```

All of the configuration options go in the general section. anon-access and auth-access control the kind of access to the repository that authenticated and nonauthenticated users have. They can each be set to either read, write, or none. The default settings are read access for anonymous users and write access for authenticated users. If you want your users to be able to authenticate themselves, you'll also have to configure a password-db, which is a relative path to a file that contains the usernames and passwords for this repository's users. The password file looks like this:

```
[users]
user = password
```

The users are listed in the users section, with the username and password separated by an equal sign (=). In this case, the only user that's defined is named user, and his password is password.

■Note The svnserve password file format stores passwords in plain text, so be sure that only the user that svnserve runs as has read access to it, to keep your users from reading each other's passwords.

The authz option allows you to use a path-based authorization file, in the same format that mod_authz_svn uses, to control who can access what portions of the repository. We'll talk more about the format of this file in Chapter 5.

The final option in svnserve.conf is the repository's realm, which is just a descriptive string presented to the user when she is asked for her username and password. It should be descriptive enough that the user can determine what username and password is appropriate, in case there are multiple repositories available on one server.

In addition to --root and --daemon, which you've already seen, svnserve has a number of other command-line options. If you're running it on a computer that has multiple network interfaces, you might need the --listen-host option to indicate the hostname or IP address of the interface the interface svnserve should listen on. Similarly, if you wish to have svnserve listen on a port other than the default (3690), you can use the --listen-port flag.

If you prefer to run svnserve out of inetd, instead of using the --daemon flag, you just need to add the appropriate line to your machine's inetd.conf file, making use of the --inetd flag to svnserve to let it know that it should use standard input and standard output instead of opening up a socket.

Another flag you might find useful is --threads, which is only present if APR supports threads on your platform. Using it will cause svnserve to run in multithreaded mode instead of forking off a new process for each connection. On systems on which threading isn't available, the --threads flag isn't available, because it's futile to present the option if it won't work. It's likewise not available on systems on which fork isn't available, because in that case threaded mode is the default anyway.

For read-write access, it's common to use svnserve in tunnel mode. Instead of using an svn:// URL, you use svn+ssh://, and Subversion will use ssh to run svnserve -t on the server. In this case, the ssh process ensures that the user is authenticated on the server. By default, the Subversion client will use ssh to execute svnserve on the remote server, but if you want to use a different command (perhaps you want to run ssh over a nonstandard port, for example), you can set the SVN_SSH environment variable to the command that should be used, or you can add an ssh = ssh -p 4747 line to the [tunnels] section of the ~/.subversion/config configuration file.

Although the only tunnel agent supported by default in the Subversion client is ssh, you can easily define your own by changing the URL syntax a bit, and either setting an environment variable or adding a configuration file entry for your tunnel agent. For example, to run your tunnel over rsh, you would set the SVN_RSH environment variable to rsh, or add a line like rsh = rsh to the config file. You would then just use a URL like svn+rsh://host/path/to/repository, and you would be using rsh to create your tunnel.

Repository Permissions

The permissions needed to perform repository operations are another instance where the FSFS back end wins in terms of ease of use. People with read-only access to the repository only require read-only access to the files making up the repository to be able to perform operations. Even people requiring write access only need the ability to create and write new files and read existing ones. Once created, a revision file in FSFS (the things in the db/revs directory) never change. Besides making FSFS repositories easier to keep secure, it also means incremental backups using rsync are very fast. As a real-world example, GCC has svn and svn+ssh access to the repository. The svn-access-method users are read-only, and thus, the svnserve daemon serving it runs as a user that only has read access to the repository. The svn+ssh users, which are the group of people we allow to perform writes, face the same problem Berkeley DB experiences regarding direct access.

   When using a Berkeley DB–driven repository, all users that directly access the repository without going through a server of some sort must have write access to the files that make up the repository. This includes pretty much everything within the db subdirectory in the repository. When you attach to a Berkeley DB database environment, your process needs to write to the database files for a variety of reasons, from taking out locks on portions of the database to writing changes out to log files before they're finally written to the actual database. This occurs regardless of whether you're actually going to make a change to the repository. Because of this requirement, it's vital that all users of your Berkeley DB–based repository have read-write access to the underlying database files. Even more insidious is the fact that when performing many actions using the repository, your client will have to write data to the repository (even if you aren't committing a change, Subversion might be storing bookkeeping data in the form of a transaction in some cases), and that will cause new Berkeley DB log files to be created. On Unix, depending on the user's umask setting, this file could be created with permissions that don't allow the other users of the repository to write to them. This will usually result in an error such as the following:

```
$ svn commit
```

```
svn: Couldn't open a repository.
svn: Commit failed (details follow):
svn: Unable to open an ra_local session to URL
svn: Unable to open repository 'file:///path/to/repos/trunk'
svn: Berkeley DB error while opening 'nodes' table for filesystem
/path/to/repos/ db: DB_RUNRECOVERY: Fatal error, run database recovery
svn: Couldn't open a repository.
svn: Your commit message was left in a temporary file:
svn:      '/home/rooneg/projects/test/svn-commit.tmp'
```

```
$ ls -l /path/to/repos/db/log.*
```

```
-rw-rw-r-- 1 svn    svn     380302 Jul 27 21:29 log.0000000001
-rw-r--r-- 1 root   svn 380302 Jul 27 21:40 log.0000000002
$
```

Unfortunately, the error message isn't especially informative. It tells you that there was a problem opening a Berkeley DB table, but there's no real indication that the cause is a permissions problem. Despite this, the permissions issue is the single most common problem people tend to encounter with their repositories, so if you ever encounter an error like this, an excellent first step to fixing it is to check the permissions on all the files in the repository's db directory.

There are a number of ways you can work around this problem, but the general idea is to ensure that the permissions on the database files are such that all users who need to access the repository have read and write access. The specifics can vary depending on what repository access method you're using. If you are accessing the repository only via ra_dav or via ra_svn through an svnserve process running in daemon mode, you just have to ensure that the user the server (either Apache or svnserve) runs under has permission to write to the files. The catch is that if you ever need to use any tools to access the repository directly, either svn via ra_local or svnadmin, or svnlook, you'll have to ensure that the repository permissions remain intact. If you're accessing the repository via ra_local or ra_svn in tunnel mode, then the process that's actually connecting to the database environment will potentially be running as any number of different users; so even if the database files start out with permissions such that everyone can write to them, if one user has a umask that is too restrictive, he could accidentally create a new log file that the other users can't write to. The usual workaround for this is to ensure that all users who need to access the repository are members of the same group and to replace either the svnserve—in the case of ra_svn—or svn—in the case of ra_local—command with a shell script that ensures the umask is correctly set. Such a wrapper script would look something like this:

```
$ cat /usr/local/bin/svnserve
```

```
#!/bin/sh
umask 002
exec /usr/local/bin/svnserve-real "$@"
$
```

This short script executes a umask 002 command and then proceeds to call the real svnserve with whatever arguments the user originally passed in.

If you're using multiple repository access methods, you'll have to take steps to make sure all of them respect the permissions on the repository. This means you'll need to replace the svn and svnserve commands with scripts that ensure the correct umask is used; you'll have to add a similar umask 002 to Apache's apachectl startup script; and, finally, you'll have to ensure that Apache runs as a user who is in the same group as your Subversion users.

In practice, though, if you use a Berkeley DB–based repository, it's probably better to standardize on one repository access method, either ra_dav, ra_svn with svnserve in daemon mode, or `ra_svn` tunneled over `ssh`, rather than supporting more than one. For either `ra_dav` or `ra_svn` with `svnserve` in daemon mode, the only time you need to worry about repository permissions is if you're accessing the repository directly, and you can usually deal with that by judicious use of `chown -R` commands. With `ra_svn` tunneled over `ssh`, you'll still need to take the precautions discussed previously, but even then at least you'll have only a single access mechanism to deal with, which reduces the amount of effort you'll spend avoiding Berkeley DB permission problems for read-only users.

Summary

In this chapter, you learned everything you need to know to administer your own Subversion repository. You learned how to create a new repository, how to back it up correctly, how to use the dump and load commands to upgrade to new versions of Subversion that alter the underlying database schema and, last but certainly not least, how to make your repository available via the network, either by using `mod_dav_svn` and Apache, or by using Subversion's custom `svnserve` server.

In the next chapter, you'll learn how to transfer your project's revision history from whatever version control system you're currently using into your new Subversion repository.

CHAPTER 4

■■■

Migrating from Other Version Control Systems

Now that you have a general idea of how to use Subversion, you're probably wondering how you might go about migrating your existing code base into a Subversion repository.

The simplest way to migrate from whatever version control system you're currently using into Subversion is just to take the latest release of your code and execute an `svn import`. In fact, you've already seen how to do this in Chapter 2.

This certainly gets you up and running as quickly as possible, but in many situations it's not acceptable. Most significant projects have accumulated a large amount of revision history, and not wanting to lose this information is understandable. Depending on what kind of version control system you're currently using, preserving that history might be easy or it might be hard. Let's take a look at the options.

Migrating a Release History

Rather than importing your entire current source tree (using `svn import`) you might consider instead importing a series of released versions of your project. This gives you some of the benefit of preserving history, in that you can at least see the evolution of various files over time, albeit at a much coarser resolution than if you actually converted the contents of your existing revision control system using a specialized tool.

The process is mildly tedious, but conceptually simple. First, you use `svn import`, which you learned about in Chapter 2, to bring the oldest version of your software into the trunk of your repository. Then, for each subsequent version, you copy the files associated with that version into a checked-out copy of the trunk. You then delete any files that no longer exist in the new version, add any new files in the new version that were not present in the old version, and deal with any renames that may have occurred by moving the new version to a temporary file-name, executing an `svn move`, and then copying the new version on top of the old one. Finally, you just `svn commit` the new version. Repeat this process for each subsequent version of the software, and you're all set.

This technique is just a special case of importing software on a vendor branch, something that's discussed in Chapter 6. In that chapter you can find examples of how to do this and information on some tools to automate the process, which can simplify things considerably.

As you can see, migrating your code into Subversion in this manner is a relatively straight-forward process, but in exchange for that simplicity you pay a price. The major problem with simply migrating over your release history is (obviously) that you lose all the revision history that makes up each of those releases. That is, you can see what changes happened to a given file between release 1 and release 2, but you miss the incremental modifications that make up that change and, more important, you miss the justifications behind those changes, which are often present in the corresponding log entries. When you go back over the revision history of a file to determine why something was done in a certain way, the reasons for making a change are often as valuable or even more valuable than the change itself.

For this reason, you probably want to make use of some other migration strategy if possible. If you don't have access to anything but the actual releases, perhaps because the actual source repository isn't accessible, or if there is no available program for converting from your old version control system to Subversion, this technique might be your only option. But if this isn't the case, you should almost certainly make use of the technique of writing a dumpfile, as all of the following converters do.

Various Migration Strategies

To migrate your revision history from your old version control system into Subversion, you'll have three tasks to complete.

First, you need some way to export your existing system's revision history. Some possible techniques for this might include writing a script to drive your existing system's client program, or making use of scripting language bindings for your existing system if they're available.

Second, you need to provide some logic that can map the existing revision history onto the Subversion model. This means breaking the existing history up into distinct revisions, mapping from any existing concepts of branches and tags into Subversion-style cheap copies, and preserving existing metadata such as RCS keywords, executable settings, log messages, or other such things. The level of complexity for this task depends on how closely your existing system matches with Subversion's way of doing things, and you'll see examples of varying complexity in the "Migrating from Perforce" section of this chapter when we explore p42svn, a Perforce-to-Subversion conversion program, and cvs2svn, a CVS-to-Subversion conversion program.

Third, you need to bring your data into a Subversion repository. This can be done in a number of ways, from driving the Subversion command-line client, to using the libsvn_fs library to directly modify a raw Subversion repository, to writing out a Subversion dumpfile that can then be loaded into an existing repository via the svnadmin load command, as you saw in Chapter 3.

The easiest way to see how these various options can be used is to simply look at some existing programs that use them, such as vss2svn, cvs2svn, and p42svn. In addition to providing you with some insight into how you would write a repository converter, this enables you to review some of the existing solutions that are out there. So if you happen to be moving from one of the version control systems that they cover, you'll see an example of how you can make use of these tools for your own repository migration.

The Subversion Dumpfile Format

As mentioned in the Chapter 3 discussion of the svnadmin dump and svnadmin load commands, Subversion makes use of a simple file format for dumping and restoring the contents of the Subversion filesystem database. This format can also be used for a number of other purposes, such as bulk-loading data into a repository. Because it's considerably simpler to create a dumpfile than it is to work directly on the filesystem, many repository conversion programs make use of the format for the final loading of their data into Subversion.

The dumpfile format is documented in the file notes/fs_dumprestore.txt, found in the Subversion source distribution. The most up-to-date data on what it contains can always be found there, but the format is reasonably simple, so a brief overview is provided here.

First, you should understand what information the dumpfile format is trying to preserve. The Subversion filesystem is essentially an array of trees. Each of these trees is a revision, and there are a number of unversioned revision properties associated with it. Each revision has a tree of nodes hanging off of it. Most of the nodes in each revision are actually just references to nodes created in earlier revisions, but in cases where a file or directory is changed in a given revision, the node that represents it will have new content. Each node may contain some versioned text, versioned properties, and possibly some history, concerning both its predecessor (i.e., which node it is a variant of) and where it is copied from.

This sounds a little complex, so let's look at a graphical example shown in Figure 4-1.

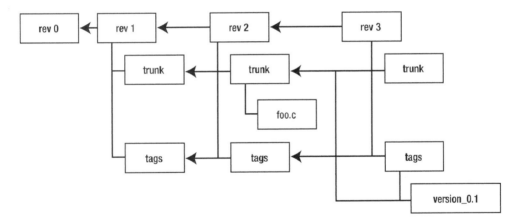

Figure 4-1. *The node structure of a subversion repository, with arrows showing which nodes are based on other nodes*

On the far left is revision 0, an empty repository. Next, there's revision 1, where the /trunk and /tags directories are created. In revision 2, the file foo.c is created inside /trunk, but /tags just refers to the same node created in revision 1. Finally, in revision 3 the directory version_0.1 is created inside /tags as a copy of /trunk. This results in a new node representing the new directory, but it just refers to the previous version of the /trunk directory, and because /trunk hasn't changed in this revision, it still refers to the version created in revision 2.

At this point the easiest thing to do is to take a look at a real example of the output of svnadmin dump, so you can get an idea of what this stuff looks like in practice. Each node in the dumpfile begins with a number of RFC 822 style headers. Some of the headers describe the data associated with the node (the number of bytes taken up by the text or property portions, for example), some indicate the action that's currently occurring (creating or removing a file or directory), and some contain information about the node itself (where and when it was copied from, for example). If the node is a directory, it will contain only headers and, potentially, properties; otherwise, it will also contain the entire contents of the file as it existed in that revision, or deltas if you used the -deltas option during the dumpfile creation.

The following is a dump of a simple repository that's only up to revision 5. It starts with the typical version and UUID headers, and then there's a node for the initial revision 0, which contains only one property, svn:date, indicating when the repository was first created. After that are four revisions, in which you create the initial repository layout (the /trunk, /branches, and /tags directories), import a source file, set a property on the file, tag the contents of the trunk as a release, and then delete the tag when you decide it isn't useful.

Let's actually look at a dumpfile and summarize the format used. The first thing is the dumpfile header, which contains a version and UUID:

```
SVN-fs-dump-format-version: 2
UUID: fbef4eb3-f2c8-0310-9138-dcbdabb51a2b
```

After the header we go straight into data for the first revision, starting with the revision properties:

```
Revision-number: 0
Prop-content-length: 56
Content-length: 56
K 8
svn:date
V 27
2003-10-05T16:00:46.069685Z
PROPS-END
```

Since revision number 0 is an empty revision, it isn't so interesting. Revision 1 is the first place any real data will appear. We start again with the revision properties:

```
Revision-number: 1
Prop-content-length: 127
Content-length: 127
K 7
svn:log
V 26
initial repository layout
K 10
svn:author
V 6
rooneg
K 8
svn:date
V 27
```

```
2003-10-05T16:05:53.652679Z
PROPS-END
```

After the revision properties we have a bunch of nodes additions for the directory nodes added in revision 1:

```
Node-path: branches
Node-kind: dir
Node-action: add
Prop-content-length: 10
Content-length: 10
PROPS-END
Node-path: tags
Node-kind: dir
Node-action: add
Prop-content-length: 10
Content-length: 10
PROPS-END
Node-path: trunk
Node-kind: dir
Node-action: add
Prop-content-length: 10
Content-length: 10
PROPS-END
```

That is all for revision 1. Revision 2 is the first revision where an actual file is added with some content. Again we start with the revision properties:

```
Revision-number: 2
Prop-content-length: 133
Content-length: 133
K 7
svn:log
V 32
initial version of hello world.
K 10
svn:author
V 6
rooneg
K 8
svn:date
V 27
2003-10-05T16:07:24.367963Z
PROPS-END
```

Now we have a node for our `hello.c` file, its text content, and its properties:

```
Node-path: trunk/hello.c
Node-kind: file
Node-action: add
Prop-content-length: 10
Text-content-length: 99
Text-content-md5: 0c1ea17162fcd46023bf6712a35dba03
Content-length: 109
PROPS-END
#include <stdio.h>
int
main (int argc, char *argv[])
{
  printf ("hello world\n");
  return 0;
}
```

That is all for revision 2. Revision 3 is going to modify a property on the `hello.c` file. But as usual it starts out with the revision properties:

```
Revision-number: 3
Prop-content-length: 114
Content-length: 114
K 7
svn:log
V 13
set eol-style
K 10
svn:author
V 6
rooneg
K 8
svn:date
V 27
2004-05-10T00:20:39.888307Z
PROPS-END
```

After the revision properties we have a node change that changes the properties set on the `hello.c` file:

```
Node-path: trunk/hello.c
Node-kind: file
Node-action: change
Prop-content-length: 36
Content-length: 36
K 13
svn:eol-style
V 2
LF
PROPS-END
```

That is all for revision 3. Revision 4 is going to copy the revision 3 trunk to the tags subdirectory. As usual we have our revision properties first:

```
Revision-number: 4
Prop-content-length: 117
Content-length: 117
K 7
svn:log
V 16
tag version 0.1
K 10
svn:author
V 6
rooneg
K 8
svn:date
V 27
2003-10-05T16:07:56.122468Z
PROPS-END
```

After the revision properties we have the node copy that copies /trunk to tags/0.1:

```
Node-path: tags/0.1
Node-kind: dir
Node-action: add
Node-copyfrom-rev: 2
Node-copyfrom-path: trunk
```

That is all for revision 4. Revision 5 is going to delete the tag we created in revision 4. For the last time (thankfully!), we have our revision properties first:

```
Revision-number: 5
Prop-content-length: 122
Content-length: 122
K 7
svn:log
V 21
deleting tag for 0.1
K 10
svn:author
V 6
rooneg
K 8
svn:date
V 27
2003-10-05T16:08:53.662110Z
PROPS-END
```

Here is our final node change, which is a delete of the tags/0.1 directory:

```
Node-path: tags/0.1
Node-action: delete
```

Well, that was long, but if you take a close look, it's not that hard to understand. Each revision starts off with a header that indicates the revision number. Then there are a few revision properties (specifically, svn:log, svn:author, and svn:date) and then some contents. When files are added, they're simply included inline as fulltext in the dumpfile, and copies and deletes are represented by headers indicating the source and destination (for copies) or path (for deletes). The format is quite readable, and as you can see, it's reasonably easy to write a program that either generates òr consumes it, depending on whether you're trying to get data into or out of a Subversion repository.

Now let's go over some of the details of the format. As mentioned, each node in the dumpfile begins with a number of RFC 822 style headers, just like you'd see in standard e-mail. The first header in each revision is always Revision-number, which indicates which revision the following nodes are a part of. All the nodes that follow are assumed to be a part of that revision, right up until another Revision-number header occurs. The last header in a node is Content-length, and after that come the contents of the node. The contents are split into two parts: the property hash and the text. The division between these parts is a single line that contains PROPS-END. If the node is a directory or a revision, only the property hash will be present; the text will be empty.

At the beginning of the dump are a few special headers that are used for globally important information that isn't associated with any specific node in the tree. First is the SVN-fs-dump-format-version header, which predictably enough tells you what version of the dump format you're looking at. The version documented here is version 2, and the only difference between it and version 1 is the addition of the next header, UUID. As you learned in the previous chapter, each Subversion repository has a UUID associated with it, so that clients can determine if they're really connecting to the same repository even if they're doing so through a different URL.

There are a number of different headers currently defined. All headers that aren't understood are ignored for backward-compatibility purposes. First, let's look at the fields associated with a node that represents a revision:

- `Revision-number`: An integer representing the number of the current revision.

- `Prop-content-length`: The number of bytes taken up by the serialized property hashtable.

- `Content-length`: The total number of bytes in the content of the node.

Then, for each node in the revision, there are the following headers, some of which are optional:

- `Node-path`: The absolute path to the item in the filesystem.

- `Node-kind`: Either `file` or `dir`. If this node is a `delete`, this header is optional.

- `Node-action`: Either `change`, `add`, `delete`, or `replace`.

- `Node-copyfrom-rev`: The revision of the copy's source if the node represents a copy. This isn't present if the node isn't a copy.

- `Node-copyfrom-path`: The path of its source if the node represents a copy. This isn't present if the node isn't a copy.

- `Prop-content-length`: The length in bytes of the node's serialized property hash. If there are no properties this is absent.

- `Text-content-md5`: The MD5 checksum of the node's text. If there is no text this node isn't present.

- `Text-content-length`: The length in bytes of the node's text. If there is no text this node is absent.

- `Prop-delta`: A Boolean flag representing whether the property contents are a delta against the previous version. Only present in dumpfiles created with the `--deltas` option.

- `Text-delta`: A Boolean flag representing whether the text contents are a delta against the previous version. Only present in dumpfiles created with the `--deltas` option.

- `Content-length`: As before, the total number of bytes in the node's content. This includes both the bytes that make up the properties and those that make up the text of the node, if any.

The properties of a node are represented by a simple serialization of key-value pairs into a text format. Keys are defined as a `K` followed by a space, the length of the key, a newline, the key, and another newline. Values are identical, but with a `V`. For example, the key "i am the key" and the value "i am the value" would look like this:

```
K 12
i am the key
V 14
i am the value
```

After the properties hash is the PROPS-END line mentioned earlier. If there's any text associated with the node, it comes after PROPS-END and is followed by a newline.

So there you have it—everything you need to know to either create a dumpfile that Subversion can read in, or process a dumpfile that someone else has created.

Migrating from Perforce

Of all the version control systems that have had conversion utilities written to allow converting their repositories into Subversion repositories, the one that provides the closest match to the Subversion model is probably Perforce. Both Perforce and Subversion have a concept of an atomic change that encompasses several files. In Perforce this is called a change, and it's pretty much directly analogous to Subversion's revision. Also, both Perforce and Subversion store branches within the same namespace as regular directory trees, with a simple copy being treated as the creation of a new branch, although in Perforce you create such a copy through either the p4 integrate or the p4 branch command, rather than Subversion's svn copy. Both systems also support similar RCS-style keyword expansion, and both have the concept of an executable file. The only place where the Perforce and Subversion models are especially different is in the handling of tags, because a Perforce tag (actually called a *label*) lives in a separate namespace rather than being just another part of the repository's directory structure, as in Subversion.

Because Perforce has such a similar data model, the process of converting a Perforce depot to a Subversion repository is actually pretty simple. There are at least two programs that have been written to do just that, and we'll take a look at both of them, as they show two very different ways to attack the problem at hand. First is the p42svn program, written by Ray Miller, which uses the Perforce Perl API to read directly from a Perforce depot and writes out the revision history in the form of a Subversion dumpfile, which can then be loaded into a Subversion repository. Second are the All Perl Changes (APC) scripts, which make use of an existing service that provides patches for each change submitted to the Perl Perforce depot and drives the svn program to convert them into a Subversion repository.

p42svn

The p42svn program is a great example of how to go about converting from an existing version control system to Subversion. It makes good use of existing technology, specifically the Perforce Perl API and the Subversion dump/restore format, to avoid having to reinvent the wheel. It quickly and cleanly maps the most commonly used Perforce commands (specifically, p4 add, p4 delete, p4 edit, p4 branch, and p4 integrate) into Subversion terminology while preserving as much of the existing Perforce metadata as is practical in the Subversion world.

The program is a simple Perl script available from the project web site at http://p42svn.tigris.org/. The relevant files are p42svn.pl and ChangeLog. Take a look at them now, and we'll take a brief tour of the source to see how it works.

p42svn Internals

Skip down to the bottom of p42svn.pl, and you'll see a section marked Main processing. This is the core of the application. It starts off by writing out the initial dump format header specified by the Subversion dumpfile format (see the svn_dump_format_version function), and then just iterates over each Perforce change for the branch it's converting. For each change, it again uses the Perforce API to retrieve additional details about it (see p4_get_change_details), such as the log entry, the author, and the date the change occurred. With this information, the beginning of the dump header for the revision can be written out (see svn_revision). Now for each action that is a part of the change, a specific conversion function is called to convert from the Perforce-style action to the equivalent Subversion dump output. This is the part of the program that is most relevant to us, so let's take a closer look at some of these conversion functions.

The p4add2svn function is a good place to start. It begins by converting the Perforce depot path into the analogous path in the Subversion repository. Then it checks for any parent paths that don't yet exist, and if there are any it creates them. Finally, it grabs the contents of the file from the Perforce depot, converts any keywords it finds from Perforce style to Subversion style (if the file is textual in nature), determines an initial set of Subversion properties from the type and content of the file, and finally writes out the file's properties and text to the dumpfile.

p4delete2svn is even simpler than p4add2svn. It simply does the depot-to-repository path conversion and then adds the appropriate headers to the dumpfile to delete the file.

Because the Subversion dumpfile format uses the fulltext of each revision, the p4add2svn function is almost exactly the same as p4edit2svn. The only difference is that it doesn't look for missing parent directories, because they already have to be there for the file to be there, and the dump output it creates has a Node-action of change instead of add.

The other two conversion functions, p4integrate2svn and p4branch2svn, are also quite similar. Both need to deal with the fact that they can be used in a few different situations in Perforce. p4 integrate can be used to create an initial branched version of a file or to move some changes from one branch of a file to another, so in the first case it needs to map to a copy, and in the second it needs to map to an edit. Similarly, p4branch2svn needs to be able to handle the fact that the file it's branching to might already exist. If it doesn't exist, it becomes a simple copy, but if it does exist, it's essentially an add on top of an existing file.

Running p42svn

To use p42svn, all you need to do is create a Subversion repository via svnadmin create, and then use p42svn to create a dumpfile holding your Perforce depot's revision history and load it into your Subversion repository via svnadmin load. The whole process looks like this:

```
$ svnadmin create /path/to/repository
$ p42svn --branch //depot/project=trunk | svnadmin load /path/to/repository
```

In this case, the contents of //depot/project in your Perforce depot will end up being placed in the /trunk directory of your Subversion repository. For more details on how to use p42svn's other options, refer to the p42svn documentation.

Limitations of p42svn

There are a couple of minor limitations to take note of in p42svn. First off, it doesn't provide a way to continue an in-progress conversion, so you really need to convert the entire branch (or depot) in one pass. Second, it keeps some data structures in memory (the %rev_map and %dirs_seen hashes, for example) that could possibly grow rather large when converting large depots. Regardless, these are minor issues that would most likely be reasonably simple to fix if they become a problem. In practice it works quite well, assuming you have direct access to the Perforce depot you're converting.

An Alternate Perforce Conversion Scheme

The APC repository shows that, in true Perl fashion, there's more than one way to do it, at least when *it* is converting a Perforce depot to a Subversion repository. The Perl source code has been kept in a Perforce depot for quite some time, but it's not especially easy to provide anonymous access to a Perforce depot, so the Perl community had to find another method of providing easy access to the revision history of its source code. The result has been the APC repository of patches. For each changeset that is submitted to the Perl Perforce depot, a corresponding patch (the output of `p4 describe -du <changeset>`) is made available via FTP and rsync, and there are a series of scripts that make it possible to apply those patches in the correct order to generate the version of the Perl source code as it exists in the Perforce depot for any given changeset number.

A number of people in the Perl community are interested in using Subversion instead of Perforce, and as a result, the system of scripts that work with the APC patches has been modified to allow it to be used to generate a Subversion repository. The APC scripts are available on CPAN in the `Perl-Repository-APC` module (see `http://search.cpan.org/dist/Perl-Repository-APC`).

The details of how the APC scripts work aren't especially interesting, mainly because they're rather specific to the Perl environment, except that they show how you can generate a Subversion repository from a Perforce depot without actually having direct access to the Perforce depot. As long as you have access to the individual changes, you can simply use a fairly mechanical process of applying the patch to a checked-out version of the code and then committing the change. It's also interesting to note that unlike `p42svn`, APC drives the `svn` binary directly, instead of generating a dumpfile. This is conceptually easier for the author of the conversion program, as there's no need to master the ins and outs of the dump format, but it's slower, as it requires the conversion program to run `svn` many times during any given run, rather than just using a single `svnadmin load` command. Now, there are certainly drawbacks to using this type of strategy for converting a Perforce depot into a Subversion repository, mainly concerning the handling of binary files (the patches that make up APC don't cover the few binary files that exist in the Perl depot; instead, the contents of those files are hard-coded into the APC scripts) and the handling of branches (the APC scripts have some custom logic to manage the various branches that exist in the Perl depot), but depending on your situation, this approach might be more practical than that of `p42svn`.

Migrating from CVS with cvs2svn

Unfortunately not all repository conversion processes are as straightforward as converting from Perforce to Subversion. CVS in particular is a good example of the other types of problems you're likely to encounter, primarily because it has a lot of problems that Subversion is specifically designed to solve, and thus there's something of a gap between their two data models. To write a conversion program you need to bridge the gap.

On the bright side, we have `cvs2svn`, a tool that handles all of this for you. It can be downloaded from `http://cvs2svn.tigris.org`. Let's take a look at what it does and how it does it.

There are two primary issues that need to be dealt with when performing this conversion. First, CVS doesn't have any kind of atomic commit concept—each file that's changed as part of a commit is changed individually. As a result, you need to use a heuristic to sort the various revisions of each RCS file in the CVS repository into Subversion-style atomic revisions. Second, CVS branches and tags are considerably different from Subversion's cheap copies, so once the changes to each individual RCS file have been sorted into Subversion revisions, extra copies need to be inserted to create the tags and branches.

cvs2svn Internals

The cvs2svn command makes a heroic attempt to go through all the contortions necessary to make this conversion work, and thus is a fantastic example of the kind of trick you need to use to do this kind of conversion. The process is divided into eight separate passes, going from the raw RCS files that make up the CVS repository to a Subversion dumpfile that can be loaded into a Subversion repository. For more details beyond those we discuss here, refer to the design-notes.txt file in the cvs2svn distribution, which covers many of the issues that cvs2svn must deal with.

In the first pass, cvs2svn uses an internal RCS parsing library to extract a summary of each revision from the RCS files. The summary includes things like a time-stamp, an MD5 digest of the log message and the author's name, the type of change, the revision number, some details about the branches and tags associated with the change, and the RCS filename. All this data is sorted by the RCS filename at this point. While extracting all this information, you also write out a file that contains the time-stamps associated with the change and the MD5 checksum, which will be used in the subsequent passes.

Given the file in pass 1, you do need to do some precursory checks about whether the branches and tags look OK. Because CVS is based on RCS files, but not quite the same, some people have been known to modify the CVS history using rcs commands. This creates problems for cvs2svn, and rather than have cvs2svn come up with a broken conversion, you want to notify the user. Assuming everything looks OK, you need to use the file written out in pass 1 to determine the appropriate time-stamp to use for each change. Because commits in CVS aren't atomic, there may be slightly different time-stamps on different parts of the same commit, so you resync them by looking for changes with the same author and log message that are less than some predefined length of time apart. This could, in theory, result in combining some changes that are really not part of the same CVS commit. But the general consensus is that if they happen that close together and it didn't seem important enough to get a real commit log, then it's probably not that big of a deal if you combine them. This pass results in a cleaned-up version of the first file you wrote out, which contains the new resynced time-stamps.

In pass 3 you will sort the CVS revisions in the data file by revision number to make life easier for pass 4.

In pass 4, you will want to move away from a flat-file storage mechanism for your information. When creating the actual SVN commits, you are going to be doing pretty random access on the revision information, so it is better to store the information in a hashtable of some sort. Pass 4 does this by copying the information to an on-disk database using one of the available hash database libraries Python supports. While processing the revision information that you have generated so far, pass 4 also makes a database of the symbolic name mappings that each revision of a file belongs to.

In pass 5 you need to group the changes into Subversion commits. This process is relatively straightforward: queuing the CVS commits sorted by time-stamp until you hit something outside the "committed at the same time" threshold. While processing these CVS commits, you will want to also discover which of the SVN commits you will be able to use for making copies of symbols and tags, in order to best "fill" a symbol or tag with the correct revisions of files, and write this data out to a file.

Next is pass 6, which is another sorting pass. This time you sort the output file of pass 5 by symbolic name in order to make it easy to search.

In pass 7 you write out a file that contains a mapping from symbolic names to the offset in the output file of pass 6 that has the data for that name. This avoids having to search for it later. A database is not used for this because they often do not do well with a large number of duplicate keys, as would be the case here.

Finally, there is pass 8, where you go over the commits you have created and write them out into a Subversion dumpfile. At the same time, you also create branches and tags. Tags are easy—they're just copies from old revisions into the tags directory that are added at the end of the dumpfile. Because CVS doesn't keep track of when tags are created, this is the best you can do. For branches it's a bit more complex. You can determine that a branch has been created when you see the first commit occurring on it, and at that point you can insert a copy that creates the branch (well, as much of it as possible anyway, as CVS branches can be created in pieces). If this hasn't created the entire branch, the remainder of it will be created via the same process later on, as commits occur on it. Of course, creating a branch isn't quite as simple as just "inserting a copy" (as you might have guessed—things with CVS are rarely simple). In many cases there are multiple different copies that you could perform to get the same result, and in those cases you try to find the smallest number of copies that would result in the final branch. This *symbolic filling* is what uses the files created in pass 5 that contain our possible sources for symbolic names. The algorithm for the actual filling is nontrivial, so you're probably better off reading the cvs2svn design document (located at `tools/cvs2svn/design-notes.txt` in the Subversion source distribution) or the cvs2svn source itself if you're really curious about the details.

Finally, in pass 8, you just load the dumpfile into a Subversion repository via the `svnadmin load` command. Now you have all the data from your CVS repository in your Subversion repository and the process is complete.

Running cvs2svn

Actually running cvs2svn is quite simple. You give it the paths to your Subversion and CVS repositories on the command line, and it takes care of the rest. Here's an example of what the entire process actually looks like:

```
$ ls /path/to/cvsroot
```

```
CVSROOT/  hello.c
```

```
$ cvs2svn -s /tmp/svnrepos /path/to/cvs/repository
```

```
----- pass 1 -----
Examining all CVS ',v' files...
```

```
myrepo/hello.c,v
Done
----- pass 2 -----
Checking for blocked exclusions...
Checking for forced tags with commits...
Checking for tag/branch mismatches...
Re-synchronizing CVS revision timestamps...
Done
----- pass 3 -----
Sorting CVS revisions...
Done
----- pass 4 -----
Copying CVS revision data from flat file to database...
Finding last CVS revisions for all symbolic names...
Done
----- pass 5 -----
Mapping CVS revisions to Subversion commits...
Creating Subversion r2 (commit)
Creating Subversion r3 (commit)
Creating Subversion r4 (closing tag/branch 'version-1_0')
Done
----- pass 6 -----
Sorting symbolic name source revisions...
Done
----- pass 7 -----
Determining offsets for all symbolic names...
Done.
----- pass 8 -----
Creating new repository 'svnrepo'
Starting Subversion Repository.
Starting Subversion r1 / 4
Starting Subversion r2 / 4
Starting Subversion r3 / 4
Starting Subversion r4 / 4
Done.

cvs2svn Statistics:
------------------
Total CVS Files:            16
Total CVS Revisions:        16
Total Unique Tags:           1
Total Unique Branches:       0
CVS Repos Size in KB:       23
Total SVN Commits:           4
First Revision Date:    Tue Jun 13 22:45:31 2006
Last Revision Date:     Tue Jun 13 22:46:24 2006
------------------
```

```
Timings:
------------------
pass 1:     0 seconds
pass 2:     0 seconds
pass 3:     0 seconds
pass 4:     0 seconds
pass 5:     0 seconds
pass 6:     0 seconds
pass 7:     0 seconds
pass 8:     1 second
total:      3 seconds total: 0 seconds
```

```
$ svn list file:///tmp/svnrepos
```

```
branches/
tags/
trunk/
```

```
$ svn list file:///tmp/svnrepos/trunk
```

```
hello.c
```

```
$ svn list file:///tmp/svnrepos/tags
```

```
version-1_0/
$
```

Using cvs2svn with RCS

As an added bonus you can also use cvs2svn to convert a standard RCS repository into a Subversion repository. The procedure is essentially the same, except RCS is somewhat simpler to convert, and thus many of the gymnastics needed for CVS don't need to be performed when converting an RCS repository.

Migrating from Visual SourceSafe with vss2svn

For those wishing to convert from Visual SourceSafe (VSS), there is a tool available called vss2svn. You can download it at http://www.pumacode.org/projects/vss2svn. This tool works somewhat similarly to cvs2svn, with the major difference being that unlike RCS, which is relatively standard and easy to parse, in order to correctly and completely convert a VSS repository, the tool authors have had to reverse-engineer the VSS database format. At one point, vss2svn was a Perl script that used the standard VSS API to extract data, but recently the decision was made to reverse-engineer the actual database format due to the limitations these APIs imposed, such as the inability to access older files that were deleted from VSS during some revision (a serious limitation). The authors believe directly using the database will enable them to make forward progress much more quickly, and the quality of the releases since they have made this decision seems to indicate this is true. As it is such a fast-moving and "young-again" project, but one that a lot of people may have use for, we refer you to the web site for instructions on how to use it.

Migrating from Mercurial or GIT with Tailor

Another newer tool in the category of conversion is Tailor. Tailor can convert between multiple types of version control systems, including the ability to convert between a number of the newer version control systems, such as GIT and Monotone. Tailor also supports incremental conversions. It can be downloaded from http://www.darcs.net/DarcsWiki/Tailor. We mention it here because it supports Subversion as both a source and a destination. To use Tailor, first generate a configuration file, like so:

```
$ tailor --verbose --source-kind cvs --target-kind svn \
        --repository /tmp/cvstest/cvsroot  \
        --module module --revision INITIAL \
        --target-repository file:///tmp/svntest \
        --target-module / module > module.tailor
```

As one might guess from the command line, Tailor has a large number of options. Let us take apart the previous command. The -kind parameters specify the type of repository for source and destination. The –repository options specify the locations of the source and destination repositories. The module options specify the name of the module to convert (in the case of CVS), and where in the target repository to put the module. Finally, the revision option specifies what revision to start the conversion from. Tailor outputs the configuration file to standard output, so we redirect it into a file. After generating the configuration file, you may wish to examine it to make sure everything is as you want it. A large number of comments about the options you can change will be put in the config file for you. Once you are satisfied, run Tailor with the configuration file to perform the actual conversion:

```
$ tailor -D -v --configfile module.tailor
```

This will create the Subversion repository specified in your config file and populate it with the data from the existing CVS repository. The Subversion repository can be incrementally updated later by running the same command again.

Where Should I Go from Here?

The obvious question here is, "Given all of these options, how should I convert my repository?" And the answer is, as usual, not obvious. If there exists a conversion program for your legacy version control system, you at least have something to try. Unfortunately, depending on what system you're converting from, you may or may not have much luck with the existing tools. Many of them are still rather new, and problems with them are far more common than I would like. So the best course of action seems to be to try whichever conversion programs exist for your legacy version control system and see how they fare with your repository. If they work, fantastic. If they don't, you have a bit of work ahead of you. Providing a simple test case to the author of the tool is probably the best way to go, assuming that you aren't comfortable with diving into the code and fixing the problem yourself.

If there's no existing program to perform your conversion, you're pretty much stuck writing one yourself. Here you have, as usual, a large number of options. You'll need to get the data that corresponds to each revision out of your existing system somehow, and then you'll have to decide on a way to get that data into Subversion, either by using the svn program from a script, by generating a dumpfile and loading it via svnadmin load, or by writing directly to a Subversion filesystem via libsvn_fs. There are pluses and minuses to each of these techniques, and which one is appropriate for your needs will depend strongly on exactly what your situation is.

Regardless of exactly how you choose to go about making your conversion, we encourage you to share your experience with the Subversion community. If you use an existing tool and it works, the author would likely appreciate an e-mail saying thanks. If you modify an existing tool, a bug report followed by a patch would almost certainly be welcome. If you have to write your own tool, be it a VCP module or a full-fledged conversion program, we strongly encourage you to consider making it available under an open source license so that others can benefit from your work, as there seems to be little point in requiring everyone to replicate the amount of work you might do to get the conversion process to work.

Summary

In this chapter you learned about several different means of converting your project from your existing version control system. If you're converting from CVS or Perforce, you now know how to use cvs2svn or p42svn, and if you're converting from some other system, you've seen enough about the Subversion dumpfile format to get you started writing your own conversion tool.

Let's move on to Chapter 5, where you'll learn how to take advantage of Subversion's Apache integration, leveraging existing Apache modules to provide more advanced authentication, fine-grained authorization, compression, and other features.

CHAPTER 5

■■■

Advanced Apache Integration

One of the major reasons Subversion makes use of Apache and mod_dav as the basis for one of its network protocols is that it allows you to leverage all sorts of existing Apache modules in order to further tweak Subversion's behavior to your taste. There are a huge number of modules available for just about everything, from compression to authentication to caching, and they let you tweak your server's behavior in a number of interesting ways. Even if there isn't a module already out there that does what you need, writing a new one is a well-documented process, and with a little work you can easily make your personal Subversion server fit into whatever mold you desire.

Before you can make use of the more advanced aspects of Subversion's Apache integration, you need to have the basics set up. If you haven't already done so, refer to the "Networking with ra_dav" section of Chapter 3 for the details.

Now that you have a basic mod_dav_svn server running, let's dive into the more advanced—and interesting—topics.

Authentication, Authorization, and Encryption

The first thing most people think about when they discover that their Subversion server is speaking a dialect of HTTP as its network protocol is "How am I going to secure this thing?" There are a number of different topics that fit into the abstract concept called *security*, and for each of these topics every user has different requirements to satisfy before he considers his server to be *secure*. While only a few of the possible techniques for securing your server are covered in this section, most share fairly similar procedures for installation and configuration.

There are three primary matters of concern when securing your mod_dav_svn configuration. The first is *authentication*, or verifying that the clients are who they say they are. The second is *authorization*, or verifying that the clients are allowed to do what they're trying to do. The third is *encryption*, or making sure that nobody else can watch what the user is doing as the data passes over the network. For each of these categories, there are a variety of options available, depending on your exact needs, and in this section those options are introduced.

mod_auth

The first type of authentication support most people encounter is mod_auth. You've already seen examples of how to use this type of authentication back in Chapter 3, but let's take a closer look:

```
<Location /repos>
  DAV svn
  SVNPath /path/to/repository
  AuthType basic
  AuthName "Example Subversion Repository"
  AuthUserFile /path/to/users/file
  Require valid-user
</Location>
```

It's just like the initial mod_dav_svn example found in Chapter 3, but with four extra lines. First, AuthType basic indicates that basic HTTP authentication should be used. Second, AuthName "Example Subversion Repository" assigns the repository a name so that users have some idea of what exactly they're authenticating against when they're asked for a username and password. Third, AuthUserFile /path/to/users/file tells Apache to use usernames and passwords found in the file at /path/to/users/file. Finally, the Require valid-user tells Apache that any valid user is allowed to access this resource.

The users file specified by the AuthUserFile line is managed via the htpasswd command, which comes with Apache. You create a new file like this:

```
$ htpasswd -c password-file rooneg
```

```
New password:
Re-type new password:
Adding password for user rooneg
$
```

This creates a file named password-file and adds a single user (rooneg) to it.

Once this file is created you can add new users by running htpasswd password-filename username and entering the password when prompted. You can change a user's password by running the same command but specifying an existing username instead of a new one.

The final bit of magic you might want to use with mod_auth is requiring a username and password for only some actions. For example, it's common to have read-only access available without an account, while requiring a username and password if a user wants to commit changes to the repository. To do that, you simply add a LimitExcept block to your repository's Location block.

```
<Location /svn>
  DAV svn
  SVNPath /path/to/repository
  AuthType basic
  AuthName "Example Subversion Repository"
  AuthUserFile /path/to/users/file
  <LimitExcept GET PROPFIND OPTIONS REPORT>
    Require valid-user
  </LimitExcept>
</Location>
```

And that's exactly what this example does. The LimitExcept block says that users are allowed to run GET, PROPFIND, OPTIONS, and REPORT HTTP commands without logging in, but to do anything else they need to have a valid username and password. Those four HTTP commands happen to be the four that are used by a Subversion client for read-only access to the repository.

For most basic uses, that's all you need to know about configuring authentication, but if your needs are more complex, you may find that you want something more than mod_auth can provide. Fortunately, there are several options available to you for just such a situation, such as mod_auth_mysql.

Authenticating Users with mod_auth_mysql

Managing your lists of users and groups via flat-text files is certainly simple, but in many situations it's just not acceptable, either because of scalability concerns or because you want to use some kind of single sign-on solution, with the login information transparently kept in sync across multiple applications. One of the ways to provide such a solution is to maintain this information in a database, such as MySQL, and use a module such as mod_auth_mysql to allow Apache to access that information instead of reading from flat files. In Apache 2.1+, there is a module included, mod_authn_dbd, which is much like mod_auth_mysql, however, it works with a lot more database systems. Because most servers still use Apache 2.0, we instead discuss using mod_auth_mysql.

mod_auth_mysql is available from http://modauthmysql.sourceforge.net/ and provides a thin layer on top of libmysqlclient to allow Apache to read usernames, groups, and hashed passwords from your MySQL database. The entire module is a single file of C code, and the installation process is trivial. See the README file for details.

Once you have the mod_auth_mysql module installed, configuring Apache to use it is quite simple. First, you need to create a MySQL database that will hold your user's information, and within that database you need to create a user_info table that will actually hold the data. The table should be created with a statement like this:

```
CREATE TABLE user_info (
  user_name CHAR(30) NOT NULL,
  user_passwd TINYBLOB NOT NULL,
  user_group CHAR(10),
  PRIMARY KEY (user)
)
```

The user_name column in this table is a unique user ID that corresponds to the username that your users give to Subversion when accessing the repository. The user_passwd column is (as you've probably guessed) the user's password, which can be stored in the following ways by setting options in httpd.conf:

- As encrypted using crypt, or with the MySQL built-in password-scrambling function PASSWORD, by setting AuthMySQLPwEncryption to scrambled.

- As an MD5/SHA1 digest by setting AuthMySQLPwEncryption to either md5 or to sha1.

- As encrypted using AES, by setting AuthMySQLPwEncryption to aes, and setting a salt using AuthMySQLSaltField. Note that using AES also *requires* that the password field be a binary large object (BLOB).

- As plain text, by setting AuthMySQLPwEncryption to none. Note this is not recommended since it results in storing the password in the database in plain text, which is considerably less secure than storing it as encrypted.

Note The size of `crypt` hashes changed after MySQL 4.1. In post-4.1, `crypt` hashes are 41 characters, and in pre-4.1, they are 10 characters. As a result, it is best to just use a `BLOB` type for the password field.

The `user_group` column contains the group the user belongs to. Here's an example of how to add a user to your `user_info` table:

```
$ mysql -h dbhost -u username -p users
```

```
Enter password:
Welcome to the MySQL monitor.  Commands end with ; or \g.
Your MySQL connection id is 25338 to server version: 5.0.22-Debian_0ubuntu6.06.2-log
Type 'help;' or '\h' for help. Type '\c' to clear the buffer.

mysql> INSERT INTO user_info
    -> VALUES ('rooneg', crypt('changeme'), 'committers');
mysql> QUIT
```

```
Bye
```

This adds a user named rooneg with a password changeme (encrypted using MySQL's built-in crypt function) in the group committers.

Once you've created your table and inserted a few users into it, you need to add something like this to your httpd.conf:

```
<Location /repos>
   [...the usual mod_dav_svn stuff...]
   AuthName "MySQL Testing"
   AuthType Basic
   AuthMySQLHost localhost
   AuthMySQLDB users
   AuthMySQLUserTable user_info
   require valid-user
</Location>
```

This assumes that your MySQL server is running on the same machine as Apache, that you're storing the user information in a database named users, and that in that database, user information is stored in a table named user_info. In addition to the various options you've already seen to control how the password is stored in the database, there are a number of other interesting ways you can configure mod_auth_mysql such that it better fits in with the rest of your infrastructure. See the README file in the mod_auth_mysql distribution for more details. Also, you should be aware that depending on what version of MySQL you're using and the hashing algorithm you use for the passwords in the database, there are a variety of different limitations on the length of the passwords you can support. See the MySQL documentation for more details.

Restricting User Actions with mod_authz_svn

After you've authenticated your clients and confirmed who exactly they are, the next step is to determine whether they are allowed to do whatever it is they're trying to do. You might assume that you can just set up different <Location> blocks for each part of your repository and define different <LimitExcept> or <Limit> requirements, depending on your needs. Unfortunately this doesn't work.

Internally, Subversion makes use of a wide variety of URLs that don't necessarily match up with the logical directory structure of your repository. So committing a change to a file inside http://svn.example.org/repos/example/trunk/ will actually involve making requests to URLs that aren't under that directory. To correctly provide access control in the face of this, you need an authorization module that has knowledge of how Subversion creates these URLs, so it can take them apart in exactly the same way mod_dav_svn does, and use that information to determine if clients are allowed to do whatever it is they're trying to do.

Fortunately, someone has already done this, so you don't have to worry too much about it. mod_authz_svn allows you to define your authorization rules in a simple text file, and it will interpret the mod_dav_svn-specific URLs and apply those rules each time someone tries to access the repository.

The primary problem with mod_authz_svn is that you're restricted to using flat files to store your access control rules. At this point there's no way to drive mod_authz_svn from a database like you can with mod_auth_mysql for authentication. That said, mod_authz_svn provides a nice example of how such a module needs to interact with Subversion, so implementing such a module is just a small matter of programming.

Assuming that you've already compiled and installed mod_dav_svn, mod_authz_svn will already be installed on your system. Enabling it is simply a matter of adding a line to httpd.conf containing LoadModule authz_svn_module modules/mod_authz_svn.so *after* the line that loads mod_dav_svn. Then you just have to add an AuthzSVNAccessFile line to your repository's Location block to indicate where mod_authz_svn should look for its config file. The Location block should look something like this:

```
<Location /repos>
  DAV svn
  SVNPath /path/to/repos
  AuthType Basic
  AuthName "Subversion repository"
  AuthUserFile /path/to/htpasswd/file
  AuthzSVNAccessFile /path/to/access/file
  Require valid-user
</Location>
```

There's one thing about this configuration that isn't immediately obvious. It has a Require valid-user line, which means that you *have* to log in before you can access the repository. If you want to allow anonymous access to your repository for some actions (such as read-only access), but you want to restrict others (such as committing changes), you can use a configuration like this:

```
<Location /repos>
  DAV svn
  SVNPath /path/to/repos
```

```
    AuthType Basic
    AuthName "Subversion repository"
    AuthUserFile /path/to/htpasswd/file
    AuthzSVNAccessFile /path/to/access/file
    Satisfy Any
    Require valid-user
</Location>
```

Notice the Satisfy Any and Require valid-user lines. When these are used together it allows anonymous users access to the repository for anything that's allowed for all users (specified as an * in the AuthzSVNAccessFile), but for anything that requires a specific user or group the client will be required to authenticate.

The config file pointed to by AuthzSVNAccessFile is, like most of Subversion's config files, in the INI format used by Python's ConfigParser module. It should contain several sections, one special section named [groups] that contains definitions for groups of users, and a number of other sections, each of which has a path specification for a name and contains users or groups and their access rights. To distinguish groups from users in the permission specifications, groups are prefixed with an @. An * can be used in the place of a user or a group as a wildcard that indicates all users have that kind of access. Access rights can be specified as r for read, w for write, rw for read-write, or nothing for no access at all. As usual, an example is probably the best way to see how this works in practice:

```
[groups]
committers = tom,dick,harry,michelle,tracey,jessica,
             mark,dave
documenters = phil,fred,rob,james
[/]
# give everyone read access to the whole repository
* = r
# and committers have read-write access
@committers = rw
[/trunk/docs]
# documentation people have read-write access
@documenters = rw
[/tags]
# phil is the release manager, so he lays down the tags
phil = rw
[/private]
# default to denying access in this section
* =
# but give committers read-write and documenters read access
@committers = rw
@documenters = r
```

And here's what this authorization configuration would look like from the user's perspective:

```
$ svn list http://svn.example.com/repos/
```

```
/trunk
/tags
/branches
/private
```

```
$ svn list http://svn.example.com/repos/private
```

```
Authentication realm: <http://svn.example.com:80> Example Repository
Password for 'bob':
Username: bob
Password for 'bob':
Authentication realm: <http://svn.example.com:80> Example Repository
Username: bob
Password for 'bob':
svn: Authorization failed
svn: PROPFIND request failed on '/repos/test/trunk'
svn: PROPFIND of '/repos/test/trunk': authorization failed (http://svn.example.com)
```

```
$ svn list --username tom  http://svn.example.com/repos/private
```

```
Authentication realm: <http://svn.example.com:80> Example Repository
Password for 'tom':
super-secret-document.txt
$
```

At first the user accesses the repository at http://svn.example.com/. Accessing this top level anonymously works fine, since there are no restrictions on that directory. Next, the user tries to list the contents of the private directory, specifying only a username on the command line. Since access to private is restricted, the user is prompted for a password. When the password doesn't match, the user is prompted for a username (the assumption is that the username might have been entered incorrectly) and a password, and when it fails again, the authorization fails and the request is rejected. Finally, the user tries to list the same directory with the username tom and enter the correct password, and because tom has access to private, the user can see the contents of private.

If you're going to use mod_authz_svn with the SVNParentPath directive, you need to be a bit careful. If you just specify raw paths such as the previous AuthzSVNAccessFile, those rules will be applied to *all* of the repositories under the SVNParentPath directory. If you want to limit the rule to a particular repository, you prefix the path with the repository name and a colon, like this:

```
[groups]
javacommitters = tom,dick,harry,michelle,tracey,jessica,mark,dave
perlcommitters = simon,casey,larry,chip
[java:/]
# give everyone read access to the whole java repository
* = r
# and the java committers have read-write access
```

```
@javacommitters = rw
[perl:/]
# everyone has read access to the perl repository
* = r
# but only the perl committers have read-write access
@perlcommitters = rw
```

In this example, there are two repositories: java and perl. Each has its own set of commiters. Both repositories are readable by anyone, but they're only writable to people in their committers group. Any other repository that's placed in the SVNParentPath directory will use the default permissions, and since specific rules are defined only for the perl and java repositories, that means that nobody will be able to access them at all. Also remember that this is the same format file that is used for svnserve's authz support. This means you can share the authz file between servers serving the same repository using different protocols.

Encrypting Traffic with mod_ssl

Now that you've learned how to authenticate your users via HTTP authentication and to restrict what they do via mod_authz_svn, the last major "security" issue remaining is the fact that all this traffic is going over the wire unencrypted. Fortunately Apache provides a solution to that problem as well by using mod_ssl to provide access to your repository via https instead of http.

Before diving into the details, we should level with you. SSL is an exceptionally complex subject, and this section covers only the most basic parts of it. For more information, we suggest you read the Apache documentation on mod_ssl, available at http://httpd.apache.org/docs-2.0/ssl/. Fortunately the default Apache installation comes with an example configuration file, ssl.conf, that covers all the configuration options you're likely to need, and the mod_ssl documentation describes these options in exhaustive detail, so we're just going to cover the basics here.

First you need to create an RSA private key with the openssl genrsa command. This key will be used by mod_ssl to encrypt the communication between your server and the clients, so without it you're not going to be able to make mod_ssl do a whole lot:

```
$ openssl genrsa -des3 -out server.key 1024
```

```
Generating RSA private key, 1024 bit long modulus
.....++++++
............++++++
e is 65537 (0x10001)
Enter pass phrase for server.key:
Verifying - Enter pass phrase for server.key:
$
```

This will leave a file named server.key in the current directory that will look something like this:

```
-----BEGIN RSA PRIVATE KEY-----
Proc-Type: 4,ENCRYPTED
DEK-Info: DES-EDE3-CBC,288C68D8DE153ABA

8MOW8XlKCmO+xb1vPNY4/q8mGH/S+NS5VBVCCYHSoh3o4JciXinsECWoldIDRkV2
rTYJS1GO+sTp71WlV8RqRzwvf3crXNR1SYbZ4QQ4d4hgO+XK58pPL3YDfOTMBoBK
QevozWFfTeO7wE2Tkv7tz4YLvoyyA/Cy7VCiNHugHd3wq+4dKEGDL1UXWt3FUZmR
Rev/nsdXX/pF+xBhFehrkSEF5LAq4+NPQO+gxdjdrdzSACizf2t1YE2CosHovwDY
IhjpDxhlLgNuyDVvXLyO8n3YPAnMO27yBsRDFllHO5pM+FT5GgbHNdI17rmOEOs6
2S7iqC3MjfdYdSl5fOYYjgADIas3t42lEFR4DZkAizLJWNqKryKn8OQEZPpb41md
6d32KG8JpMYXJ+W/TvRBKBFc8ViOqKCuBXgCyv6LmeT1twVvtlBGOjnN2cBPWDhv
1e/MLreMOo23AS71BqPlHcJEwqZXKrQhvmu3w9RNpyR37yh7E5ZoVEQteTosPuIe
XrGA+5pKQ84NsB5/iexpBit4IDIaAnGAKDZ5+IUElKTOYNUOc6KCqIfzF++O86oM
XLhSMMIknD8ewMk1gMhsAOPPXJw8yT2HRLO/+GtK7zHOuxGDLgxdn+xXSiD+nI+1
/bup6H9OCqEaWwNDgKeNLZFJIJjOfhiF6AYGYVJJAqBW6mZj/G4SEWp8FY8AqJt+
SimbUHwnCOP+ZaItBYc34ggsel1xd6lChbJ6j49MpHBsjOkFRK2IKfhROheTjgbC
RJC3OI9AFLrO+mk1jOCuR3RaK6jwleUqcYYse+nNnpPDNteXiQaPLw==
-----END RSA PRIVATE KEY-----
```

Note that you'll need to remember the passphrase you provided while creating the key.

Next you need to create a Certificate Signing Request (CSR) from the key, with the command openssl req. You'll have to enter a number of pieces of information during this process, which will be used to create a Distinguished Name for your certificate. When prompted for the Common Name, you want to enter the Fully Qualified Domain Name of the server (e.g., svn.example.com). Once you have a CSR, you can send it off to a certificate authority (CA), who will sign it and send you a certificate. Generating a CSR using OpenSSL looks like this:

```
$ openssl req -new -key server.key -out server.csr
```

```
Enter pass phrase for server.key:
You are about to be asked to enter information that will be incorporated
into your certificate request.
What you are about to enter is what is called a Distinguished Name or a DN.
There are quite a few fields but you can leave some blank
For some fields there will be a default value,
If you enter '.', the field will be left blank.
-----
Country Name (2 letter code) [AU]:
State or Province Name (full name) [Some-State]:
Locality Name (eg, city) []:
Organization Name (eg, company) [Internet Widgits Pty Ltd]:
Organizational Unit Name (eg, section) []:
Common Name (eg, YOUR name) []:svn.example.com
Email Address []:
Please enter the following 'extra' attributes
to be sent with your certificate request
A challenge password []:
An optional company name []:
$
```

Now you send the CSR off to a CA and wait for it to send you your certificate. Exactly how long this takes and how much it costs will depend on your CSR, but just to give you an idea, in October 2006 VeriSign was charging $1,790 for a 128-bit key that would last for two years, and it took up to two days to get an order filled. Of course, if you think VeriSign is overpriced, you can use a vendor such as Comodo (http://www.instantssl.com/) and get something similar for around $80.

What do you get for all of this? An SSL certificate that mainstream browsers such as Internet Explorer and Firefox will recognize. If you only care about Windows desktops that are under your control, and you have a Windows 2003 domain and Microsoft Certificate Server, you probably already have a CA that is recognized by all your desktops. In that case, you can simply get Certificate Server to sign a certificate for you, and it will work for all of your desktops.

Of course, it's quite likely that you don't need a certificate that's signed by a CA. If only a few Subversion clients are going to access your repository, it's perfectly reasonable to create a self-signed certificate, which you can do with another openssl command. Note that the Common Name you enter when creating your self-signed certificate needs to be the same as your Subversion server's hostname. Creating a self-signed certificate using OpenSSL looks like this:

```
$ openssl req -new -key server.key -x509 -out server.crt
```

```
Enter pass phrase for server.key:
You are about to be asked to enter information that will be incorporated
into your certificate request.
What you are about to enter is what is called a Distinguished Name or a DN.
There are quite a few fields but you can leave some blank
For some fields there will be a default value,
If you enter '.', the field will be left blank.
-----
Country Name (2 letter code) [AU]:
State or Province Name (full name) [Some-State]:
Locality Name (eg, city) []:
Organization Name (eg, company) [Internet Widgits Pty Ltd]:
Organizational Unit Name (eg, section) []:
Common Name (eg, YOUR name) []:svn.example.com
Email Address []:
$
```

Now you have two files: server.key, which is your certificate's key, and server.crt, which is your actual signed certificate. You need to copy them someplace Apache can find them. By default, that should be conf/ssl.key/server.key and conf/ssl.crt/server.crt, but if you want to put them somewhere different, you can just change the values for SSLCertificateKeyFile and SSLCertificateFile in the ssl.conf file.

Next, double-check that the ServerName directive in your VirtualHost block matches the Common Name you used for your certificate, and that the Listen directive in ssl.conf matches the one in httpd.conf. If either of these things isn't correct, you won't be able to access your server over SSL.

You then need to start the server via `apachectl startssl`, as in the following example. The server will ask you to enter your certificate passphrase on the terminal before it starts up, and once you do, it will be up and running, listening on port 443:

```
$ apachectl startssl
```

```
Apache/2.0.48 mod_ssl/2.0.48 (Pass Phrase Dialog)
Some of your private key files are encrypted for security reasons.
In order to read them you have to provide us with the pass phrases.
Server quicksilver:443 (RSA)
Enter pass phrase:
Ok: Pass Phrase Dialog successful.
$
```

Finally, just point a web browser at your server using the `https` schema, and if everything is working properly, you'll access your server over SSL. If you'd like a more manual method of verifying this you can use something like `openssl s_client -connect localhost:443 -state -debug`. This is basically the SSL version of telneting to port 80 on your server. You can just type in an HTTP request (such as `GET / HTTP/1.0`), and in addition to a lot of debugging information, you'll get back your server's index page.

Of course, if you don't want to have to enter a passphrase every time you start your server (and, honestly, that would be a pain), after you generate your RSA key you can remove the passphrase, like this:

```
$ cp server.key server.key.save
$ openssl rsa -in server.key.save -out server.key
```

```
Enter pass phrase for server.key.save:
writing RSA key
$
```

If you want to require that your clients always access the repository via SSL, which is a perfectly reasonable requirement if your repository contains sensitive data, you just need to add an `SSLRequireSSL` directive to your repository's `Location` block:

```
<Location /repos>
  DAV svn
  SVNPath /path/to/repos
  <IfDefine SSL>
    SSLRequireSSL
  </IfDefine>
</Location>
```

Most likely your Subversion installation already supports SSL. To confirm this simply use the `svn --version` command. The results should look like this:

```
$ svn --version
svn, version 1.4.0 (r21228)
   compiled Sep 20 2006, 13:48:20

Copyright (C) 2000-2006 CollabNet.
Subversion is open source software, see http://subversion.tigris.org/
This product includes software developed by CollabNet (http://www.Collab.Net/).

The following repository access (RA) modules are available:

* ra_dav : Module for accessing a repository via WebDAV (DeltaV) protocol.
  - handles 'http' scheme
  - handles 'https' scheme
* ra_svn : Module for accessing a repository using the svn network protocol.
  - handles 'svn' scheme
* ra_local : Module for accessing a repository on local disk.
  - handles 'file' scheme
$
```

Note that the section in the previous output about ra_dav indicates that it supports both the http and https URL schemas. If https isn't listed in the output, you aren't using a version of Neon (the WebDAV client library that Subversion uses) that supports SSL.

If you don't see https mentioned in that output, you'll have to configure Neon to include SSL support via the OpenSSL library. You simply pass the --with-ssl flag to Neon's configure script during the build process. If, for some reason, your OpenSSL libraries are located in an odd place and Neon can't find them, you might also need to add a --with-libs=/path/to/libs option to tell Neon where they are. If you're building Subversion with the version of Neon that's shipped in the source tree, you can simply use these arguments when you call Subversion's configure script, and it will automatically pass them on to Neon's configure. Once you have a version of Neon that supports SSL, you'll be able to access repositories over https:// URLs just like you would for http:// URLs.

At this point, you can start accessing your repository over SSL, and the traffic between your client and server will be encrypted. Depending on how your server's certificate is signed, your clients might need to confirm that the server's certificate is valid before Subversion will accept it. This is similar to confirming an SSH server's identity. A fingerprint is presented along with the Distinguished Name of the server. If the fingerprint matches what you know it should be (this should always be confirmed by verifying the fingerprint with the server administrator), you can accept it, either temporarily (which means it will be considered valid until the next time Subversion tries to connect to the server) or permanently (in which case it will be stored in your ~/.subversion/auth/svn.ssl.server directory and you won't be asked to confirm it the next time you access this server). The whole process looks something like this:

```
$ svn co https://svn.example.co/repos/trunk wc
Error validating server certificate for 'https://tor-svn.freehaven.net:443':
 - The certificate is not issued by a trusted authority. Use the
   fingerprint to validate the certificate manually!
Certificate information:
 - Hostname: svn.example.com
 - Valid: from Aug 16 20:51:46 2006 GMT until Aug 13 20:51:46 2016 GMT
 - Issuer: svn.example.com
 - Fingerprint: 11:34:5c:b1:c4:12:76:10:86:ce:df:69:3d:06:a9:57:fa:dc:c9:29
(R)eject, accept (t)emporarily or accept (p)ermanently? p
Checked out revision 1.
```

```
$ svn info wc | grep ^URL
```

```
URL: https://svn.example.com/repos/trunk
$
```

Of course, if you are the server administrator, you'll need to get the fingerprint from the certificate directly, so that you can give it to your users. This can be accomplished with the openssl command:

```
$ openssl x509 -sha1 -noout -fingerprint < server.crt
```

```
SHA1
Fingerprint=11:34:5c:b1:c4:12:76:10:86:ce:df:69:3d:06:a9:57:fa:dc:c9:29
$
```

Giving your users the fingerprint in advance when they're prompted to validate it will allow them to verify that the fingerprint the server sends them matches the one they were given, confirming that they're connected to the correct server. Naturally, confirming this each time you access the server would get tedious, so when you indicate to Subversion that you want to accept the certificate permanently, it will no longer prompt you in the future, at least as long as the server uses the same certificate.

Compression

Because of Subversion's integration with Apache, users can take advantage of another popular module called mod_deflate, an Apache module that provides support for compressing HTTP traffic. Now it turns out that svndiff, the binary diff format Subversion sends back and forth over the network, already intrinsically provides a measure of compression, but there are still some savings to be gained by compressing the non-svndiff portions of the traffic. WebDAV's wire protocol contains a fair amount of XML text, which can be compressed quite easily by Apache and uncompressed at the other end by Neon, Subversion's HTTP client library. Even better, once you enable compression on your server, it will transparently work for clients that support it, and those that don't will simply continue using the uncompressed form.

mod_deflate isn't included in the default set of modules compiled with Apache, so depending on how you installed Apache, you may not have it installed. If it isn't there, you can enable it by passing --enable-deflate to configure when building Apache.

Once you've installed the module, enabling mod_deflate in Apache is just a matter of adding a SetOutputFilter DEFLATE directive to your repository's Location block in httpd.conf. The most basic configuration would look something like this:

```
<Location /repos>
  DAV svn
  SVNPath /path/to/repos
  SetOutputFilter DEFLATE
</Location>
```

Now this will work just fine for Subversion clients accessing the repository, but if you're going to want to deal nicely with other clients (for example, the different varieties of web browsers out there), you might want a more complex arrangement, where you only turn on compression for certain mime types, depending on both the type of browser you're serving data to and the type of data you're serving. There are numerous examples of how to do this in the Apache online documentation, located at http://httpd.apache.org/docs-2.0/mod/mod_deflate.html.

Configuring your Subversion client to support compression is even easier than configuring it in Apache. In most cases Neon will automatically detect the presence of zlib (the library that contains the actual compression code) and turn it on automatically. To verify this you can run neon-config --libs:

```
$ neon-config --libs
```

```
-L/usr/local/lib -lneon -lssl -lcrypto -lz -lxml2 -lz -liconv -lm
$
```

Note the presence of -lz in the list of libraries you should link against when using Neon.[1] That means that Neon was built with compression support, and thus it expects you to link in zlib when you're using it in a program. As a result, any Subversion that is built with this version of Neon will have compression support turned on.

If you don't see an -lz in that line, it's likely that Neon was unable to find the zlib libraries on your system when it was built, and just as with the SSL libraries, you probably have to pass --with-lib=/path/to/libs to configure so that Neon can find it correctly.

Once both Apache and Subversion have been configured to use compression, that's all there is to it. As a part of normal operations, Subversion will advertise to Apache that it's able to accept compressed data, and Apache will notice this and start compressing things before sending them back to the client.

---

1. Through some quirk of autoconf, -lz appears to be in the list twice. In your installation, it might only turn up once—the important thing is that it's there.

DAV Autoversioning

You might be interested to know that tools from prominent vendors such as Apple and Microsoft can communicate with WebDAV servers. For example, Mac OS X's Finder can mount a WebDAV server as a network drive, as can Microsoft's Web Folders. It's awfully tempting to take such tools, put them in the hands of untrained users who would normally be terrified of version control systems, and allow them to edit content in a Subversion repository through a much friendlier interface.

And, amazingly, it even works. Sort of . . .

It's remarkably easy to access the HEAD revision of your repository via a WebDAV tool. For example, we can mount `http://svn.collab.net/repos/svn/trunk` as a network share on a PowerBook by simply selecting Go ➤ Connect To Server in the Finder and typing in the URL. It appears on the desktop and we can browse the repository via the same interface we use to browse the local filesystem. Everything's nice and simple, right up until we try to edit a file.

By default, accessing a Subversion repository via a generic WebDAV client will provide you with read-only access. The reason for this is simple: WebDAV doesn't provide everything Subversion requires to make a change to the repository. Subversion actually uses a set of extensions to WebDAV called DeltaV, which provides support for concepts related to version control. To make a change to something in a Subversion repository, you can't just start issuing PUT requests like you would with a generic WebDAV server; you have to take several more steps first. Unfortunately, while there are a lot of WebDAV clients in the world, there aren't very many DeltaV clients yet, and it's almost certain that your WebDAV-enabled tool doesn't know how to speak DeltaV.

Now in some situations—for instance, when you have a nontechnical user who wants to access a repository via a tool that supports WebDAV—it may be perfectly reasonable to say "the hell with it" and just live without all the extra stuff that DeltaV gives you, such as the ability to easily access previous revisions of the versioned files or the ability to enter custom log messages when committing changes. To do that, you can just add the SVNAutoversioning directive to your repository's Location block in httpd.conf. This tells Subversion that any WebDAV client that has authenticated correctly (assuming you're using some kind of authentication) can write to the repository without having to support the full DeltaV specification. Internally, it translates generic WebDAV write requests into the underlying DeltaV requests that mod_dav_svn expects. Your Location block should now look something like this:

```
<Location /repos>
  DAV svn
  SVNPath /path/to/repos
  SVNAutoversioning On
</Location>
```

When someone uses a non-Subversion WebDAV client to commit a change to the repository, a log message will be automatically generated, and you'll end up with logs that look something like this:

```
------------------------------------------------------------------------
r500 |  rooneg | 2003-06-08 09:56:24 -0400 (Sun, 08 Jun 2003) | 2 lines
Autoversioning commit:  a non-deltaV client made a change to
/trunk/README
------------------------------------------------------------------------
```

This isn't perfect. It means that whenever someone uses a WebDAV client to write to a repository via SVNAutoversioning, it will result in a number of separate revisions, rather than one atomic change like you would get with a Subversion client. The autogenerated log messages mean that there's no record of why the change was made in the commit logs. But despite these drawbacks, it does allow a WebDAV client to write to a Subversion repository, and depending on your needs that might be enough for you.

Logging

If you take a look at the Apache log files generated by subversion using HTTP, you will see a very large number of requests, with no easy way to tell what is actually going on. In fact, if you are getting multiple operations from the same addresses, it will be almost completely unintelligible. Fortunately, there is a way to have a higher level of logging.

Subversion 1.3 and above include a feature that enables you to log the high-level Subversion operation that is occurring during a set of requests. This is done by setting an Apache environment variable named SVN-ACTION when mod_dav_svn is processing a Subversion request. Using this in logs only requires that you use a custom logging directive that includes this environment variable.

For example, to log a time-stamp, an SVN action, and a username to a log file named logs/svn_logfile, the following custom log directive would suffice:

```
CustomLog logs/svn_logfile "%t %{SVN-ACTION}e %u" env=SVN-ACTION
```

Using custom log files instead of trying to interpret the mess of DAV requests that will be in the regular log files is highly suggested to maintain sanity.

Repository Browsing

A neat side-effect of using Apache and http to serve a Subversion repository is that you can browse it easily using just a web browser. If you simply browse to the URL for your repository, your web browser will display the directory listing, as if it was any other directory. Browsing to URLs to files in the repository will also do the obvious thing of showing or downloading that file, depending on the svn:mime-type property.

This functionality is deliberately rather limited, because mod_dav_svn is not a repository browsing application, it is an access method for the Subversion client. The only concession made is that you can specify an XSLT style sheet to be used to display the data and make it slightly prettier. This is done by adding an SVNIndexXSLT directive to the repository configuration in Apache. The option specified to the directive is the URL of the style sheet to use. The actual transformation and display using the style sheet is done on the client side, not the server side, so the browser needs to support XSLT in order for the directive to have any effect on that user's display.

Again, be aware this method has its limitations. In particular, it will always display the latest revision of whatever you ask for; there is no URL that will enable you to show an older version. For true repository browsing, you should be using a third-party tool. It is still cool to be able to pass around URLs to things such as design documents, and have them automatically access the latest version that is in the repository without any trouble.

Common Issues with mod_dav_svn

One common complaint with mod_dav_svn is that if no auth module is used, speed of commands such as log are still slower than svnserve (though it may still be quite fast). A major reason for the speed difference is that mod_dav_svn doesn't know whether any authorization modules are loaded. It therefore has to ask Apache to check authorization for every path involved in the log operation, to ensure that nobody gets access to data that they shouldn't. If you aren't using authorization at all in your repository, you can get a large speedup on log (and other) operations by inserting an SVNPathAuthz off in the Location block for your repository.

Another common problem is an uncooperative HTTP proxy server between the client and the server. If you're getting odd error messages trying to access your repository, and you're behind a proxy, it's quite likely that the proxy is messing something up. Subversion makes use of quite a few HTTP commands above and beyond those found in standard HTTP 1.1, and there are quite a few proxy servers out there that freak out when they see a command they don't understand.

Specifically, you should make sure that your proxy server supports at least the following HTTP commands:

- *From HTTP 1.1*: GET, HEAD, POST, PUT, DELETE, OPTIONS, TRACE, and CONNECT

- *From WebDAV*: LOCK, UNLOCK, PROPFIND, PROPPATCH, COPY, MOVE, and MKCOL

- *From the DeltaV extensions to WebDAV*: CHECKIN, CHECKOUT, UNCHECKOUT, VERSION-CONTROL, REPORT, UPDATE, LABEL, MERGE, MKWORKSPACE, BASELINE-CONTROL, and MKACTIVITY

■**Note** Astute readers will note that Subversion doesn't actually make use of all the previous commands at this time. That said, in the future, as more WebDAV compatibility work is done, it's likely that they'll be used, so making sure your proxy server works with all of them is probably a good idea.

If you can't work around your uncooperative proxy server, you might find that switching from http to https or running your http server on a nonstandard port might allow you to side-step the proxy server. The Subversion project's own server, http://svn.collab.net/, listens for HTTP traffic on both port 80 and port 81 for just this reason. Of course, it also might send you right into an uncooperative corporate firewall that blocks traffic on ports it doesn't know are safe, in which case you're stuck trying to fix the proxy server, but it's still worth a shot.

Finally, if you really think you've found a bug, it may be useful to get a dump of the requests going back and forth across the network. To do this, you can set the neon-debug-mask variable in your client's servers config file to the combination of the NE_DBG values in Neon's ne_utils.h header. For example, if you're using Neon 0.25.5 and you set neon-debug-mask to

130 (i.e., NE_DBG_HTTP plus NE_DBG_HTTPBODY), Neon will dump the HTTP headers and request bodies to the standard error stream whenever Subversion makes a request across the network. In order to make this information a bit more useful, you might also want to set `http-compression` to `false`, so that HTTP compression is disabled and the traffic is readable to the human eye.

Summary

In this chapter, you saw a bit more of what you can do with mod_dav_svn. You can now provide flexible authentication support via various different Apache modules such as mod_auth or mod_auth_mysql, limit access to various parts of your repository to specific users or groups, secure your connections via SSL with mod_ssl, compress your traffic via mod_deflate, and allow non-Subversion WebDAV clients to access your repository. You can also log high-level Subversion operations to your Apache log file. Finally, you learned a bit about the common pitfalls of working with mod_dav_svn and how to diagnose and avoid them.

Armed with this knowledge, you're now ready to learn about some of the more abstract issues that confront Subversion users. In Chapter 6 you'll take a look at some "best practices" that will help you make better use of Subversion in your daily life.

CHAPTER 6

■■■

Best Practices

To get the most out of Subversion, you'll find that it's best to adapt your development style slightly so that it fits better with how Subversion is designed to work. None of the best practices discussed in this chapter are required to use Subversion, but by following some or all of them, you'll find that Subversion becomes more useful, because you'll be working with it instead of against it.

The main thing you should keep in mind is that while version control software such as Subversion is certainly useful for a number of purposes, its primary reason for existence is to make it easier for you to do your job as a developer by improving communication between software developers. This communication can take several forms, ranging from letting you know about changes other developers are making and helping you to merge your uncommitted work with their latest changes, to allowing you to look back in time to determine how a part of your system worked in a previous version and how and why it evolved into its current form. Most of the best practices discussed in this chapter are about making it easier to use Subversion to enable this kind of communication. Specifically, we'll discuss how to produce changes that are easy to understand and ways to easily work with branches, techniques for creating vendor branches, use of test suites, and methods for making a release of your software, and, finally, how to make effective use of hook scripts.

Before we jump into these best practices, it's important to consider some issues regarding how changes are incorporated into a project. Some projects follow a *stable trunk* policy, where all new development is done on a branch, and that branch is merged into the mainline development branch only after it has been proven to work. Others prefer a more freewheeling style, where most development occurs in the trunk, and branches are used only in special cases.

Both of these development styles are perfectly valid, and there are good arguments in favor of each. It's up to you to determine which policy you use for your project, but for the rest of this chapter, we'll be assuming an *unstable trunk* style, mainly because Subversion (and CVS before it) tends to lend itself to such a policy.

That said, virtually all of the best practices we discuss here can be easily modified so that they apply equally well to a stable trunk style as they do to an unstable trunk style. Simply remember to apply changes to your development branch first rather than to the trunk directly, and insert a separate step where you merge the changes into the trunk after they've been approved.

Now let's get started on the rest of the chapter.

Choosing a Repository Layout

A good repository layout is essential to managing a development process, as it enables people to find the code, releases, and so on, that they are looking for. As a result, one of the most important things to get right when starting to use Subversion in your organization is to pick a good repository layout. For single projects, the standard trunk/branches/tags repository layout works great. In other words, the root of your repository should look like this:

```
branches
tags
trunk
```

This layout is standard across almost all single-project Subversion repositories and is instantly familiar to anyone who has used Subversion before. However, what to do in the case of multiple projects is not so clear. There are two basic schools of thought on the subject, the first being to do the following:

```
branches
            project1
            project2
tags
            project1
            project2
trunk
            project1
            project2
```

The second is to do this:

```
project1
            branches
            tags
            trunk
project2
            branches
            tags
            trunk
```

Each of these layouts has its advantages and disadvantages. The first layout works well when the projects share dependencies or are part of the same larger unit. It has the advantage that the top level of the repository still looks familiar, and it is easy to perform common tasks such as tagging a release of all the subdirectories of the trunk at once. On the downside, it is a bit harder to move things around. In particular, if you want to split these projects into separate Subversion repositories at some point later, it will be tricky to do so without some advanced dumpfile filtering. If you want to change the repository layout back to something like the standard layout after the move, that will also require some advanced dumpfile filtering. It also makes fine-grained authentication a bit harder, simply because the projects share a common root directory.

The second layout works well when the projects don't have much in common and are just separate projects sharing the same repository. This layout makes splitting the repository into separate single-project repositories, with the standard single-project layout, easy as cake. It also makes it clear that the projects contained in the repository really are separate and makes specifying different permissions for them easy. On the downside it is not easy to tag or branch all of the projects at once, because they need to be placed into separate directories. There is a tool to do these multiple copies as a single commit called `mucc`, however most people are not aware of it, or how to use it. This nice tool can be found in the `contrib/client-side` directory of the Subversion distribution.

Whichever layout you choose, just make sure you have considered the trade-offs in each before creating your repository. Otherwise you are bound to need to reorganize your repository layout later in ways that are not pleasant to perform.

Avoid Locking Mergeable Files

Development organizations that started off using version control systems that require locking, as well as organizations that are new at using source code control, sometimes get the wrong idea. They believe that if they do not force their developers to use a lock-modify-unlock model, chaos will ensue. The unfortunate reality is that forcing developers to use this model doesn't do anything except cause lost productivity.

Locking is often used to solve the social problem of synchronizing work with others. Rarely do technical solutions to these kinds of social problems work, and locking is no exception. Source code is malleable, and requiring that only one person be able to work on a given piece of it at a time just means other people who need to work on that piece can't get their work done. Synchronizing work with others so you can all be on the same page as to who is doing what is something best left to communication by e-mail, instant messaging, or phone, not by forcing locking of files in a version control system.

In addition, changes to the same file by multiple developers rarely conflict, and when they do, resolving them is a relatively easy process, because Subversion is a system built to be able to merge files and handle conflicts. This is not to say that you should never lock any files. In fact, graphics files, and other files that can't be merged with standard merging tools, should be locked before editing. But please don't hurt your developers by forcing them to lock source code. It is unlikely to actually help whatever problem you are trying to solve.

Committing Changes

Ultimately the whole point of using a version control system is to commit your changes into it so that your project's history is preserved and, more important, so that the rest of your team has access to your work. If you don't do that, you might as well be editing a local copy of the source code and making backup copies manually, because you'd actually get more functionality from that than you'd get with Subversion if you never used `svn commit`. With that in mind, the first set of practices you're going to examine concern the things you should think about when using `svn commit`.

Commit Early, Commit Often

First, when using Subversion in your development work, you need to try to structure your changes so that they can quickly be committed to the repository. The longer your change is sitting in your working copy, the more dangerous it becomes for a number of reasons. First off, the repository, almost by definition, is safer than your local working copy. It's almost certainly running on more capable hardware that's less likely to suffer a disk failure. And even if the repository does fall victim to such a failure, you're almost certainly going to be in a better position when it comes to recovering from that failure, because you probably have better backups for your repository than you do for your developer's home directories. The sooner you commit that change and get it out of your working copy, the less likely you are to lose the change because of some problem outside your control.

Furthermore, migrating the change from your working copy into the repository means that you no longer have to worry about another developer making a change that conflicts with your work. Subversion's update-merge-commit style of development means that the task of merging committed changes with in-progress changes falls on the developer making the change, and every time you update, you risk having to take time to perform such a merge manually. Even if Subversion can handle the merge automatically, you still need to verify that it did so correctly and that your in-progress change is still valid with the new code base. Finally, merging changes tends to become harder as time goes on and the code base drifts farther and farther from the one you started making the change to, so if you can make sure your changes are reasonably young, you'll probably have an easier merge process waiting for you. So, in general, it's in your own best interest to commit sooner, simply so you don't have to waste your time merging your changes into a new version in the repository.

Now, that last reason may sound a bit selfish, but is it really? By committing your change quickly, you lessen the risk of having to merge your changes, but you increase the chances that another developer will have to do the same thing, right?

Yeah, that's definitely true, but it's not a sufficient reason to avoid following this general rule, because even if your change results in a merge for one of your coworkers, he'll still be better off if you commit sooner. The sooner you get your change into the repository, the sooner the rest of the developers on your team will see the change. Now, in many situations, there may be some sort of code review of your changes prior to the commit, and that's all well and good for a variety of reasons, but there's nothing quite like forcing other people to use the code for uncovering bugs, and the sooner those bugs are found, the better off everyone is. Once again, we're back to the idea that you should try to get your change into the repository as quickly as possible.

Make Small, Atomic Changes

Committing your changes to the repository as quickly as possible is obviously a good idea, but as with many good ideas there's a downside to it. Having your change in the repository means that all of a sudden that bug you introduced is no longer just going to screw up your day by forcing you to track it down once you've become aware of it. It now has the potential to ruin your whole team's day, because they're all just as likely as you to find it and spend most of their day trying to figure out what they just broke, only to eventually learn that it's *your* committed change that broke things, not *their* uncommitted changes.

With this in mind, it's easy to talk yourself out of committing your changes, since if you wait just a little longer and stare at the diff one more time, you'll be able to see that critical bug that could totally ruin everyone's day and make you look like an idiot in front of your entire team, right? Well, it might feel that way sometimes, but in general, it just isn't true. There's always one more bug, and Murphy's Law ensures that you won't see it until after you commit anyway.

This being the case, it seems prudent to try to structure your changes so that the chance for that big, catastrophic, embarrassing bug cropping up at the worst possible time is minimized. The best way to do this, in our opinion, is to make your changes small and focused.

A small change offers a number of advantages. First of all, it encourages you to make better use of Subversion's built-in commands. It's considerably easier to view the diff associated with the addition of a particular feature or a particular bug fix if you can simply run `svn diff svn://svn.example.org/repos/project -r 133:134` than it is if you have to include the path to each and every file associated with that part of the change, because the actual commit includes a whole lot of changes to other files that are unrelated to the bug in question. Heck, in some cases, you can't even do that because the commit made unrelated changes within a single file, so there's no way to see just the portion of the change that's relevant to the issue at hand.

This may seem like a rather minor problem, but it turns into a big deal when you consider how it applies to `svn merge`. If you later want to merge a particular bug fix from the trunk back to a previous release branch, or if you want to roll back a particular change, it's much easier to do so if the change is limited to a particular revision. If the change is spread out over multiple revisions, you can end up needing multiple invocations of `svn merge` to get them all. Or even worse, if a single revision has more than one change, you're stuck extracting the change manually, either by manually selecting which files within a revision need to be reverted, or by running the merge and then going through files and manually fixing the portions of the change that don't need to be reverted. Any way you slice it, this isn't something that's a whole lot of fun to deal with, and it can be easily avoided by making each revision contain exactly one complete atomic change, which can be easily viewed in a diff, easily merged from one branch to another, and easily rolled back in case the hypothetical catastrophic bug happens to occur in this particular change.

Beyond the issues associated with `svn merge` and `svn diff`, keeping your changes small and self-contained has another less tangible benefit: your changes will often be small enough to be understood. It's far easier to comprehend the implications of a diff consisting of just a few hundred lines spread across five files than a significantly larger diff spread across two dozen files. This comes into play on both the side of the developer making the change and on the side of the developers reviewing the change. So if you keep your changes small and self-contained, you're more likely to do a good job coding and less likely to introduce new bugs, and the people reviewing your changes are more likely to be able to give you useful commentary because they'll actually be able to digest the changes and comment on them within a reasonable amount of time.

Use Meaningful Log Messages

Keeping a change small and self-contained isn't the only thing you can do to make it easy for other developers to understand it. An even simpler thing you can do is to write a useful log message. If your commit has a useful log message associated with it, your reviewers will find it that much easier to dive in and provide useful feedback and, more important, it will become possible to look back at the history of your code base and determine not just what was changed, but why it was changed. Subversion records the *what* portion of the history automatically, so you don't need to worry about that at all; but if you want the *why* to exist beyond the moment you type `svn commit`, you'll have to put it there yourself.

Just in case it isn't obvious what the difference is between a *bad* log message and a *good* log message, here is an example:

```
Fixed Bug.
```

This is quite clearly a poor log message. All it says is that a bug was fixed. There's nothing to indicate how the bug showed up in the program, what the underlying problem actually was, or how it was found. Sure, much of this can probably be inferred by looking at the diff for the revision, but as time passes, doing that becomes harder and harder because you'll be less likely to remember the context in which the change was made. Here is an example of an ideal log message:

```
Fix issue #1729.  Now we don't crash because of a missing file.
* get_editor.c
  (frobnicate_file): Check that file exists before frobnicating,
  Take an absolute path instead of a relative one.
* do_thing.c
  (frobnicate_things): Update calls to frobnicate_file.
```

The details of the problem being fixed are spelled out. The specific changes made to each file are mentioned and, better yet, the name of the functions that were modified are listed, making it that much easier to search through the logs later to determine what changes modified those particular functions. Finally, an issue number (presumably from a bug-tracking system) is mentioned, so you have a place to look for more information about the context for this commit.

Don't Break the Tree

The entire "commit early, commit often" development methodology is centered on the idea that you can integrate your changes with those that the other developers on the project are making. This hinges on the assumption that whatever you're working on can be broken up into atomic, bite-sized changes that result in a working system. Each change needs to leave the tree at approximately the same level of usability it was in before the change, or at an even better level.

Breaking your source tree, either by making it unable to build or by making the results of the build unusable, is the cardinal sin of software development. It takes a problem that could have affected just a single developer and forces the entire community of developers to deal with it. In a bad case, it can result in hours or days of wasted effort or, even worse, a situation in which some developers in the community avoid updating their working copies so that they don't have to deal with the consequences of a particular change. If the developers aren't updating, nobody is testing the latest changes to the code base (and with good reason, since it doesn't work because of the breakage), and you've sacrificed almost every benefit of committing your changes into the repository.

So now you have a dilemma. On one hand you have the need to get your changes into the tree, and on the other hand you absolutely have to avoid breaking the tree because it will have consequences that nobody wants to deal with. As usual, it becomes a question of trade-offs.

You need to find a way to minimize the risk that comes with making a change and still get your work into the repository quickly enough to reap the benefits mentioned in the previous few sections.

Unfortunately, avoiding this kind of breakage isn't always possible. Sometimes you need to make changes that are too large to split into coherent pieces that don't break the tree. In these cases, when you truly need to make an earth-shattering change that will leave your source tree broken for an extended period of time, you might want to consider doing development on a branch instead of in the trunk.

Branching and Merging

Techniques for working with multiple development branches and merging changes back and forth between them are some of the hardest things to learn when working with a version control system. Let's take a look at some ways to make it easier.

When to Branch

The ability to branch cheaply and easily is a good thing, and much of the work that's gone into Subversion's repository design centers on making it possible to do just that. Subversion makes the act of creating a new branch as cheap and easy as making a simple copy, with a single command that takes a constant amount of time and space in the repository. This is a huge improvement over systems such as CVS, where the time and space penalty incurred by creating a branch is proportional to the number of files on the branch.

Of course, just because it's easy to do doesn't mean you should start making branches without a good reason. Creating a new development branch is a nontrivial act. You're taking the majority of the problems that come with doing extended amounts of development work in your local working copy and duplicating them inside the repository. This means that you're splitting the attention of your development team between the main development work taking place in the trunk and your new development work taking place on the branch. You're forcing yourself to undergo the pain associated with merges, both in merging changes from the trunk out to your branch while you're working on the branch, and in merging your changes from the branch to the trunk when you're finally done.

Previously we said that the whole point of using Subversion is to commit your changes into the repository. We'd like to revise that statement a bit: the whole point is to commit your changes into the trunk of the repository where people will use them. Doing development on a branch means that there are several more steps between when you commit the change on the branch and when your change finally makes its way into the trunk where it can be really useful. So if you can possibly avoid doing your work on a branch, you should, in the interest of reducing the total amount of required work.

Note that this argument holds true only for branches that are being used for development work. There are certainly other uses for branches, such as stabilizing your code base before a release, that aren't necessarily subject to the same kinds of problems. We'll discuss release branches later in this chapter in the "Releases" section.

The bottom line is that you should do your development work on a branch only when you absolutely have to. Some good reasons might be that your work is going to take some time to complete, or that it will render the source tree unusable for other unrelated development work, or that it is experimental and you're not sure if it will ever be used in the trunk. In each of these cases, the pain of doing your development on the branch is outweighed by the fact that doing so reduces the inconvenience your change will cause other developers working on the project. The question you need to ask yourself before deciding to work on a branch is, will the pain I'm causing myself pay off in the end by making life easier for the rest of the team? If the answer is yes, perhaps you should be working on a branch.

Making Merges Easier

Whenever you're making changes on a branch, there are a few simple things to keep in mind that will make your eventual merge process considerably easier.

First, it is highly recommended to use a tool such as `svnmerge.py` (which is available in the `contrib/client-side` directory of the Subversion distribution) to manage your merges. Tools such as `svnmerge.py` know how to track what has been merged already to your branch, how to block revisions from being merged, and how to automatically generate nice commit messages for your merges. It really makes merging relatively painless.

Second, you want to keep the amount of change you introduce on the branch to the absolute minimum. The more you change, the more likely it is that you'll introduce a conflict between your change and other changes happening on the trunk, and that means the merge will be more complicated. One way to reduce the amount of change is to limit yourself to meaningful changes only. For instance, avoid making whitespace-only changes that, although they might make the code look nicer, really don't change what the program itself does. Making sweeping changes to a file's indenting style or something like that will almost certainly result in a conflict with any other change that happens to that file on the trunk.

Third, you can reduce the difficulty of your eventual merge by breaking it up into smaller merges. As changes are made on the trunk, you can merge them into your branch, rather than waiting until your change is finished and merging them all at once. This allows you to handle the conflicts as they occur, giving you more time to think about what needs to be done and decreasing the chance of an incorrect merge. If you wait until you've finished with your change, there might be multiple independent changes on the trunk that need to be merged with your change, and multiple independent changes will almost always be more difficult to merge at once than if you handle them one at a time.

Finally, before moving a change from the branch to the trunk, always merge outstanding changes from the trunk to the branch first and commit them to the branch. Then, the only changes remaining on the branch should be the ones you are trying to move to the trunk. Doing this merge ensures you are testing the final result of your changes only, and can therefore compare your results directly to the trunk that you are going to merge the change into. Of course, if you're merging changes from the trunk into the branch as you go, this final merge from trunk to branch is considerably smaller; but no matter how large the merge is, it's still a good idea.

Planning for svn switch

The `svn switch` command is perhaps the best technique Subversion provides for making sure your eventual merges are as easy as possible. To take advantage of `svn switch`, only branch small portions of the tree, instead of something as large as the entire trunk. Performing a switch of only a portion of the working copy enables the rest of your working copy to track the trunk (or whatever other revision is checked out), without having to perform merges to keep it up-to-date. As a result, you are left only having to merge the portion you actually branched and care about, instead of the entire tree.

What do you need to do to make this work? Well, technically, nothing special. You just have to create a branch, check out the trunk, and then switch the portions of the tree you wish to modify over to the branch. In practice, this works much better if you follow solid software engineering practices and keep the interdependencies between your software's subsystems to a bare minimum. If you're modifying a single library, it will be considerably easier to switch the contents of that library over to the branch and limit your modifications to those files if the rest of the source tree interacts with that library only via a well-defined interface that doesn't need to change. Unfortunately, if you do end up having to modify the interface, much of the benefit of svn switch will be lost, as you'll have to modify all the code that makes use of the interface, which almost certainly stretches into areas of the tree that other people are working on, increasing the amount of merging that needs to be done.

To further simplify the process of making use of svn switch, you might want to try keeping each independent subsystem of your project in a separate subdirectory, as it is simpler to switch an entire directory over to the branch than it is to switch each file over by hand. A good example of this can be seen in the Subversion source tree itself. The various libraries are broken out into subdirectories, and when development is done on a branch, the modifications can often be restricted to a single subdirectory, which allows svn switch to be more easily employed.

Vendor Branches

Aside from using branches for development and for releases, as we cover later in the "Releases" section, the third most common reason for using branches is for integration of software that is developed externally to your organization. The general idea behind a vendor branch is to provide a branch of development that contains unmodified versions of externally developed software, so that upgrades of that software can be done without local modifications getting in the way. Some version control systems (notably CVS) have specific support for these kinds of *vendor branches*. Subversion doesn't offer any specific vendor branch support, but it's sufficiently flexible to allow you to have access to much the same functionality.

At first, once you've imported an unmodified version of the vendor's software, you can simply copy a version of it into your development tree. Going forward, you make whatever modifications are needed to the version in your development tree, leaving the version on the vendor branch untouched. Later, as the vendor releases new versions of code, you can import them into the vendor branch and use the vendor branch to ease the job of merging the vendor's changes into your development branch.

How to Maintain a Vendor Branch

Maintaining a vendor branch is reasonably simple, although it might not seem like it at first glance. Let's go over the basic procedure so you can see exactly how it's done.

Say you're making use of the CPAN (Comprehensive Perl Archive Network) Perl module Mail::SimpleList to maintain some local mailing lists, and you want to make some changes to the module while still keeping track of new releases. Keeping a vendor branch in your repository that holds the versions released on CPAN is a perfect way to do this.

First, you simply need to create a location in your repository to hold the vendor branch. Personally, we tend to use a top-level directory named vendor, which holds a directory for each piece of software we're tracking. If you're following the same convention, the first thing you'd do to bring Mail::SimpleList into your repository on a vendor branch is to create those directories:

```
$ svn mkdir svn://example.com/repos/vendor/mail-simplelist \
        -m "new directory for vendor branches"
```

```
Committed revision 1.
```

Next, you import the current version of the software into a directory under your vendor branch. We usually use a directory named current:

```
$ tar zxvf Mail-SimpleList-0.90.tar.gz
```

```
Mail-SimpleList-0.90/
Mail-SimpleList-0.90/examplefilter.pl
Mail-SimpleList-0.90/t/
Mail-SimpleList-0.90/t/podtohelp.t
Mail-SimpleList-0.90/t/acceptance.t
Mail-SimpleList-0.90/t/alias.t
Mail-SimpleList-0.90/t/lib/
Mail-SimpleList-0.90/t/lib/FakeMail.pm
Mail-SimpleList-0.90/t/lib/FakeIn.pm
Mail-SimpleList-0.90/t/aliases.t
Mail-SimpleList-0.90/t/base.t
Mail-SimpleList-0.90/Changes
Mail-SimpleList-0.90/MANIFEST
Mail-SimpleList-0.90/lib/
Mail-SimpleList-0.90/lib/Mail/
Mail-SimpleList-0.90/lib/Mail/SimpleList/
Mail-SimpleList-0.90/lib/Mail/SimpleList/PodToHelp.pm
Mail-SimpleList-0.90/lib/Mail/SimpleList/Aliases.pm
Mail-SimpleList-0.90/lib/Mail/SimpleList/Alias.pm
Mail-SimpleList-0.90/lib/Mail/SimpleList.pm
Mail-SimpleList-0.90/META.yml
Mail-SimpleList-0.90/Makefile.PL
Mail-SimpleList-0.90/Build.PL
Mail-SimpleList-0.90/README
```

```
$ svn import Mail-SimpleList-0.90 \
          svn://example.org/repos/vendor/mail-simplelist/current \
          -m "import Mail::SimpleList 0.90."
```

```
Adding          Mail-SimpleList-0.90/Build.PL
Adding          Mail-SimpleList-0.90/Changes
Adding          Mail-SimpleList-0.90/examplefilter.pl
Adding          Mail-SimpleList-0.90/lib
Adding          Mail-SimpleList-0.90/lib/Mail
Adding          Mail-SimpleList-0.90/lib/Mail/SimpleList
Adding          Mail-SimpleList-0.90/lib/Mail/SimpleList/Alias.pm
Adding          Mail-SimpleList-0.90/lib/Mail/SimpleList/Aliases.pm
Adding          Mail-SimpleList-0.90/lib/Mail/SimpleList/PodToHelp.pm
Adding          Mail-SimpleList-0.90/lib/Mail/SimpleList.pm
Adding          Mail-SimpleList-0.90/Makefile.PL
Adding          Mail-SimpleList-0.90/MANIFEST
Adding          Mail-SimpleList-0.90/META.yml
Adding          Mail-SimpleList-0.90/README
Adding          Mail-SimpleList-0.90/t
Adding          Mail-SimpleList-0.90/t/acceptance.t
Adding          Mail-SimpleList-0.90/t/alias.t
Adding          Mail-SimpleList-0.90/t/aliases.t
Adding          Mail-SimpleList-0.90/t/base.t
Adding          Mail-SimpleList-0.90/t/lib
Adding          Mail-SimpleList-0.90/t/lib/FakeIn.pm
Adding          Mail-SimpleList-0.90/t/lib/FakeMail.pm
Adding          Mail-SimpleList-0.90/t/podtohelp.t
Committed revision 2.
```

```
$ svn list svn://example.org/repos/vendor/mail-simplelist/current
```

```
Build.PL
Changes
MANIFEST
META.yml
Makefile.PL
README
examplefilter.pl
lib/
t/
$
```

Now, you simply tag the current directory so you can refer to this version in the future, and then you copy a version of it into the trunk so you can make whatever local modifications you want:

```
$ svn copy svn://example.org/repos/vendor/mail-simplelist/current \
        svn://example.org/repos/vendor/mail-simplelist/0.90 \
        -m "tag version 0.90 of Mail::SimpleList."
```

```
Committed revision 3.
```

```
$ svn copy svn://example.org/repos/vendor/mail-simplelist/vendor \
          svn://example.org/repos/trunk/mail-simplelist \
          -m "bring version 0.90 of Mail::SimpleList into the trunk."
```

```
Committed revision 4.
$
```

At this point you can check out the trunk, make whatever changes you want, and commit them to the trunk. Your local changes remain confined to the trunk, while the vendor branch remains exactly as it was when you imported it. Everything continues like this until a new version of Mail::SimpleList is released.

Once a new release comes out, you're faced with the task of importing it on the vendor branch and merging the changes into your modified version in the trunk. First, you check out the current directory from the vendor branch:

```
$ svn co svn://example.org/repos/vendor/mail-simplelist/current current
```

```
A   current/t
A   current/t/podtohelp.t
A   current/t/aliases.t
A   current/t/lib
A   current/t/lib/FakeMail.pm
A   current/t/lib/FakeIn.pm
A   current/t/acceptance.t
A   current/t/alias.t
A   current/t/base.t
A   current/META.yml
A   current/lib
A   current/lib/Mail
A   current/lib/Mail/SimpleList.pm
A   current/lib/Mail/SimpleList
A   current/lib/Mail/SimpleList/Alias.pm
A   current/lib/Mail/SimpleList/PodToHelp.pm
A   current/lib/Mail/SimpleList/Aliases.pm
A   current/MANIFEST
A   current/Makefile.PL
A   current/Changes
A   current/Build.PL
A   current/examplefilter.pl
A   current/README
Checked out revision 10.
$
```

Now, you apply the changes between the two vendor versions to your working copy:

```
$ tar zxvf Mail-SimpleList-0.91.tar.gz
```

```
Mail-SimpleList-0.91/
Mail-SimpleList-0.91/lib/
Mail-SimpleList-0.91/lib/Mail/
Mail-SimpleList-0.91/lib/Mail/SimpleList/
Mail-SimpleList-0.91/lib/Mail/SimpleList/Alias.pm
Mail-SimpleList-0.91/lib/Mail/SimpleList/PodToHelp.pm
Mail-SimpleList-0.91/lib/Mail/SimpleList/Aliases.pm
Mail-SimpleList-0.91/lib/Mail/SimpleList.pm
Mail-SimpleList-0.91/t/
Mail-SimpleList-0.91/t/lib/
Mail-SimpleList-0.91/t/lib/FakeIn.pm
Mail-SimpleList-0.91/t/lib/FakeMail.pm
Mail-SimpleList-0.91/t/acceptance.t
Mail-SimpleList-0.91/t/aliases.t
Mail-SimpleList-0.91/t/podtohelp.t
Mail-SimpleList-0.91/t/base.t
Mail-SimpleList-0.91/t/alias.t
Mail-SimpleList-0.91/README
Mail-SimpleList-0.91/examplefilter.pl
Mail-SimpleList-0.91/Build.PL
Mail-SimpleList-0.91/META.yml
Mail-SimpleList-0.91/Makefile.PL
Mail-SimpleList-0.91/MANIFEST
Mail-SimpleList-0.91/Changes
```

```
$ cd current
$ cp -r ../Mail-SimpleList-0.91/* .
$ svn status
```

```
M     t/acceptance.t
M     META.yml
M     lib/Mail/SimpleList.pm
M     lib/Mail/SimpleList/Alias.pm
M     lib/Mail/SimpleList/Aliases.pm
M     Changes
M     README
$
```

OK, so this was a simple import. You just copied the contents of the new release of Mail::SimpleList right over your checked-out copy of the previous version. svn status shows you that a few files have been modified, and if you compare them to the version from version 0.91 of Mail::SimpleList, you'll see that your working copy is now an exact replica of the new version. At this point you might also need to deal with tasks such as adding new files that didn't exist in the previous version, removing files that were removed in the new version, and renaming (via svn move) files that have been renamed. This is a reasonably simple process, but it can take some time, depending on the size of the project in question. Luckily there is an easier solution that will be mentioned later on in this section, that involves a script called svn_load_dirs.pl.

Once you're sure that you have your working copy in a state that best matches the new version of the software, you can commit it to the repository and tag the new release:

```
$ svn commit -m "import version 0.91 of Mail::SimpleList."
```

```
Sending        Changes
Sending        META.yml
Sending        README
Sending        lib/Mail/SimpleList/Alias.pm
Sending        lib/Mail/SimpleList/Aliases.pm
Sending        lib/Mail/SimpleList.pm
Sending        t/acceptance.t
Transmitting file data .......
Committed revision 11.
```

```
$ svn copy svn://example.org/repos/vendor/mail-simplelist/current \
          svn://example.org/repos/vendor/mail-simplelist/0.91 \
          -m "tag version 0.91 of Mail::SimpleList."
```

```
Committed revision 12.
$
```

The last step in importing the new version is to merge the changes from the newest version into your version in the trunk:

```
$ svn checkout svn://example.org/repos/trunk/mail-simplelist trunk
```

```
A  trunk/t
A  trunk/t/podtohelp.t
A  trunk/t/aliases.t
A  trunk/t/lib
A  trunk/t/lib/FakeMail.pm
A  trunk/t/lib/FakeIn.pm
A  trunk/t/acceptance.t
A  trunk/t/alias.t
A  trunk/t/base.t
A  trunk/META.yml
A  trunk/lib
A  trunk/lib/Mail
A  trunk/lib/Mail/SimpleList.pm
A  trunk/lib/Mail/SimpleList
```

```
A  trunk/lib/Mail/SimpleList/Alias.pm
A  trunk/lib/Mail/SimpleList/PodToHelp.pm
A  trunk/lib/Mail/SimpleList/Aliases.pm
A  trunk/MANIFEST
A  trunk/Makefile.PL
A  trunk/Changes
A  trunk/Build.PL
A  trunk/examplefilter.pl
A  trunk/README
Checked out revision 12.
```

```
$ cd trunk
$ svn merge svn://example.org/repos/vendor/mail-simplelist/0.90 \
          svn://example.org/repos/vendor/mail-simplelist/0.91
```

```
U  t/acceptance.t
U  lib/Mail/SimpleList.pm
U  lib/Mail/SimpleList/Alias.pm
U  lib/Mail/SimpleList/Aliases.pm
U  META.yml
U  Changes
U  README
```

```
$ svn diff | more
```

```
[ ... make sure the changes are good ... ]
```

```
$ svn commit -m "merge changes from version 0.91 into trunk."
```

```
Sending        Changes
Sending        META.yml
Sending        README
Sending        lib/Mail/SimpleList/Alias.pm
Sending        lib/Mail/SimpleList/Aliases.pm
Sending        lib/Mail/SimpleList.pm
Sending        t/acceptance.t
Transmitting file data .......
Committed revision 13.
$
```

Of course, this merging process might not always go as smoothly as it did in this example. Depending on the local changes you've made, you might have to deal with conflicts each time you import a new upstream version of the software. In general, it's probably a good idea to minimize the number of local changes you maintain, using the same techniques discussed in the section "Branching and Merging." Assuming your local changes are generally usable, it is also a good idea to try to get them accepted by the upstream maintainer whenever possible.

Automating the Vendor Import Process

Since the process of importing a new release into your vendor branch is fairly mechanical and kind of tedious, some thought has gone into finding ways to automate it. One of the results of thinking about automation is the svn_load_dirs.pl script, which is available in the contrib/client-side directory of the Subversion distribution. svn_load_dirs.pl automates much of the process of checking out the current version you have in your vendor branch; comparing it to the new version of the software; figuring out what files have been deleted, moved, and renamed; and committing the results to the vendor branch and optionally tagging them.

As you might expect, svn_load_dirs.pl works by checking out the current directory (or whatever directory you tell it to use) from your vendor branch and then comparing the contents with the directory tree you're importing. It looks for files that have been added and removed and tries to determine whether any of them were renamed. Renames are performed using svn move and the remaining changes are handled with svn add or svn delete. The script will ask for confirmation from the user before making any of these changes.

svn_load_dirs.pl is pretty simple to use, so we'll just leave you with an example of how you would perform the import of a Mail::SimpleList version 0.91 with this script:

```
$ tar zxvf Mail-SimpleList-0.91.tar.gz
```

```
[ ... lots of output ... ]
```

```
$ svn_load_dirs.pl -t 0.91 \
                 svn://example.org/repos/vendor/mail-simplelist \
                 current \
                 ./Mail-SimpleList-0.91
```

```
[ ... lots of output ... ]
$
```

The -t 0.91 means that the resulting import should be tagged as 0.91. The root directory to use for the import is svn://example.org/repos/vendor/mail-simplelist, the directory within the root that should hold the import is /current, and ./Mail-SimpleList-0.91 is the directory tree to import.

Releases

If you never actually release your software to your users, all the version control techniques in the world aren't going to do you much good. With that in mind, let's look at how Subversion can help you out with the release process.

Making a Release Branch

The first step in the process of making a release of your project should always be to make a release branch. A *release branch* is a branch created from your development trunk once you determine that all the goals for your release have been reached. After the release branch has been created, all testing of the release should be done on the branch, and development work can continue on the trunk. The majority of the developers can turn their attention to working on the next phase of the project, while those who are tasked with making the release can feel free to take their time testing the branch without worrying about holding up development work.

If testing goes well, the branch can simply be tagged and a release can be created. If testing doesn't go well, the people making the release can simply inform the rest of the team about the problem. Once a fix is found, the developers commit it to the trunk, and someone working on the release can merge it into the release branch and start the testing process again. The process continues until testing confirms that the release is stable enough for tagging.

A typical procedure for making a release might be as follows. First, a branch is made from the trunk:

```
$ svn copy svn://example.org/repos/trunk \
          svn://example.org/repos/branches/release-1.0 \
          -m "create release branch"
```

```
Committed revision 2064.
$
```

At this point a test release is created from the branch, using the same procedure that the final release will use. That release is then tested to ensure that it meets all the requirements of the release process. If any problems are found, they can be fixed on the trunk and then merged into the branch.

```
$ svn merge -r 2070:2071 svn://example.org/repos/trunk .
```

```
M main.c
```

```
$ svn commit -m "merge fix for issue #175 into the release branch."
```

```
Sending        main.c
Transmitting file data .
Committed revision 2080.
$
```

Whenever problems like this are found and fixed, a new test release should be created from the branch and resubmitted for testing. This routine repeats until a release is created with no showstopper bugs. At that point, the branch can be made into a tag and the final release version of the software is created from the branch:

```
$ svn cp svn://example.org/repos/branches/release-1.0 \
        svn://example.org/repos/tags/1.0 \
        -m "tag version 1.0"
```

```
Committed revision 2090.
$
```

Notice that once the release branch is created, only those developers working on the release (and in many groups, this could be a single person rather than a team) modify it. This ensures that the people responsible for making the final release are always aware of the state of the release, and thus can be sure of exactly what they're releasing. The remaining developers can continue working on the trunk, out of the way of those making the release, only interacting with them when a problem is found and a fix needs to be merged into the branch for the release.

Finalizing the Release

The final steps in creating a release of your software should always be creating a tag for the release (based on the release branch, assuming you're using one) and then creating your final distribution (tarball, installer, or whatever) based on that tag. Once the tag is created, the release is finalized, and if a problem is found, a new release needs to be created if you want to fix it. This ensures that everyone has a consistent view of exactly what constitutes that particular release. It's vitally important later on that people who download the packaged version and people who grab the contents of the tag as soon as you create it are talking about the same exact contents when they're reporting bugs. If you later delete and recreate the tag, you'll always be wondering which version of the release people are referring to.

Rolling the Distribution

Once you've created the tag for your release, all you have to do is create the final tarball (or ZIP file, or whatever). Generally, you won't want to include an entire Subversion working copy in your tarball (if only because the vast majority of your users are unlikely to want to pay the disk space and bandwidth penalty involved in downloading a tarball full of administrative directories), so those will have to be removed somehow.

A simple way to do this is to use the `svn export` command to pull down the contents of your release tag. In addition to simplifying the process of getting a clean tree without any administrative directories, this allows you to ensure that the contents of your release are exactly the same as the contents of your tag, reducing the chance that you might accidentally release a tarball that contains some kind of local change.

To further ensure that your releases are reproducible right out of the repository, consider scripting your release process, so that the entire act of rolling a tarball based off of the tag can be easily replicated at any time. Any time you can remove the chance for user error to enter into the process, you probably should do so, as errors in the final result of your release process will reflect poorly on the entire development team.

After the Release

Once you've sent your release out into the world, it's important to be able to accumulate useful bug reports from your users about its contents. Among the most important bits of information you need from your users for a bug report to be useful is exactly what version of your software they're using. In addition to simply embedding your release's version in the tag, the release distribution, the change log, and other such places associated with the release, consider making use of svn:keywords to embed version information directly into the files that make up your product. It's considerably easier to debug a problem if your users can easily answer the question "So in exactly what version of Module.pm were you seeing this again?" Making it as easy as possible for your users to answer that question will improve the odds that your developers can get the information they need to do their jobs.

If you do this correctly, your users don't necessarily even need your source code to tell you what version of your code was used to create the final executables and libraries they're using. It's somewhat common practice these days to embed revision keywords right in the final executable code of a program. The process, which we'll now demonstrate for C code, is really quite simple.

First, each C file in the program should have the svn:keywords property set to the appropriate value for the keywords you wish to embed in the program (in this case Id). Then, within each C file, you embed a static character buffer that consists of a string containing the keyword. When the final program is compiled, the keyword strings are still part of the program (or library), and they can be extracted with a program such as strings or ident. The following is an example of using the Id keyword and then extracting the results with ident:

```
$ cat main.c
```

```
static const char id[] = "$Id: main.c 3 2003-11-16 02:57:30Z rooneg $";
extern void function(void);
int
main (int argc, char *argv[])
{
  function ();
  return 0;
}
```

```
$ cat function.c
```

```
#include <stdio.h>
static const char id[] = "$Id: function.c 3 2003-11-16 02:57:30Z rooneg $";
void
function (void)
{
  printf ("hello world\n");
}
```

```
$ svn pget svn:keywords main.c function.c
```

```
main.c - Id
function.c - Id
```

```
$ cc -c main.c
$ cc -c function.c
$ cc -o program main.o function.o
$ ./program
```

```
hello world
```

```
$ ident program
```

```
    $Id: main.c 3 2003-11-16 02:57:30Z rooneg $
    $Id: function.c 3 2003-11-16 02:57:30Z rooneg $
$
```

As you can see, with a little effort you can take the information Subversion makes available in its various keywords and place it in your final distribution, whether it consists of source code or binary executables, so that your users can extract all the information you'll need to know when diagnosing a problem.

Automated Testing with Subversion

Although there's no direct relationship between version control software and regression testing, there is a strong indirect relationship worth exploring. A strong base of testing infrastructure for your project allows you to make better use of your version control software. In this section, we discuss some ways you can build that infrastructure and how making use of it during development will help you better use Subversion.

■**Note** Regression testing is the process of using automated tests to ensure bugs that have been fixed in a piece of software do not reoccur later in a newer version of that software.

You Need a Test Suite

Many of the best practices we've discussed in this chapter rely on developers having enough confidence in their work that they can commit changes into the repository relatively quickly. There are only two ways developers can make commits quickly enough to be able to take advantage of everything Subversion has to offer: either the project needs to be very small and thus it can be manually tested in a reasonable amount of time, or there have to be enough automated tests that developers can have a reasonable amount of faith that their newest bug fix doesn't break something else.

This implies that to use Subversion (well, to use it effectively) on anything other than a trivial project, you'll have to build an automated test suite of some sort. Countless tools are available to help you do this. Because this book isn't about unit testing tools, we're only going to go as far as to mention a few significant points you should keep in mind while building your testing infrastructure. The tests should be easy to run, with the bare minimum number of manual steps required to make them work. Ideally, they'll be integrated into your build system, and as soon as a developer checks out a new working copy, she should be able to immediately build, run, and test the software, just by running one or two commands. The harder you make it to run the tests, the less useful they'll be, for the simple reason that developers are both human and lazy, and if it's at all difficult to run the tests, they won't do it. Once the developers are in the habit of checking in changes without running the tests, you've lost any advantage you had from having tests in the first place, and you've put yourself in danger of losing the ability to make rapid changes to your code base.

Another matter to keep in mind is that the output of the tests needs to be useful and easy to understand. Ideally the test suite should produce no output at all if nothing is broken, and if there is a problem, the test suite should pinpoint exactly what tests are failing. You should be able to run small subsets of the test suite manually, without running the rest, and if at all possible the test suite should produce output as tests are being run, because when a test run takes 15 or 20 minutes, it's really irritating to have to sit there and see nothing but a blank screen until the whole thing finishes.

The goal here is to build a culture. Developers should view breaking the tests with as much fear as they do breaking the build. Once they do, you'll find that the added confidence the developers gain from the presence of a test suite will allow them to more quickly solve the problems they're working on.

Don't Rely on Your Users to Run the Test Suite

Unfortunately, even if you've made it easy to check out a working copy, build the code, and run all the tests, and even if you build a developer culture in which breaking the tests is as horrific a mistake as breaking the build, that won't be enough. No matter what you do, you'll end up with developers checking in changes without running the tests. It's unavoidable. It isn't because you have bad developers on your team, it's just that you have human developers on your team, and they make mistakes.

So what can you do about it? Run the tests for them, that's what.

Running automated builds and tests regularly, either continuously or whenever a change is committed, is the only way to be sure your developers aren't messing up. So what you need is an automated tinderbox: a system that downloads, compiles, and tests your source on a variety of systems, and that mails the results of that build to your developers. This tinderbox can run periodically, kicking off a new build every few hours or, if your system can be built and tested quickly enough, you might want to simply have a `post-commit-hook` that kicks off the builds on your test systems.

However you set up this system, the idea is simple. Since the problem is that developers are human and fallible, you remove them from the equation as much as possible, automating everything you can. You automate the process of version control not because it can't be done manually, but because it's simply too error-prone to do it that way. This is just another example of the same thing.

Making Good Use of Hook Scripts

Another useful feature of Subversion that's easy to overlook is the ability to hook into the life cycle of the various ways a client can modify the repository via a hook script. Used correctly this technique allows you to link all sorts of external tools into your repository, gives you a huge amount of flexibility to control what ends up in your repository in the first place, and lets people know what ends up there and when.

Notifying the Rest of the Team

The simplest and most vital role for a hook script is to notify the development team of changes to the repository. Traditionally this is done via a `post-commit-hook` script, which sends an e-mail to a mailing list. A number of example scripts are available in the `tools/hook-scripts` directory of the Subversion distribution, including `commit-email.pl`, which is a reasonably simple Perl script, and `mailer.py`, which is a more complex script written in Python that does a slightly better job of composing useful messages but requires the Subversion Python bindings (discussed in Chapter 8).

What's important here isn't so much what tool is used to actually send the e-mail, but that there is some notification sent to your developers to inform them that a commit has occurred. You need to try to ensure that your developers hear about a change before they actually receive that change in their working copy via `svn update`. This facilitates communication between the team, encourages code reviews, and generally makes sure that changes are discussed rather than just allowed to slip into the source tree unnoticed. More discussion leads to a higher quality source base, and that's the entire point of this exercise, isn't it?

Enforcing Project Standards

Aside from notifying developers of changes, the primary use for hook scripts is to ensure that changes being made to the repository conform to project standards. These standards can include limiting commits to various parts of the tree to certain users, disallowing changes to the contents of directories that are used as tags, or ensuring that a change being committed follows the project's rules concerning filenaming conventions or other such matters.

The specifics of what your `pre-commit-hook` script looks for are, of course, up to you, but you should keep a few things in mind when designing it. First, the script needs to be able to work pretty quickly. Looking over the names of any added files and verifying that they match the project's conventions is probably OK, but actually checking out the code, applying the changes, and running the unit tests is almost certainly going to be a problem. If your hook script takes too long, you risk having your client's connection time-out while waiting for it to complete, which is something you really want to avoid. Second—and this is even more important—your hook script absolutely *cannot* modify the transaction that is being built in the repository. The reason for not being allowed to modify the transaction is simple: there is no way to propagate the change back to the client performing the commit, which would result in the client having an out-of-date working copy that it believes is up-to-date. In general, while you could try to modify certain parts of the in-progress commit (specifically the revision properties that are being built up, such as the log message for the commit), it's likely to be tricky, and it's almost certainly a better idea to just reject anything that doesn't fit your criteria and to require the user to fix the issue and recommit.

Make Backups

The final best practice we're going to mention is so simple that it's quite easy to forget: make backups of your repository. Specifically, you should make periodic backups of the entire contents of your repository, either via `svnadmin hotcopy` or `svnadmin dump`, as discussed in Chapter 3. If something should happen to make your repository unusable—for example, a hard disk crash—you'll want to be able to restore it in the minimum amount of time.

Additionally, you should ensure that the backups are stored on a different machine than your primary Subversion server, so that in the event of a problem that renders the machine itself useless, you can restore service by placing the repository on a new machine. If at all possible, you should probably try to store your backups in a completely different physical location than your primary repository, so that even a catastrophic event that renders the building unusable wouldn't keep you from restoring access for your users.

There's no limit to how paranoid you can be regarding the contents of your repository, so have a solid plan for making backups and restoring service from them should it become necessary. Finally, be sure to test that procedure every so often to ensure that nothing has changed to make your backup and restore procedures invalid. A little time invested up front can save you *a lot* of trouble down the road if disaster strikes.

Summary

As you've learned, Subversion provides you with a lot of freedom, and in this chapter we discussed some of the proven ways to use that freedom to make your development process easier. It's likely that not all these best practices will apply directly to your particular development project, but you'll find that many of them do, and you'll almost certainly find that applying them where possible makes your job easier in the long run.

In the next chapter, you'll learn about other ways to make better use of Subversion by using third-party tools that integrate with Subversion in various ways. From command-line shell integration, to web-based repository viewers, to full-fledged IDE integration, third-party tools play an important role in a Subversion-based development process.

■ ■ ■

## CHAPTER 7

Integrating Subversion with Other Tools

Right from the very beginning, Subversion was designed to make it as easy as possible to integrate with other tools. This mindset is apparent in several regards.

First, the Subversion command-line client is designed so that its output is both easy for humans to understand and reasonably simple for machines to parse. When the two goals are in conflict, the human side wins out, of course, as the client is first and foremost a tool for a user to interact with Subversion. That said, in general you will find that the Subversion developers have been quite good about making it simple for tools to read the output of the commands. This results in a number of third-party tools that work with Subversion by simply calling out to the svn program from time to time.

Second, Subversion has been implemented primarily as a collection of libraries, written in highly portable C code. This means it's reasonably simple for almost any language to interact with Subversion directly by calling in to the Subversion libraries via the standard techniques for calling C code from whatever language they're written in. In some cases, higher-level wrappers have already been written that allow you to make use of the Subversion libraries from other languages without having to interact directly with the C-level code.

More details about how to make use of this part of Subversion are presented in Chapter 8, but for now let's take a look at some of the ways people have managed to integrate Subversion into other tools.

Command-Line Tab Completion

Although Subversion's command-line tools were designed to be more user-friendly than those of its predecessor, CVS, there are still a rather large number of individual subcommands (30 at last count). While this is less than other version control systems, it's still a lot, and it's not always easy to remember exactly what the commands are and which options go with each one.

For many people, this might mean spending a lot of time using the svn help command or reading books like this one; but if you're a Bash or Zsh user, there's a better way to keep on top of things. These shells come with powerful programmable tab completion abilities, which can be configured to intelligently complete different commands in different ways. Conveniently, tab completion rules for Subversion are available, allowing your shell to give you context-sensitive hints about what subcommands and options are valid in a given situation.

Setting up the tab completion support for Bash is accomplished by enabling support for extended globbing[1] and programmable completion, and then sourcing the tools/client-side/bash_completion file from the Subversion distribution:

```
$ shopt -s extglob progcomp
$ . tools/client-side/bash_completion
```

Now when you type in **svn** and the beginning of your command and then press Tab, Bash will try to complete the command for you. If you have show-all-if-ambiguous turned on in your .inputrc, the output will look something like this:

```
$ svn p<TAB>
```

```
pdel      pget      praise    propedit  proplist  pset
pedit     plist     propdel   propget   propset
$ svn p
```

And if you begin to type in an option to the subcommand and press Tab again, Bash will try to complete the option, like this:

```
$ svn praise -<TAB>
```

```
--config-dir      --non-interactive      --revision      --xml
--help            --no-auth-cache        --username      -h
--incremental     --password             --verbose       -r
$ svn praise -
```

As you can see, this makes it much easier to learn the various subcommands when you're first getting started. Even if you're an experienced Subversion user, this feature can greatly speed up your ability to work with the subcommands that you don't use on a daily basis.

To make use of the Subversion tab completion support in Zsh, you don't have to do anything special. It's been part of the default configuration since version 4.0.8, so just upgrade to that version if you haven't already and you'll be all set.

---

1. Globbing is the process of expanding a pattern describing a set of files (such as foo*) into the actual list of files (foo1, foo2, foo3).

Emacs Version Control and psvn.el

In addition to making it easier to interact with Subversion from the command line, the Subversion team has done substantial work on making it more convenient to work with Subversion from within various text editors. The most notable example of this is GNU Emacs.

There are two primary ways to use Subversion from within Emacs. If you're interested in a lightweight interface, consider the vc-svn module, which allows Subversion to be used alongside CVS, RCS, and SCCS as part of the generic Emacs version control (vc) package. For those looking to access more Subversion-specific functionality, the psvn package is available. psvn provides a full-featured interface to Subversion's functionality. Both vc-svn and psvn are written in pure elisp and call out to the svn binary to do the actual work of interacting with Subversion.

The steps for installing vc-svn vary, depending on the version of Emacs you're running. For GNU Emacs versions 21.2, 21.3, and 21.4, you need to copy the file contrib/client-side/vc-svn.el from the Subversion tarball into a directory in your Emacs load-path and add SVN to the vc-handled-backends list. For example, our .emacs file has the following lines in it:

```
(setq load-path (cons "~/.elisp/" load-path))
(add-to-list 'vc-handled-backends 'SVN)
```

Since we have a copy of vc-svn.el sitting in the ~/.elisp directory, this allows our Emacs to use the vc-svn back end whenever we edit a file that's within a Subversion working copy.

For versions of GNU Emacs newer than 21.4, vc-svn.el is already included in the core Emacs distribution, so you don't have to do anything to make it work. For versions of GNU Emacs older than 21.2, or any version of XEmacs, you're out of luck with vc-svn. vc-svn requires a refactored version of the vc package that makes it possible to write simple plugins for new version control systems. The refactored version was released in version 21.2 of GNU Emacs and hasn't yet been ported to XEmacs.

Once you've made sure SVN is in your vc-handled-backends list, you can verify that vc-svn is working by opening a versioned file in your working copy. In the Emacs status line, you'll notice a section that says something like SVN-105, where SVN indicates that the file is under Subversion's control, the hyphen indicates that the file hasn't been modified, and 105 is the revision in which the file was last changed. When you edit the file, the hyphen will change to a colon (:), to indicate that the file has local modifications.

In addition to providing a handy status indicator, the vc plugin offers a number of commands. For details on what's provided by vc, you can consult the vc documentation, but for the time being we'll outline some of the most useful commands:

- C-x v i calls svn add on the file you're currently editing.

- C-x v = executes svn diff on the file you're currently editing and shows the result in a new buffer.

- C-x v u reverts any local changes to the file you're editing.

- C-x v v checks in your changes to the file (it pops up a new buffer for you to enter the log message, and you type **C-c C-c** when you've finished writing the commit log and want to run the commit).

Unfortunately, vc-svn is hamstrung by the requirements of the vc interface, which was designed for version control systems such as RCS and SCCS. It has no concept of committing multiple files at the same time, among other things, and thus isn't able to use all of Subversion's capabilities. For that, you need psvn.

Installing psvn is even easier than installing vc-svn. You simply copy the file contrib/client-side/psvn/psvn.el from the Subversion distribution into a directory in your Emacs load-path and add a (require 'psvn) line to your .emacs configuration file. Once it's installed, execute M-x svn-status in Emacs and give it the path to your working copy. The screen that appears should look something like this:

```
svn status for directory ~/Hacking/plucene/SVN-Log-Index/
0 files marked
        43   43 rooneg      .
  M     43   36 rooneg      Build.PL
        43    3 rooneg      MANIFEST.SKIP
        43   36 rooneg      MANIFEST
        43   30 rooneg      META.yml
        43   27 rooneg      Makefile.PL
        43   36 rooneg      README
        43   42 rooneg      bin
  M     43   42 rooneg        sli
  ?             ?          index
        43   43 rooneg      lib
        43   43 rooneg        SVN
        43   43 rooneg          Log
        43   43 rooneg            Index.pm
        43   38 rooneg      t
        43   14 rooneg        01use.t
        43   34 rooneg        02basics.t
        43   38 rooneg        03bugs.t
```

As you can probably guess, the screen pretty much matches the output you normally see from svn status. In this case, the working copy is at revision 43, with the various files having been last changed in a number of prior revisions. The index directory is unversioned, and the bin/sli and Build.PL files have been modified.

To use psvn to interact with your working copy and repository, you simply go to the *svn-status* buffer and run the commands defined by psvn. Each of the available commands is listed in the SVN menu, and they're self-explanatory. In most cases, you can just move the cursor over the file you want to target and press the key for the command. The results of your command, if any, will show up in a new buffer. If you want to perform a command that targets multiple targets, use the m and u commands to mark and unmark the targets, and then press the key for the command. Pressing Enter will bring up the file or directory under the cursor in a new buffer.

Some useful commands include g, which refreshes the screen by running svn status; U, which runs svn update; =, which runs svn diff on a single file; * u, which runs svn diff on the marked files; and, for Emacs-savvy users, E, which runs Ediff on a single file. You can also use a to svn add a file; + to run svn mkdir; and R to use svn move. Essentially all of the commonly used Subversion commands are right at your fingertips, all within Emacs.

Note that psvn tends to run svn status in the background to implement a number of its commands, so depending on the size of your working copy, you may find psvn more responsive if you display only a subset of your working copy by giving M-x svn-status a subdirectory within your working copy. The h command will allow you to jump back and forth between the various directories you've given to M-x svn-status within a given session.

Ant Integration

In the Java world, it has become increasingly common to manage a project's build process with Ant (http://ant.apache.org/). Ant provides a simple XML language for describing the actions that should occur during the build, and an API for writing extensions to the core Ant functionality in Java. As with just about every other tool used in software development, the standard reaction of a software developer is, of course, to see whether version control software can be integrated into Ant. As you might expect, it can be, via the svnAnt project, an offshoot of the Subclipse project, which we will discuss later in the section "Eclipse."

To install svnAnt, you simply need to download a release from the svnant directory of the Documents & Files section of the project's web site, located at http://subclipse.tigris.org/. After unzipping the release, you'll find three JAR files in the lib directory: svnant.jar, svnClientAdapter.jar, and svnjavahl.jar. Simply add those JAR files to the classpath in your Ant build file, and you're ready to go. If possible, svnAnt will try to use the Java Native Interface (JNI)–based JavaHL bindings to make direct use of the Subversion libraries from Java, but if it can't find them, it's perfectly capable of making use of the command-line client instead.

The svnAnt project provides ample documentation, so there's little need to rehash that information here. Instead, here are a few examples of how to do some common tasks you might want to automate via Ant.

First, consider the following fragment of an Ant build file that checks out a project, builds it, and runs the unit tests. This might be used to provide some kind of automated unit testing:

```
<target name="smoke" depends="checkout,build,test" />
<target name="checkout">
  <svn>
    <checkout url="http://svn.example.com/repos/project/trunk"
              destPath="project" />
  </svn>
</target>
<target name="build" depends="checkout">
  <exec dir="project"
        executable="ant"
        output="build.log"
        resultproperty="buildresult">
    <arg value="build"/>
  </exec>
</target>
<target name="build-notify"
        depends="build"
        if="buildresult">
```

```
  <mail from="testers@example.org"
   tolist="notification@example.org"
   subject="Build failure"
   files="build.log"/>
<target>
<target name="test" depends="build" unless="buildresult">
  <exec dir="project"
        executable="ant"
        output="test.log"
        resultproperty="testresult">
    <arg value="test"/>
  </exec>
</target>
<target name="test-notify"
        depends="test"
        if="testresult">
  <mail from="testers@example.org"
   tolist="notification@example.org"
   subject="Test failure"
   files="test.log"/>
<target>
```

Second, here's a fragment of an Ant build file that automates the process of tagging a release:

```
<target name="release.tag">
  <svn>
    <copy srcUrl="http://svn.example.com/repos/project/trunk"
          destUrl="http://svn.example.com/repos/project/tags/${version}"
          message="${commit.message}" />
  </svn>
</target>
```

You would probably use this during the release process after the user has already set the ${version} variable in the build.xml file, with the ${commit.message} property being passed in via the command line.

As you can see, the svnAnt Ant plugin provides access to almost any Subversion command you might want to run, allowing you to automate a number of tasks within the familiar context of your Ant build files.

Web-Based Repository Interfaces

Despite the fact that mod_dav_svn lets you browse the HEAD revision of your Subversion repository via a web browser, a common request on the Subversion mailing lists is for a more polished web-based interface, one that includes the ability to view previous revisions, log messages, the differences between various revisions, and various other things. The Subversion developers have steadfastly refused to add that kind of functionality to mod_dav_svn itself, since its job is to provide clients with a way to access the repository, not to present the perfect web front end to users.

Fortunately, the various language bindings for the Subversion libraries provide more than enough access to the repository's internals to allow you to write such a tool, and at least two such tools are available to you. For those who prefer Python, the ViewVC program has been extended to allow it to browse Subversion repositories. For those who are more Perl inclined, the SVN::Web module provides a convenient way to access your repository via the Web. We'll cover both tools in more detail in the sections that follow.

ViewVC

ViewVC (`http://www.viewvc.org/`) started off life as a port of CVSWeb to Python. Greg Stein, one of the core Subversion developers, wanted to add some features to CVSWeb but found it to be somewhat difficult given that CVSWeb is written in rather complex and hard-to-understand Perl. He decided it would be faster to simply rewrite the software in Python, and ViewVC was born. Later, when people started requesting a web-based front end for Subversion, several of the ViewVC developers worked to abstract out the CVS-specific code in ViewVC and added an alternate back end that talks to a Subversion repository via the Subversion Python bindings.

ViewVC works by directly accessing your Subversion repository via the Python bindings for `libsvn_fs`. As a result, you'll need to install the Python bindings for the Subversion libraries before you can make use of ViewVC. See the Chapter 8 section "Using Subversion from Python" for details on how to perform this installation. Once you've installed the Python bindings, you can proceed with the ViewVC installation.

The first thing you need to do to install ViewVC is to get a copy of it. ViewVC can be downloaded at `http://www.viewvc.org`, and any version 1.0 or greater will do (the latest is 1.0.2).

Once you've downloaded a copy of ViewVC, the installation and configuration steps are actually quite simple. First, run the `viewvc-install` script from the top level of the downloaded copy. This will prompt you for a directory to install into, and it will install everything ViewVC needs into that directory. Within the installation directory is a file named `viewvc.conf`, which holds the configuration options for your ViewVC installation. You can tweak a number of options here, but the two that are most important to you are `svn_roots` and `root_parents`. The option `svn_roots` contains a comma-separated list of repositories, where each repository consists of a name, a colon, and the full path to the repository. `root_parents` is a path to a directory that contains Subversion repositories, just like the `SVNParentPath` directive used when configuring `mod_dav_svn`. Finally, you may want to set the `default_root` parameter to indicate the name of the repository that should be shown by default.

Here's a simple example of the Subversion-specific parts of `viewvc.conf` from our own ViewVC installation. It's configured to show two Subversion repositories, one that holds our development work and one that holds our writing, with the default being the development repository:

```
[general]
svn_roots = writing:/home/repos/writing,
            dev:/home/repos/dev
default_root = dev
```

As we mentioned in Chapter 2, when using a BDB repository, the `mod_dav_svn` module presents several issues regarding programs that are run as part of or by a web server and the permissions on the Berkeley DB files that make up a Subversion repository. If the user the web server is running as doesn't have read-write access to the files making up the repository, you'll see errors that look something like this when you first try to access the repository:

```
An Exception Has Occurred
Python Traceback
Traceback (most recent call last):
  File "/Users/rooneg/Hacking/tmp/viewsvn/lib/ViewVC.py", line 2722, in main
    request.run_ViewVC()
  File "/Users/rooneg/Hacking/tmp/viewsvn/lib/ViewVC.py", line 257, in run_ViewVC➥
self.rootpath, rev)
  File "/Users/rooneg/Hacking/tmp/viewsvn/lib/vclib/svn/__init__.py", line 268, in➥
__init__
    self.repos = repos.svn_repos_open(rootpath, self.pool)
SubversionException: ('Berkeley DB error while opening environment for filesystem➥
/tmp/repos/db:\nPermission denied', 160029)
```

In this case, you must ensure that the ViewVC executing user has read-write access to the
repository, or use an FSFS-based repository. Once you do, you'll see something like Figure 7-1.

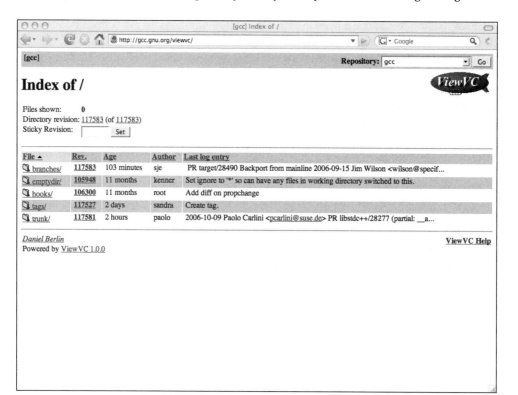

Figure 7-1. *ViewVC viewing a directory*

As Figure 7-1 shows, the first thing you see when using ViewVC to examine a repository is its directory view. From this view, you can move forward and backward to see the state of this directory at any given revision, navigate to subdirectories by clicking their names, and view the history of a given file by clicking its filename, as shown in Figure 7-2.

Figure 7-2. *ViewVC viewing a file*

To view the contents of a file, you can either go to the log history page and click the Download link or, from the directory view, you can click the revision number to view the log message from that revision and the file contents on one screen. Figure 7-3 shows an example.

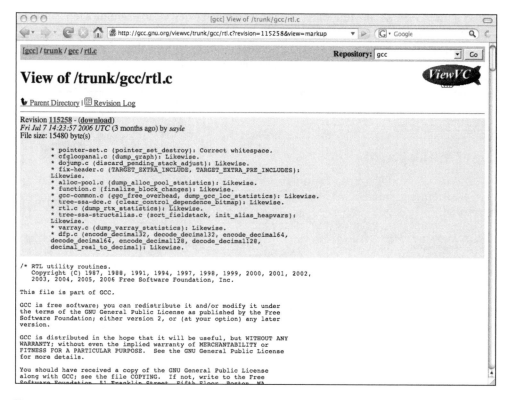

Figure 7-3. *ViewVC viewing a revision of a file*

From the file history view, you can also click the revision numbers to see a screen that shows what files changed in that revision along with the log message, as shown in Figure 7-4; and you can also view the difference between various revisions.

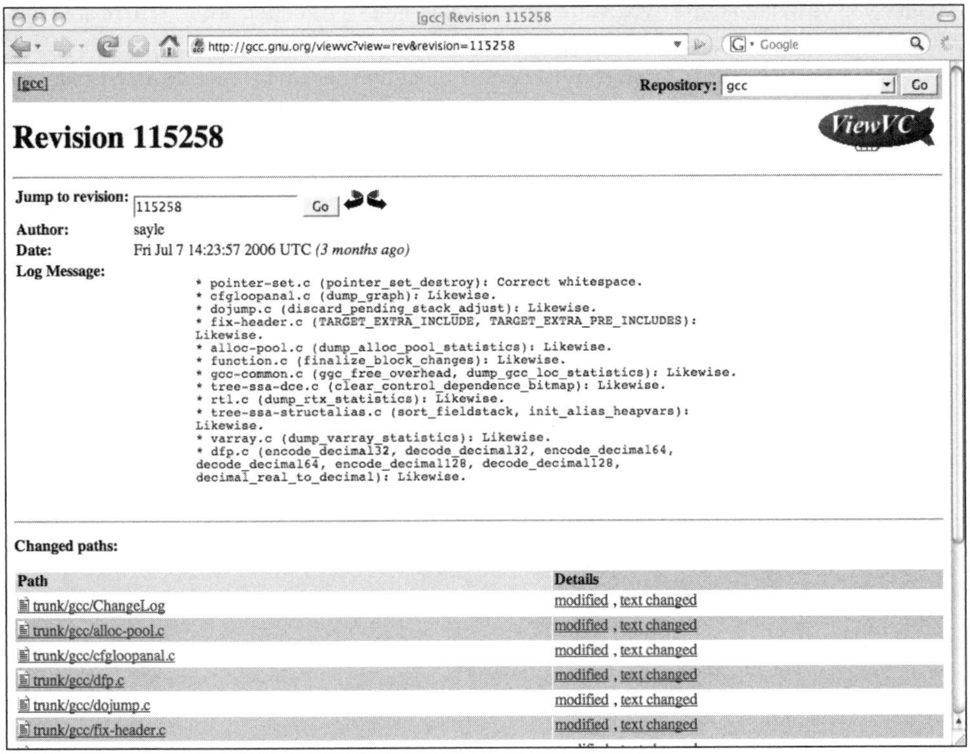

Figure 7-4. *ViewVC viewing an entire revision*

SVN::Web

If you prefer Perl to Python, or if you simply want a web-based repository viewer that isn't hampered by the fact that it must support version control systems other than Subversion, SVN::Web might be for you.

Once you have the Subversion Perl bindings installed, as described in the "Using Subversion from Perl" section of Chapter 8, installing SVN::Web is much the same as installing any other Perl module. You can either download the tarball from CPAN, and as the root user execute `perl Makefile.PL && make && make install`, or you can start the CPAN shell by running `perl -MCPAN -e shell` and run the command `install SVN::Web`. The second technique has the advantage of being able to download and install SVN::Web's various prerequisites; so unless you like the idea of downloading and installing a large number of Perl modules by hand, you should probably do it that way.

Once you've installed the SVN::Web Perl modules, go to a directory where you're able to run CGI programs via your web server and run the `svnweb-install` program. `svnweb-install` will write out an `index.cgi` file that runs the web application, a `config.yaml` file that holds the configuration information for your SVN::Web installation, and a `templates` directory that contains templates to control the look and feel of the various pages SVN::Web shows to the user. Next, you can add your repositories to the `config.yaml` file like this:

```
repos:
  test: '/path/to/test'
  test2: '/path/to/test2'
reposparent: '/path/to/repositories'
```

As with ViewVC, you can either configure each repository individually or you can configure a `reposparent` path, which is a directory that holds a number of repositories.

Once you've configured SVN::Web, you should see something like Figure 7-5 when viewing the repository in a browser.

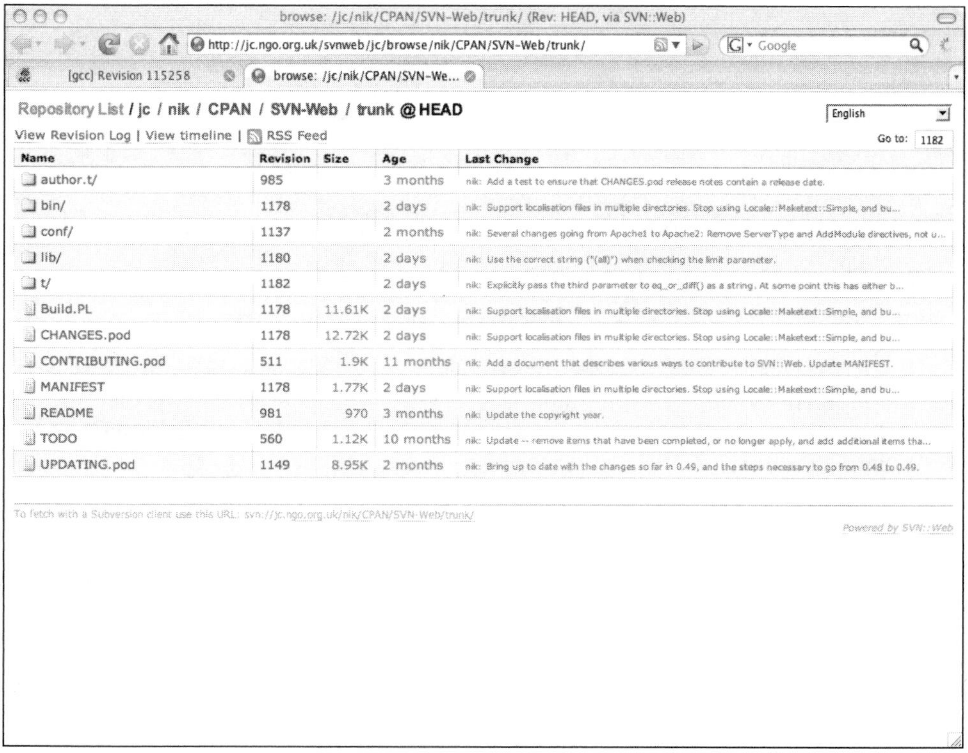

Figure 7-5. *SVN::Web viewing a directory*

This is SVN::Web's directory view. From here, you can view the history of the directory by clicking the View Revision Log link, or you can view the history of a particular file by clicking the filename links, as shown in Figure 7-6.

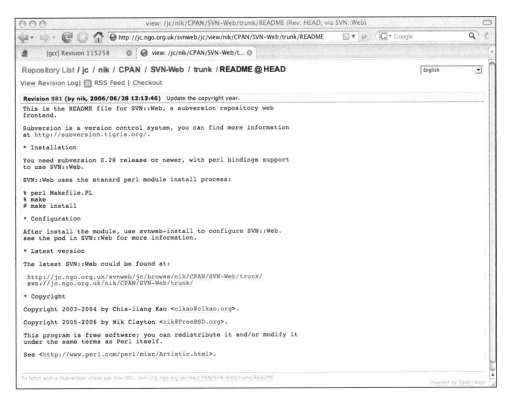

Figure 7-6. *SVN::Web viewing the history of a file*

Here in the history page, you can view differences between various revisions of a file, check out various revisions of a file, access RSS feeds for the log of this particular file or directory (via the RSS Feed link), and, perhaps most interesting, view a screen describing the changes in a given revision by clicking the Revision N link (where *N* is the revision number), which displays a screen like the one in Figure 7-7.

Figure 7-7. *SVN::Web viewing a revision*

From here, you have easy access to all the files and directories associated with a particular change, as well as to their revision histories and the log message.

As with ViewVC, SVN::Web works by accessing your repository directly, so you'll need to deal with all the same problems relating to file permissions and database files that you would with mod_dav_svn and ViewVC if you are using BDB.

Besides SVN::Web and ViewVC, there are a number of other web-based repository viewers, including WebSVN (http://websvn.tigris.org) and Chora (http://www.horde.org/chora). Each one has its own strengths and weaknesses, but most are customizable enough to make anyone happy.

Trac

Relatively recent to the world of Subversion (compared to the "plain" web-based repository viewers) is an all-singing, all-dancing, integrated product known as Trac. Trac provides a repository viewer, a wiki, and an issue tracker, all with a relatively unified interface. It is very easy to set up, and provides most, if not all, of what smaller projects want in one place, with a very nice interface. Links between each piece of Trac are natural, making it easy to link source code from the wiki and bug tracker, and refer to bugs from the source code/check-ins or the wiki. People seem to really like the integrated approach Trac offers, as it has become incredibly popular. Trac's underlying source code control system is Subversion, which is why we list it here. You can find it at `http://trac.edgewall.com/`.

IDE Integration

While the Unix developers of the world are generally comfortable using a standard text editor such as vi or Emacs for editing their source code, and the command-line `svn` tool for their version control, in many other environments, an integrated development environment (IDE) such as Visual Studio or Eclipse is more common. Fortunately, the users of several such systems have been able to provide Subversion integration for their IDE, so with a bit of luck, your IDE of choice may work relatively well out of the box with Subversion.

IntelliJ

Some Java developers swear by IntelliJ as a Java IDE. If you are one of them, there is TMate, a plugin that adds Subversion browsing and version control to IntelliJ. It can be found at `http://companions.jetbrains.com/tmate`.

Eclipse

Eclipse (`http://www.eclipse.org/`) is a Java-based IDE that intends to be a platform for building specialized development tools. As a result of Eclipse's extensible design and open source style of development, a number of different projects have been started to provide an Eclipse plugin for Subversion. At this book's publication time, the most mature example of this kind of plugin was provided by the Subclipse project, which makes use of the Subversion JavaHL bindings, which use JNI to call into the native Subversion libraries from Java code (Subclipse can also fall back to using the pure JAVA JavaSVN or the command-line client if these libraries are not available).

For more details on how to download, install, and use Subclipse, you can refer to the Subclipse web site at `http://subclipse.tigris.org/`.

Visual Studio

Those of you living in the world of Microsoft's .NET Framework are probably wishing for some way to integrate Subversion with Visual Studio .NET. The AnkhSVN project provides you with just that, integrating nicely with the 2002, 2003, and 2005 versions of Visual Studio .NET by using Managed C++ to bridge the gap between the plugin, which is written in C#, and the native Subversion libraries, which are written in C.

For more details on downloading, installing, and using AnkhSVN, you can refer to the project's web site at `http://ankhsvn.tigris.org/`. If you find AnkhSVN doesn't work for you, there is another VisualStudio .NET plugin called VisualSVN, which can be found at `http://www.visualsvn.com`.

TortoiseSVN

Like Trac, Tortoise doesn't really fit into any other category, which is why it has its own heading. TortoiseSVN is a Windows shell extension that provides Subversion support. In simple terms, it allows you to work with Subversion repositories directly from the Windows Explorer interface, which makes it very familiar to people used to manipulating files and directories in Windows. It also provides a large number of graphical utilities for diffing, merging, and browsing, on top of the Explorer support. A lot of people, developers and nondevelopers alike, swear that TortoiseSVN is the greatest thing since sliced bread. We're not Windows users, but if we were, we'd check it out at `http://tortoisesvn.net`.

Summary

In this chapter, you saw various ways to use third-party tools with Subversion, from command-line shells, to build tools, to web-based repository viewers, and all the way up to full-fledged IDE support. While some of these methods are implemented by having the tool call the Subversion command-line interface, most make use of the Subversion libraries directly.

In the next chapter, you'll learn to make use of those libraries in your own programs. You'll no longer be limited to tools that already have support for Subversion; instead, you'll be able to create your own.

CHAPTER 8

■■■

Using the Subversion APIs

A significant design goal of Subversion has always been that the core functionality of the software is implemented in a series of C libraries, and the applications the user uses (such as svn or svnadmin) are thin wrappers around those libraries. This has a number of benefits, both for the developers and for the users.

The developers benefit because this kind of design results in a much cleaner code base, with clear divisions between the various bits of functionality that make up Subversion. A new developer can then jump into this code base with a minimum amount of effort, because for a number of different tasks, the developer needs to understand only a single library, as opposed to the entire system. This stands in stark contrast to the CVS code base, in which there is no separation of functionality, and new features or bug fixes often require the developer to touch a disturbing amount of the code base.

The users benefit because the availability of these libraries results in a number of other programs being able to interoperate with Subversion. It's considerably easier to make your IDE, scripting language, or GUI client link into the Subversion libraries than it is to reimplement all that functionality yourself; and it's much more reliable than calling out to the command-line client and parsing the output to determine what the result of the command is, as is commonly done with CVS. This ability to easily use Subversion's code in your own program has resulted in a number of alternate client implementations, such as RapidSVN (http://rapidsvn.tigris.org/), TortoiseSVN (http://tortoisesvn.net/), and many others listed on Subversion's web site (http://subversion.tigris.org/links.html#clients). More important for the purposes of this chapter, it has allowed the creation of bindings for a number of alternate languages, such as Perl and Python. The result is that now you don't have to know how to write C code in order to make your program work with Subversion.

Subversion Source Documentation

Before diving into any of the details of the Subversion libraries, it's worth pointing out that this chapter gives only a basic overview—just enough to get you started. The Subversion project uses Doxygen to create API documentation directly from the public header files, so the best place to go for the details on how any of the various functions work is that documentation. You can build the documentation yourself by running make doc-api in the top level of the Subversion distribution. The output will be placed in the doc/doxygen directory. If you don't have access to the Doxygen program, you can always find the most recent documentation at http://svn.collab.net/svn-doxygen/.

Just so you're not surprised when reading the Subversion source code, Listing 8-1 presents an example of the Doxygen markup.

Listing 8-1. *Doxygen Markup*

```
/** Write a pretty-printed version of @a string to @c FILE @a f.
 *
 * @a pool is used for all temporary memory allocation.
 */
void output_function (FILE *f, const char *string, apr_pool_t *pool);
```

The first thing to notice is that the comment starts with /** instead of the usual /*. This indicates that it is a comment that Doxygen should parse. The arguments to the function are then marked up with @a markers, so that Doxygen can find them and highlight them in the final HTML documentation it outputs. Finally, anything that is a literal quotation from some kind of code, such as FILE in the example, is marked up with @c for similar reasons. The markup is reasonably nonintrusive, yet it allows nice HTML documentation to be generated easily.

Another thing to be aware of before diving in and writing your own code that takes advantage of Subversion's libraries is the versioning rules used by the Subversion developers. When a new version of Subversion is released, you can be sure that as long as it uses the same major version number (i.e., the *1* in 1.0.5 and 1.1.0), code compiled against the earlier version will continue to work with the latter version. The reverse isn't necessarily true, though, as new functions may have been added in the 1.1.*x* series of releases that aren't present in the 1.0.*x* series. So it's safe to change versions, either by upgrading to a new release or downgrading to an older one, as long as you stay within the same minor version number (1.0.*x*, for example). There are similar rules for client/server compatibility. A new release of Subversion never breaks compatibility with older clients as long as the client and server share the same major version number. Newer clients may depend on features only present in newer versions of the server, but they'll always behave reasonably when used against an older version of the server. These rules are documented in detail in the "Release Numbering, Compatibility, and Deprecation" section of the HACKING file, which is online at http://subversion.tigris.org/hacking.html. If you're going to be making use of the Subversion libraries in your own program, it's a good idea to read that section of the documentation.

How the Libraries Fit Together

As mentioned, Subversion is implemented as a collection of C libraries that together make up the various applications generally referred to as *Subversion*. At the lowest level you'll find libsvn_subr, which just provides various utility routines used by the rest of the libraries. Implemented on top of libsvn_subr is libsvn_delta, which contains code for performing binary diffs between arbitrary files, and code for performing diffs between two directory trees, both of which Subversion uses in a number of different places.

The remaining libraries can be split into three major groups. The first group consists of the libraries used to implement the client applications. These consist of libsvn_client, which provides the high-level interface to the system that most client programs use; libsvn_diff, which libsvn_client uses to do textual diffs and merges between plain text files; and libsvn_wc, which is used to manage the client's working copy on disk.

The second group consists of the libraries associated with the repository itself. At the lowest level is libsvn_fs, which is a loader for the underlying filesystem libraries. libsvn_fs_base implements the FS API using Berkeley DB, and libsvn_fs_fs implements it using FSFS's flat file mechanism. On top of that is libsvn_repos, which adds in things such as the various hook scripts that get executed when you access the repository.

The third group, located in between the client libraries and the repository libraries, is known as the *repository access libraries*. The repository access libraries are designed as an interface, presented by libsvn_ra, and a number of implementations of that interface, currently libsvn_ra_local, which talks directly to the repository via libsvn_repos; libsvn_ra_svn, which talks to the repository via a custom protocol and a custom server, svnserve; and libsvn_ra_dav, which talks to the repository via a WebDAV dialect using mod_dav_svn.

Actually, if you look at the libraries installed along with your Subversion installation, you might also see a few more, for example, libsvn_swig_perl and libsvn_swig_py. These libraries contain glue code for the Perl and Python language bindings, and we'll discuss them in more detail later on.

Anyway, that's an awful lot of libraries, so you'll probably get a better understanding of them from the illustration in Figure 8-1.

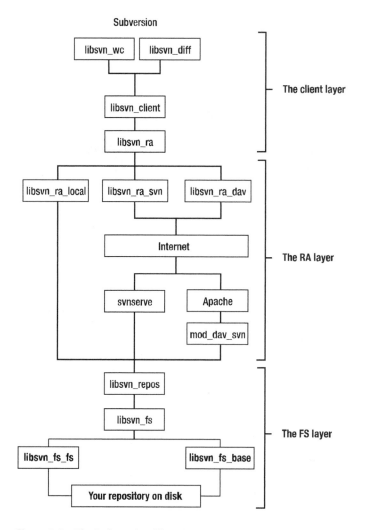

Figure 8-1. *The Subversion libraries*

■**Note** `libsvn_subr` and `libsvn_delta` don't show up in Figure 8-1 because they're used in so many places that including them would just make the diagram cluttered and difficult to understand.

APR and the Core SVN Libraries

Before you can start using the more interesting Subversion libraries (`libsvn_client`, `libsvn_ra`, or `libsvn_repos`, most likely), you'll need to learn about two bits of code: the Apache Portable Runtime (APR), and the utilities found in `libsvn_subr`. The APR is the way Subversion handles the problem of needing to be able to run on a variety of different operating systems. Additionally, it contains a collection of common data structures used throughout Subversion. On top of the APR libraries is `libsvn_subr`, which provides other low-level data structures and utility functions used everywhere in the Subversion libraries.

APR

Subversion's connection with Apache has been a topic of conversation for some time, and for many people the most interesting part of that connection is the use of the Apache HTTP server as one of Subversion's server processes. But at least from the point of view of a developer, it's Subversion's use of the APR that's far more significant.

During the development of version 2 of the Apache HTTP server, a huge amount of effort went into splitting out as much of the platform-specific code from the server as possible and placing it into a separate portability library, the APR. The Apache HTTP server has always been known for its portability, and with the creation of the APR, that same portability is now available to anyone who wants it. As a result of using APR, Subversion is able to run on any platform APR has been ported to, at least in theory. In practice, this means that Subversion runs on pretty much any variety of Unix, as well as on Win32 systems.

In addition to the obvious portability gains, APR provides Subversion with a number of useful data structures. Subversion makes heavy use of APR's memory pools, hash tables, variable-length arrays, and a number of other data structures; so before you can make use of the Subversion libraries in your own code, you'll have to become conversant in their use.

Startup and Shutdown

Before you can begin using any APR functionality, you need to initialize APR's internal data structures by calling `apr_initialize()`. Similarly, after your program is finished, but before it exits, you need to call `apr_terminate()`, which is generally done by making use of the `atexit()` function. There is a utility function, `svn_cmdline_init`, which will take care of this setup for free. If you don't use `svn_cmdline_init`, the initialization code generally looks something like Listing 8-2.

Listing 8-2. *Setting Up APR*

```
int
setup_apr (void)
{
  apr_status_t err = apr_initialize ();
  if (err)
    {
      return EXIT_FAILURE;
    }

  if (atexit (apr_terminate) < 0)
    {
      return EXIT_FAILURE;
    }
  return 0;
}
```

Now that we've gotten that out of the way, let's move on to the more interesting parts of APR.

Memory Pools

A significant problem in most C code is management of memory and other resources. Because it has no built-in destructors or exception-handling functions, it's considerably easier to forget to free memory or close filehandles and sockets than in other languages such as C++; and garbage collectors, while available for C, have their own set of issues. The APR provides the apr_pool_t data structure as a means of dealing with these issues. Instead of manually allocating memory with malloc() and deallocating it with free(), all memory is allocated within apr_pool_t objects via functions such as apr_pcalloc(), and when the programmer knows that none of the memory allocated within the pool is needed, the pool can be cleared. Similarly, filehandles, sockets, and other resources can associate cleanup functions with the pool, which will be called when the pool is cleared. As a result of having this system at her disposal, the programmer is able to think about resource allocation at a higher level than in most C programs.

The best way to learn to make use of memory pools is by seeing an example of how they're used. Listing 8-3 shows a function that looks over a number of files, determines which are important, and returns an array of strings containing NULL entries for files that aren't important and the path to the files that are. In the process, it also makes good use of APR pools, and thus provides a useful example.

Listing 8-3. *Using APR Pools*

```
#include <svn_pools.h>

/* given a file number, return its path */
char * find_file (int i, apr_pool_t *pool);

/* returns 1 if a given file is important, 0 if it is not. */
int is_important (const char *file, apr_pool_t *pool);

/* look through files numbered 0 up to maximum.  for each one that is important,
   put its filename in the array we will return, otherwise leave its slot
   in the array as NULL. */
char **
find_important_files (int maximum, apr_pool_t *pool)
{
  int i;

  /* allocate an array of char *'s to hold potentially important files */
  char ** important_files = apr_pcalloc (pool, sizeof(char *) * maximum);

  /* create an iteration pool */
  apr_pool_t *subpool = svn_pool_create (pool);
```

```
  for (i = 0; i < maximum; ++i)
    {
      svn_pool_clear (subpool);

      /* get a file, allocated in subpool */
      char *file = find_file (i, subpool);

      if (is_important (file, subpool))
        {
          /* if file is important, strdup it into the main pool so it will
             persist beyond this iteration so we can return it. */
          important_files[i] = apr_pstrdup (pool, file);
        }
    }

  /* clean up our subpool so that the resources can be reused in the future */
  svn_pool_destroy (subpool);

  return important_files;
}
```

Let's take a look at what's happening here. First, each function in the example takes as an argument an apr_pool_t, which is used for all memory allocation instead of the standard C malloc() or free() functions. Next, you use svn_pool_create() when you need to create a new pool. This is actually a Subversion-specific wrapper around the underlying apr_pool_create() function, but it's used in all of Subversion's code for a variety of reasons, so you should use it instead of going directly to the APR function. It takes a single argument, which is the parent pool for the pool you're creating. If the parent pool is NULL, a new top-level pool will be created. Most important, whenever there's a potentially unbounded amount of allocation occurring (such as within the for loop) a subpool is used. This keeps you from allocating a ridiculous amount of memory, which is how a *memory leak* manifests itself with pools. Sure, the memory eventually gets cleaned up when the top-level pool is destroyed, but if you use up all your machine's memory and get terminated by the operating system's out-of-memory killer, that's little comfort. Finally, when an item needs to persist longer than the loop, it's simply duplicated into the main pool. The calling function will clear or destroy that pool when it is done with the resources allocated within it.

Note that you've seen two ways of dealing with a pool once the resources allocated within it are no longer needed. First is svn_pool_clear(), which indicates that you're done with the memory you allocated within it, and it can be reused. To minimize the number of times the operating system's memory allocator is called, this memory is not actually freed; it sticks around so that you can use it again the next time you allocate something from the pool. If you're really finished with the pool and don't want to use it ever again, you use the second function, svn_pool_destroy(), which will return the memory allocated to the pool to its parent pool or, if there is no parent pool, to the operating system. Note that svn_pool_destroy() does not actually reclaim memory, it just enables it to be reused. As with svn_pool_create(), both of these functions are wrappers around the underlying APR functions, apr_pool_clear() and apr_pool_destroy(), primarily provided for debugging purposes. As before, you should use the Subversion wrappers rather than directly using the APR functions.

In both cases, cleanups that are associated with the pool will be called, so filehandles and other nonmemory resources associated with the pool will be returned to the operating system. Both functions also recurse into the pool's subpools, so if you clear or destroy a parent pool, all its subpools will be destroyed.

Throughout the life of the Subversion project, several "best practices" for using memory pools have become clear. First, you should pass a pool to every function and use it for all allocation. The only case in which you can use the native malloc() and free() functions is when they're needed to interoperate with some external library that requires them. Second, don't put a memory pool in an object and then use that memory pool for allocations related to that object. It might be tempting to embed a pool in a data structure and use it for allocation associated with that object, but it leads to unbounded allocation of memory, which is never a good idea. It is, however, common to embed a memory pool in an object to be able to free the memory pool when the object is no longer needed, and this is a perfectly normal thing to do. Outside of needing to free memory pools when the object is no longer needed, you should make use of the pool passed to each function for allocation, creating subpools for temporary allocations and destroying them when you're done with that memory. In cases in which you might allocate unbounded amounts of memory, make use of iteration pools for everything that doesn't need to outlive the current iteration of the loop, and clear the pool as soon as possible.

More information on the Subversion team's current thoughts on how to best make use of memory pools can be found in the HACKING file.

While it might seem odd at first to be allocating memory without explicitly freeing it, soon it becomes clear that this style of programming is considerably less error-prone than manual memory management; and with a little practice you'll find it simplifies your code, which is always a good thing.

Error Checking

The other part of APR that requires a little getting used to is the way it handles error conditions. All APR functions that can possibly fail return an apr_status_t value, which is defined in apr_errno.h. The apr_status_t values are split into several categories. First is everyone's favorite status code, APR_SUCCESS, which is always defined as zero, so you can do things like the error checking in Listing 8-4.

Listing 8-4. *Error Checking with APR*

```
void
parse_file (const char *filename, apr_pool_t *pool)
{
  apr_file_t *file;
  apr_status_t err;

  err = apr_file_open (&file, filename, 0, APR_OS_DEFAULT, pool);
  if (err) {
    /* couldn't open the file, so handle the error somehow */
  } else {
    /* it succeeded, so we continue on parsing the contents of the file */
  }
}
```

Next are the APR error values, which start at `APR_OS_START_ERROR` and account for anything that can cause an APR function to fail. The names of these values all begin with `APR_E` and are defined in `apr_errno.h`. Then there are the status codes, starting at `APR_OS_START_STATUS`, which don't indicate either success or failure but are returned when `APR_SUCCESS` doesn't make sense. All these status codes are named starting with `APR_`. Next is a range of error codes reserved for applications that use APR, with values starting at `APR_OS_START_USERERR`. Subversion's own error codes are defined within this range. Finally, there is `APR_OS_START_SYSERR`, the beginning of the range of values used for system-specific errors. All these constants are defined in `apr_errno.h`, along with documentation on their semantics. Generally, though, you shouldn't need to worry about them unless you're writing an application that makes heavy use of APR and you want to define your own error codes. If you're doing that, consult the APR documentation for the details.

If you read the preceding paragraph closely, you may have picked up on something a little odd. There are two ranges of error codes that can result when an APR function fails: the errors that come from the operating system via `errno` or some other system-specific means, and the range defined by APR explicitly. This is done because for speed reasons APR wants to be able to return `errno` values directly, without passing through some kind of translation layer; but for portability it needs some way to return an appropriate value on a system that doesn't have the appropriate `errno` code. This works in your favor speedwise because most of the time code only cares if an error occurs; and it's reasonably rare to want to programmatically check for specific kinds of errors. Since the platform-specific `errno` value is returned directly, there's no need to take the time to translate into an APR-specific error code unless you actually need to do so.

So when you do care about the specific type of error code that's been returned, how do you figure out what kind of error it is? Here's another place where APR helps you out. It turns out that different operating systems have different error codes that can logically be mapped back to the same `errno` value. For example, Windows and OS/2 have a few hundred different error codes, but POSIX defines only about 50. This means you end up needing to convert the platform-specific value back to a canonical APR representation, which is done by a series of `APR_STATUS_IS` macros defined in `apr_errno.h`. In some cases, a macro might just be a simple comparison, but in many situations (check out `APR_STATUS_IS_ENOENT` for a good example), it might involve several different possibilities.

In summary, you can count on APR always returning `APR_SUCCESS`, which is equal to zero, when a function succeeds. In all other cases, it will return a nonzero `apr_status_t`; but if you want to check for a particular kind of error, you need to use the `APR_STATUS_IS` macros defined in `apr_errno.h`.

Hash Tables

A more conventional part of the APR library is its hash table data structure, `apr_hash_t`. You've certainly encountered hash tables before, so we won't spend too much time on them; but they're used in a number of places throughout Subversion, so the API deserves a mention.

An `apr_hash_t` is created with the `apr_hash_make()` function. Once you have one, you can add or remove items in the table with the `apr_hash_set()` function. The function accepts a pointer to the key, the size of the key (which may be `APR_HASH_KEY_STRING` to indicate that the key is a pointer to a null-terminated string), and a pointer to the value, which can be `NULL` to indicate that the item should be removed. Retrieving values from the table is accomplished with the `apr_hash_get()` function, which takes a pointer to the key and the length of the key, just like `apr_hash_set()`. If you want to iterate over all the key-value pairs in the hash, you can make use of an `apr_hash_index_t` and the `apr_hash_first()` and `apr_hash_next()` functions.

It's probably easiest to look at an example of how this all works. Listing 8-5 just runs through all the common functions for working with APR's hash tables.

Listing 8-5. *Using APR Hash Tables*

```
void
demonstrate_hash_tables (apr_pool_t *pool)
{
  /* create an empty hash table */
  apr_hash_t *hash = apr_hash_make (pool);

  /* add some items */
  apr_hash_set (hash, "foo", APR_HASH_KEY_STRING, "bar");
  apr_hash_set (hash, "baz", APR_HASH_KEY_STRING, "zot");

  {
    apr_hash_index_t *idx;
    const void *key;
    void *val;

    /* iterate over them */
    for (idx = apr_hash_first (pool, hash); idx; idx = apr_hash_next (idx))
      {
        /* and print them out */
        apr_hash_this (idx, &key, NULL, &val);
        printf ("key = '%s', val = '%s'\n",
                (const char *) key, (const char *) val);
      }
  }

  {
    /* get a specific value */
    void *val = apr_hash_get (hash, "foo", APR_HASH_KEY_STRING);
    if (val)
      {
        /* do something with it */
      }
  }

  /* remove the item at "foo" */
  apr_hash_set (hash, "foo", APR_HASH_KEY_STRING, NULL);
}
```

This example includes all the major things you're likely to want to do with a hash table. First, a hash table is created with apr_hash_make(). Then, apr_hash_set() is used to insert several entries into the hash. Next, apr_hash_first() and apr_hash_next() are used to iterate over the values in the hash, and apr_hash_this() is used to retrieve the current value so it can be printed out. apr_hash_get() is then used to retrieve a specific value from the hash, and finally, apr_hash_set() is used with a NULL value to remove an element.

Note that this example uses APR_HASH_KEY_STRING for the calls to apr_hash_set() and apr_hash_get(), which only works because the keys are const char *s. If they were not, the size of the key would have to be passed instead. As a final note about hashes, while they have their own pools, they do not own either the keys or the values.

Variable-Length Arrays

The last APR data structure you generally see in the Subversion API is the variable-length array, which you access through an apr_array_header_t. An array can be allocated via apr_array_make(), which takes as its arguments a pool, the number of items to initially allocate, and the size of the items to allocate. Then items can be added to it via apr_array_push() and removed via apr_array_pop(). If you push on more items than the array has room for, more space will be allocated; and if you pop off more than are stored in the array, NULL will be returned. Unlike most other APR data structures, apr_array_header_t isn't opaque, so to iterate over it you should look at its nelts and elts members. As usual, an example makes the use clearer (see Listing 8-6).

Listing 8-6. *Using Variable-Length Arrays*

```
void
demonstrate_apr_arrays (apr_pool_t *pool)
{
  /* make an array with 2 slots in it */
  apr_array_header_t *array = apr_array_make (pool, 2, sizeof (char *));

  /* push two strings onto the array */
  (*(char **) apr_array_push (array)) = "foo";
  (*(char **) apr_array_push (array)) = "bar";

  /* push another one on, this causes the extra spot to be allocated */
  (*(char **) apr_array_push (array)) = "baz";

  /* iterate over them */
  for (int i = 0; i < array->nelts; ++i)
    {
      printf ("%s\n", ((char **) array->elts)[i]);
    }

  {
    /* try to pop off the lastitem */
    char **item = apr_array_pop (array);
    if (item)
      {
        /* use it */
      }
  }
}
```

This example covers all you need to know to make use of APR's variable-length arrays. First, `apr_array_make()` is used to create the array, and then `apr_array_push()` is used to add items to the array. It's worth noting that the interface to `apr_array_push()` is a little strange. It returns a `void *` pointer; and to actually insert your item into the place in memory it has specified for you, you need to cast to a pointer to whatever you're storing (in this case, the array holds `char *`s, so `apr_array_push()`'s return value should be cast to a `char **`), and then dereference it to actually do the final assignment. Then the array's `nelts` and `elts` members are used to iterate over the array and to actually access its contents. Finally, `apr_array_pop()` is used to remove the last item in the array and returns a pointer to the location used to store the item.

A number of other functions are provided for working with these arrays, all of which are declared and documented in `apr_tables.h`, but the ones just described are the most commonly used.

More Information on APR

This concludes our whirlwind introduction to the most significant parts of the APR API as applied to use by a Subversion application. However, we haven't even scratched the surface regarding what is available. For more information, including the APR API documentation, refer to the APR web site at `http://apr.apache.org/`.

libsvn_subr

In any sufficiently large C application, there's generally a need for a number of utility functions—code that isn't directly related to the main purpose of the application, but that is nonetheless required by it. In Subversion that code lives in `libsvn_subr`, and you'll need to become familiar with it to make use of the other more interesting libraries. In this section we cover enough of the contents of `libsvn_subr` that you'll be able to understand the Subversion code that uses it. Specifically, we deal with error objects, UTF-8 conversion functions, revisions, counted strings, and generic stream objects.

Error Objects

The first notable feature of the Subversion libraries you're likely to notice is their use of the `svn_error_t` structure. Any Subversion function that can fail returns a pointer to an `svn_error_t`, which is defined in `svn_types.h`, as shown in Listing 8-7.

Listing 8-7. *The svn_error_t Structure*

```
typedef struct svn_error_t {
  /** APR error value, possibly SVN_ custom err */
  apr_status_t apr_err;

  /** details from producer of error */
  const char *message;

  /** ptr to the error we "wrap" */
  struct svn_error_t *child;
```

```
/** The pool holding this error and any child errors it wraps */
apr_pool_t *pool;

/** Source file where the error originated.  Only used if @c SVN_DEBUG. */
const char *file;

/** Source line where the error originated.  Only used if @c SVN_DEBUG. */
long line;
}
```

When a function succeeds, it returns SVN_NO_ERROR, which is defined to be zero, for the same reasons that APR_SUCCESS is. In all other cases, it returns a pointer to an svn_error_t object that describes the problem that occurred.

If there's an underlying APR-level error, the apr_err field will be set to the apr_status_t that the APR function returned; otherwise, it will hold one of the SVN_ERR_ constants defined in svn_error_codes.h. The message field holds a character string that gives more information about exactly what went wrong; and if you want a generic description of the error, you can get one via the svn_strerror() function. If the error is returned in response to another lower-level error, the child field will point to the underlying error structure, so the code that eventually deals with the error (perhaps by presenting a summary of what went wrong) needs to be able to deal with a potential chain of errors, not simply one.

The pool field points to the apr_pool_t that the error was allocated from. This is an exception to the rule regarding not giving objects their own pool, and it's done because error objects often need to persist longer than the pool being used for allocation when they are created. As a result, it's necessary to call svn_error_clear() on svn_error_ts when you're done with them, or you'll end up with a memory leak.

If you want to create your own errors (perhaps you're implementing a callback function for which you need to use one of Subversion's APIs, and it's defined to return an svn_error_t *), you can use svn_error_create(), which accepts an error code (either from APR or svn_error_codes.h), a pointer to a child error (or NULL if there is none), and an error message to display to the user. It returns a pointer to an error object that can be returned to the calling function. Similarly, you can use svn_error_createf(), which uses a printf()-style format string and a variable number of other arguments to create the error message for the user.

Since use of svn_error_ts tends to result in large numbers of functions that all return pointers to svn_error_ts, a number of convenience macros have been provided to simplify your code. SVN_ERR(), the most common of these, takes an expression that returns an svn_error_t *, checks to see if it returns SVN_NO_ERROR, and if it doesn't, returns the error to its calling function. For cases in which you want to include some extra information in the case of an error, SVN_ERR_W() does the same thing but with a message string as the second argument, which will be used to create an error that wraps around the error returned by the function you're calling. Listing 8-8 shows how this all works.

Listing 8-8. *Subversion Error Handling*

```
/* an example function that returns svn_error_t's in various ways*/
svn_error_t *
function_that_might_fail(apr_pool_t *pool)
```

```
{
  /* first, the most generic way of dealing with an error.  if this function
     returns any kind of error at all, SVN_ERR will immediately return that
     error to our calling function and let it deal with it. */
  SVN_ERR(another_function_that_might_fail(pool));

  if (something)
    {
      /* this case is similar, but instead of just using SVN_ERR, we use
         SVN_ERR_W, which allows us to specify a message that will be wrapped
         around any error that is returned.  so if this function returns
         an error, we'll create a new error, with "the first case" as its
         message and the error we're going to wrap as its parent.  when
         the calling function receives the chain of errors, it will have both
         the lower-level error message that indicates that this function
         failed and our more specific error message wrapped around it, which
         indicates some more detail about how it was being used when it did
         fail. */
      SVN_ERR_W(a_third_function_that_might_fail(pool),
              "the first case");
    }
  else if (something_else)
    {
      /* in this case, we aren't reacting to an error we received from a
         function we called, instead we're returning an error we create
         ourselves. */
      return svn_error_createf (SVN_ERR_BAD_URL,
                                NULL,
                                "got bad URL '%s'",
                                bad_url);
    }
  else
    {
      /* finally, we have the case where we're calling a function that returns
         an error, but we don't particularly care if it failed or not.  perhaps
         we're already recovering from another error, and subsequent problems
         aren't really unexpected.  in this case, we need to use svn_error_clear
         to destroy it, or we'll get a memory leak. */
      svn_error_t *err = a_function_that_might_fail_but_we_dont_care(pool);

      svn_error_clear(err);
    }

  return SVN_NO_ERROR;
}
```

So there you have it: the four major ways to deal with errors in Subversion code. You either simply return the error to your calling function, return it to your caller with more information added, create your own error and return it, or clear out the error with svn_error_clear().

It's perhaps easiest to think of svn_error_ts as C++-style exceptions implemented in C. Once you get used to using them, you'll find that they can carry large amounts of information about exactly what's going on; but to use them correctly, you need to be aware of them at all times. So while they do simplify some parts of error handling, you still need to stay on your toes.

UTF-8 Conversion Functions

To allow some measure of internationalization, Subversion's interfaces have been defined such that all strings they manipulate are UTF-8 encoded. This means that whenever you call a Subversion function that takes some sort of string as an argument, you have to convert it from your native locale's representation into UTF-8 before calling the function, and then convert the results from UTF-8 back to your native locale's representation when you output it for your user, unless your locale's encoding is UTF-8, in which case you've got it easy. You may already have access to code that can do this conversion for you, either via your operating system or the scripting language you're working in, but if you don't, you can always use the same ones Subversion uses internally, which are found in svn_utf.h.

For converting C-style null-terminated strings from your native locale into UTF-8, you need to use the svn_utf_cstring_to_utf8() function. To reverse the procedure, you can use svn_utf_cstring_from_utf8(). Both functions work about as you would expect, taking a pointer to a char *, where they store the result of the transformation as the first argument, the C string to convert as the second argument, and an apr_pool_t to use for allocations as the third argument. Listing 8-9 shows what the general process looks like.

Listing 8-9. *UTF-8 Conversion Functions*

```
svn_error_t *
call_some_subversion_function(const char *native_path, apr_pool_t *pool)
{
  const char *utf8_path, *result_of_operation, *native_result;

  SVN_ERR (svn_utf_cstring_to_utf8 (&utf8_path, native_path, pool));

  SVN_ERR (some_svn_function (&result_of_operation, utf8_path, pool));

  SVN_ERR (svn_utf_cstring_from_utf8 (&native_result,
                                      result_of_operation, pool));

  printf ("the result is %s\n", native_result);

  return SVN_NO_ERROR;
}
```

Revisions

As you might expect with a version control system, the concept of a revision is rather central to many of Subversion's APIs. There are two different representations of a revision that you'll need to be aware of going forward, one that's quite specific and is used for representing the revision as it exists in the repository, and one that's more flexible and is suitable for representing revisions as they come from the user.

First is svn_revnum_t, which is simply an integer. When Subversion returns a revision to you, such as after performing a commit, this is the form the revision will be in. svn_revnum_t is defined in svn_types.h, along with some convenience macros to simplify working with svn_revnum_ts in your code. You'll probably find both SVN_INVALID_REVNUM and SVN_IS_VALID_REVNUM useful for determining whether a particular svn_revnum_t is valid, and SVN_REVNUM_T_FMT useful for formatting svn_revnum_ts via printf()-type functions.

While it's certainly possible to work with Subversion while referring to revisions via raw svn_revnum_ts, most people wouldn't find that very satisfying. It's considerably nicer to be able to use symbolic names such as HEAD, BASE, or PREV, or even to refer to the revision via a date, in addition to being able to use a raw number such as svn_revnum_t. To make this possible, Subversion uses another representation for a revision whenever it's being passed in by the user. This representation, svn_opt_revision_t (defined in svn_opt.h), includes a kind flag, which is of type enum svn_opt_revision_kind, and a value union, which can either contain an svn_revnum_t number (to be used when kind is set to svn_opt_revision_number), or an apr_time_t date (to be used when kind is set to svn_opt_revision_date). To obtain an svn_opt_revision_t that corresponds to one of the symbolic names (HEAD, BASE, PREV, etc.), you simply set kind to one of the other values in the enum (svn_opt_revision_head, svn_opt_revision_base, svn_opt_revision_prev, etc.). If no revision information is specified by the user, you should set kind to svn_opt_revision_unspecified.

Counted Strings

At various times, usually when dealing with property values, it's useful to be able to pass data around as *counted strings* (meaning a buffer and a count that indicates how long the buffer is), rather than simply working with standard C null-terminated strings. This allows you to work with data that's not necessarily null-terminated or has embedded null values, which can be necessary at times. For this reason, Subversion provides two special data types: svn_string_t and svn_stringbuf_t. Both are defined in svn_string.h and obey two rules. First, the end of the data is null-terminated, so str->data[str->len] will always be zero. This doesn't mean that there can't be embedded null values within the data buffer, but the rule is still useful when passing the data to functions that expect C strings. Second, the functions provided for manipulating these data structures explicitly use the length to determine where the end of the data is, so you can work with data that contains embedded null values.

svn_string_t is a simple counted string, consisting of a data pointer and a length. It's the most basic counted string type Subversion uses, and it can't be modified. A number of utility functions are defined in svn_string.h for creating, copying, comparing, and searching svn_string_ts, but they're simple enough that even an example is overkill, and Subversion's own Doxygen documentation provides more than adequate information about how to use them.

svn_stringbuf_t is a slightly more complex structure than svn_string_t, and its complexity comes from the fact that it can be modified after it's created. If you've ever programmed in Java, the difference between svn_string_t and svn_stringbuf_t is analogous to the difference between java.lang.String and java.lang.StringBuffer.

As with svn_string_t, svn_stringbuf_t is defined in svn_string.h, and there you can find numerous functions for creating, modifying, examining, and otherwise manipulating them. Again, these functions are self-explanatory, so no example has been provided.

Generic Streams

In many situations, Subversion needs to function on potentially large amounts of data without holding it all in memory at any one time. To facilitate this, a generic stream object, svn_stream_t, is used. The opaque stream object itself along with various functions that operate on instances of that object are declared in svn_io.h.

WHAT'S A BATON?

Many of Subversion's APIs include references to *baton* objects. These are void * arguments that are passed into Subversion's functions, usually along with a callback function of some sort. The baton gives the caller a way to include a pointer to whatever kind of data the callback function will need access to. When Subversion calls the callback later on, it will pass the baton in as one of the callback's arguments. The callback then casts the baton back to whatever data type the user originally passed in and makes use of the data in whatever way is appropriate. In other APIs, these kinds of arguments are often called void *ctx or void *userdata, but in Subversion they are called *batons* because they're passed around a lot.

A generic stream can be created with svn_stream_create(), which takes a baton argument that will be passed to the svn_read_fn_t, svn_write_fn_t, and svn_close_fn_t function pointers associated with the stream via svn_stream_set_read(), svn_stream_set_write(), and svn_stream_set_close(). If you want to reset the baton, you can use svn_stream_set_baton(). Once you have a stream, you can use functions such as svn_stream_read() and svn_stream_readline() to read data from it, svn_stream_write() and svn_stream_printf() to write to it, and svn_stream_close() to close it when you're done with it.

That's probably not entirely clear, so Listing 8-10 presents an example of how to create an svn_stream_t that returns zeroed-out data when you read from it. This isn't a particularly useful type of stream, but it does show you enough of the API that it's a good example.

Listing 8-10. *A /dev/zero Stream*

```
static svn_error_t *
dev_zero_read (void *baton,
               char *buffer,
               apr_size_t *len)
{
  int i;

  for (i = 0; i < *len; ++i)
    {
      buffer[i] = 0;
    }
```

```
    return SVN_NO_ERROR;
}

svn_stream_t *
make_dev_zero_stream (apr_pool_t *pool)
{
    /* note that we don't need to store any specific data for use by our read
       callback, so our baton is NULL */
    svn_stream_t *stream = svn_stream_create (NULL, pool);

    svn_stream_set_read (stream, dev_zero_read);

    return stream;
}
```

This code sets up a generic stream with a read function that fills in whatever buffer you pass it with zeros. From this example, you can clearly see how to implement your own stream that returns whatever data you wish, such as reading some specialized compressed format or pulling data out of a database; and with a bit more work you can use svn_stream_set_write() and svn_stream_set_close() to add specialized behavior when the user writes data to the stream or tries to close it.

If you're just looking for a way to use a function that takes an svn_stream_t, and you don't want to go through the trouble of implementing your own stream type, you can get a generic file-backed stream with svn_stream_from_aprfile(), or one that wraps an svn_stringbuf_t with svn_stream_from_stringbuf(), or one that wraps stdout with svn_stream_from_stdout(). In most cases, these should be sufficient to allow you to call a given Subversion function without having to jump through the hoops necessary to define your own stream.

The Client Library

libsvn_client provides the highest-level interface to the Subversion libraries, sitting on top of libsvn_wc and lisvn_ra to give you control over both the working copy and the repository. This is the level in which all of the svn subcommands are implemented, and as a result, once you've learned the command-line client, you've already learned much of what you need to know about this library. In general, for a given subcommand in the command-line client, there's a corresponding function that implements the guts of the command. For example, for svn add, the implementation is found in svn_client_add().

In this section, we explain how to make use of many commonly used functions in libsvn_client and give you enough information to figure out how to use the rest of libsvn_client's functions yourself. There is also an example minimal client in the Subversion source code distribution, at tools/example/minimal_client.c, which can be used as a reference to do things discussed in this chapter.

Common Aspects

To make use of the majority of the functions in libsvn_client, you'll need to become aware of some of the conventions followed by its functions.

The first thing you need to do before using any of the functions in `libsvn_client` is to set up the client context, which is encapsulated in the `svn_client_ctx_t` structure. `svn_client_ctx_t` is a structure that contains common bits of data and callback functions that are used through `libsvn_client`. This includes the client's configuration, the data structures used for handling authentication, and callbacks for tasks such as notifying the client of things that are happening, obtaining commit log messages from the client, and determining whether the client has cancelled the current operation. Instead of the rest of the API being filled with a number of different function arguments, these arguments are combined into a single structure, which is then passed to all the functions in the same way.

Before you can fill in the `svn_client_ctx_t` with your application's functions, you need to allocate one. To do this, you need to use the `svn_client_create_context()` function. This is provided as a safeguard against some future version of the Subversion libraries changing the size of the `svn_client_ctx_t` structure. If you allocate the structure in your own code and a new version of `libsvn_client` is released that changes the size of the structure, your application will most likely crash because it will pass in an `svn_client_ctx_t` that's smaller than `libsvn_client` expects. Using `svn_client_create_context()` to do the allocation for you prevents this from occurring.

Once you've created an `svn_client_ctx_t`, the first thing you'll probably want to put in it is your user's configuration information. Reading the user configuration is not required, but it is highly recommended. To read the user configuration, first call `svn_config_ensure()`; this will make certain that the initial configuration files are written out if they don't already exist. Next, call `svn_config_get_config()` to parse the configuration into the `svn_client_ctx_t`'s `config` hash. If you want to manually override any of the client's configuration options by setting the values in the hash to something other than what is read out of the user's configuration files, this would be the time to do it.

Before your application can do much of anything, you'll need to be able to authenticate yourself in some way, which means you'll have to build up an `svn_auth_baton_t` (which is stored as the `auth_baton` member of the `svn_client_ctx_t`) that knows how to figure out your username, password, and potentially other interesting bits of information that the repository might need to authenticate you. The process for doing this is a bit long, but hopefully the following information will clarify it.

A number of authentication providers are defined in `svn_auth.h`, each of which knows how to retrieve some kind of information about you. For example, the `svn.simple` provider knows how to retrieve your username and password via a prompt function, which is all that many authentication mechanisms (such as HTTP basic authentication, or the CRAM-MD5 authentication used by `svnserve`) require. Alternatively, the `svn.username` type only retrieves your username, since that's all that accessing a repository over `ra_local` requires. For more complicated scenarios such as SSL authentication, there are more complicated providers, such as `svn.ssl.client-cert`.

Building an authentication provider is tricky, as its API is a bit complicated; so `libsvn_client` provides functions to do the hard part for you. You simply implement a callback function to handle the task of prompting the user for information and pass it in to the function that builds the provider, and `libsvn_client` will take care of the tricky parts. You build up an `apr_array_header_t` that holds all of your providers, and then use `svn_auth_open()` to initialize the authentication baton with them. When `libsvn_client` encounters a situation where it needs to authenticate you, it will call your prompt functions as needed until it's able to authenticate, eventually returning an error if it exceeds the number of retries you specified when creating the providers.

In retrospect, that doesn't sound all that simple, so let's review an example (see Listing 8-11) of how to set up the svn.simple and svn.username providers so that the various Subversion APIs can make use of them to determine the user's username and password when needed.

Listing 8-11. *Using Authentication Providers*

```
/* prompt the user for a username and password */
static svn_error_t *
simple_prompt_callback (svn_auth_cred_simple_t **cred,
                        void *baton,
                        const char *realm,
                        const char *username,
                        svn_boolean_t may_save,
                        apr_pool_t *pool)
{
  svn_auth_cred_simple_t *ret = apr_pcalloc (pool, sizeof (*ret));
  size_t len;
  char *line;

  /* tell the user what the repository realm is, so he knows what username
     he should enter. */
  if (realm)
    printf ("Realm: %s\n", realm);

  /* if we were passed a username, that means subversion had one cached for
     this realm already, so use that. */
  if (username)
    ret->username = apr_pstrdup (pool, username);
  else
    {
      /* we didn't have a username, so prompt the user to enter one. */
      printf ("Username? : ");

      /* read in the username the user entered */
      line = fgetln (stdin, &len);

      /* assuming the user entered something copy it into our final
         svn_auth_cred_simple_t structure so we can return it. */
      if (line)
        {
          ret->username = apr_palloc (pool, len);
          snprintf (ret->username, len - 1, line);
        }
    }

  /* now we do the same thing for the user's password... */
  printf ("Password? : ");
```

```
  line = fgetln (stdin, &len);

  if (line)
    {
      ret->password = apr_palloc (pool, len);
      snprintf (ret->password, len - 1, line);
    }

  /* return the svn_auth_cred_simple_t by reference. */
  *cred = ret;

  return SVN_NO_ERROR;
}

/* similar to the previous function, but just prompts for a username */
static svn_error_t *
username_prompt_callback (svn_auth_cred_username_t **cred,
                          void *baton,
                          const char *realm,
                          svn_boolean_t may_save,
                          apr_pool_t *pool)
{
  svn_auth_cred_username_t *ret = apr_pcalloc (pool, sizeof (*ret));
  size_t len;
  char *line;

  if (realm)
    printf ("Realm: %s\n", realm);

  printf ("Username? : ");

  line = fgetln (stdin, &len);

  if (line)
    {
      ret->username = apr_palloc (pool, len);
      snprintf (ret->username, len - 1, line);
    }

  *cred = ret;

  return SVN_NO_ERROR;
}

/* build authentication providers that use our prompting functions and add
   them to a client context. */
static svn_error_t *
set_up_auth (svn_client_ctx_t *ctx, apr_pool_t *pool)
```

```
{
  svn_auth_provider_object_t *provider;

  /* create an array to hold our two providers. */
  apr_array_header_t *providers
    = apr_array_make (pool, 2, sizeof (svn_auth_provider_object_t *));

  /* create the svn.simple provider. */
  svn_client_get_simple_prompt_provider (&provider,
                                         simple_prompt_callback,
                                         NULL, /* the baton goes here */
                                         2, /* number of times to retry */
                                         pool);

  /* add it to the array. */
  APR_ARRAY_PUSH (providers, svn_auth_provider_object_t *) = provider;

  /* create the svn.username provider. */
  svn_client_get_username_prompt_provider (&provider,
                                           username_prompt_callback,
                                           NULL, /* the baton goes here */
                                           2, /* number of times to retry */
                                           pool);

  /* add it to the array. */
  APR_ARRAY_PUSH (providers, svn_auth_provider_object_t *) = provider;

  /* now that we've got the array of providers, use them to create our auth
     baton. */
  svn_auth_open (&ctx->auth_baton, providers, pool);

  return SVN_NO_ERROR;
}
```

Here you can see two very simple prompt functions, one that tries to retrieve both a username and password (if the username isn't already known), and one that retrieves a username. Then you use svn_client_get_simple_prompt_provider() and svn_client_get_username_prompt_provider() to wrap those prompt functions up into providers, which are then stuck in an array and passed in to svn_auth_open() to initialize your svn_auth_baton_t. If you want to provide support for other kinds of authentication, such as those used for SSL, you would build additional providers, as documented in svn_auth.h.

Most of the libsvn_client functions need to provide information on what they're doing to the calling application so that the application can pass that information on to the user, possibly by printing something out to the screen or updating a display or whatever else might be appropriate. As you might have guessed, this functionality is provided via a callback function/baton pair that the calling application places in the context structure. The caller provides a function of type svn_wc_notify_func2_t as the notify_func2 member of the client context; and for every significant action that occurs, the function will be called.

As usual with callback functions, the notification function is passed a void pointer (the notify_baton2 member of the client context) that holds application-specific data, and a pointer to some callback-specific structure. In this case, the pointer to structure passed is an svn_wc_notify_t structure. Generally, the path member of the structure will indicate the file or directory this call pertains to, the action member will indicate what's occurring, and the kind member will tell you what type of node the path refers to (i.e., if it's a file or a directory). The remaining members (mime_type, err, lock_state, lock, content_state, prop_state, and revision) are specific to the various different actions.

Listing 8-12 shows an example of a notification callback that would be appropriate for a call to svn_client_update().

Listing 8-12. *Using Notification Callbacks*

```
static void
notification_callback (void *baton,
                       const svn_wc_notify_t *notify, apr_pool_t *pool)
{
  switch (notify->action)
    {
      case svn_wc_notify_update_add:
        printf ("Adding %s\n", notify->path);
        break;

      case svn_wc_notify_update_delete:
        printf ("Deleting %s\n", notify->path);
        break;

      case svn_wc_notify_update_update:
        /* if this were real, we'd also pay attention to property changes,
         * which would mean we'd also be printing stuff out for directories,
         * but for this example only files will be enough.
         */
        if (notify->kind == svn_node_file)
          {
            if (notify->content_state == svn_wc_notify_state_conflicted)
              printf ("Conflict at %s\n", notify->path);
            else if (notify->content_state == svn_wc_notify_state_merged)
              printf ("Merged %s\n", notify->path);
            else if (notify->content_state == svn_wc_notify_state_changed)
              printf ("Updating %s\n", notify->path);
          }
        break;

      case svn_wc_notify_update_completed:
        printf ("Updated to %" SVN_REVNUM_T_FMT "\n", notify->revision);
        break;
```

```
        default:
          break;
    }
}

svn_error_t *
set_up_notification (svn_client_ctx_t *ctx, apr_pool_t *pool)
{
  ctx->notify_func2 = notification_callback;

  ctx->notify_baton2 = NULL;

  return SVN_NO_ERROR;
}
```

Most notification callbacks end up looking something like this. A switch statement allows you to specify different behavior for each notification action, and when it's appropriate for the action you received, you check the other arguments to determine what you should tell the user.

A number of libsvn_client's functions can take some time to complete, because they're working on a large amount of data, or because they're communicating with the server over a network, or both. As a result, users occasionally wish to cancel such long-running commands before they complete. To make this possible, the svn_client_ctx_t contains a cancellation callback and baton (see Listing 8-13), which are used periodically during long-running tasks to determine whether the user has cancelled the operation. You simply fill in the cancel_baton member of the client context with a function pointer of type svn_cancel_func_t (defined in svn_types.h), and optionally set the cancel_baton member to whatever you would like to be passed to your cancellation function whenever it's called. As your libsvn_client function goes about its work, it will periodically call cancel_func, which should return an error of type SVN_ERR_CANCELLED when it determines that the user has cancelled the operation.

Listing 8-13. *Setting Up Cancellation Support*

```
static volatile sig_atomic_t been_cancelled = FALSE;

static void
signal_handler (int unused)
{
  been_cancelled = TRUE;
}

svn_error_t *
cancellation_callback (void *baton)
{
  if (been_cancelled)
    return svn_error_create (SVN_ERR_CANCELLED, NULL, "Caught signal");
  else
    return SVN_NO_ERROR;
}
```

```
svn_error_t *
set_up_cancellation (svn_client_ctx_t *ctx, apr_pool_t *pool)
{
  apr_signal (SIGINT, signal_handler);

  ctx->cancel_func = cancellation_callback;

  /* in a more complex application with multiple operations in progress at
   * once, we'd set this to whatever data the callback would need to look at
   * to determine if the action this context is being used for was cancelled.
   */
  ctx->cancel_baton = NULL;

  return SVN_NO_ERROR;
}
```

This is almost exactly what the svn program uses for its cancellation support. A signal handler is set up so that if the user tries to exit the program by pressing Ctrl+C, a flag (been_cancelled) will be set, and the cancellation callback periodically checks to see if the flag has been set to TRUE. If the flag has been set to TRUE, the callback returns an error and the command in progress will be stopped.

As you've probably noticed, a number of Subversion's subcommands can cause a commit to be performed on the repository. These commands are implemented by separate functions within libsvn_client, but they share some common characteristics. First, they take as their first argument a pointer to a pointer to an svn_client_commit_info_t, which will be filled in with the results of the commit once it's performed. This includes such information as the revision that the commit created, the server-side date that the commit occurred on, and the username of the author of the commit. Second, they all make use of the log_msg_func2 and log_msg_baton2 members of the svn_client_ctx_t structure to obtain a log message for the commit. log_msg_func2 is of type svn_client_get_commit_log2_t, and it returns a log message either via the log_msg argument, which the function can set to point to the log message itself, or the tmp_file argument, which the function can set to point to the filename of a temporary file that contains the log message. In either case, the log message must be in UTF-8 encoding, with linefeed line endings. The function is also passed commit_items, which is an array of svn_client_commit_item2_t structures that describe the items being committed, and finally the function is passed a pointer to the log_msg_baton2 from the svn_client_ctx_t, so it has access to application-specific data.

Listing 8-14 presents a short example of how to set up your own log message baton and callback.

Listing 8-14. *Log Message Callbacks*

```
struct message_baton {
  const char *message;
  const char *file;
};
```

```
svn_error_t *
get_log_message (const char **log_msg,
                 const char **tmp_file,
                 const apr_array_header_t *commit_items,
                 void *baton,
                 apr_pool_t *pool)
{
  struct message_baton *mb = baton;

  if (mb->message)
    *log_msg = apr_pstrdup (pool, mb->message);
  else if (mb->file)
    *tmp_file = apr_pstrdup (pool, mb->file);
  else
    return svn_error_create (SVN_ERR_CL_BAD_LOG_MESSAGE, NULL,
                             "User did not specify a log message");

  return SVN_NO_ERROR;
}

svn_error_t *
set_up_log_message_callback (svn_client_ctx_t *ctx,
                             const char *log_msg,
                             const char *tmp_file,
                             apr_pool_t *pool)
{
  struct message_baton *mb = apr_pcalloc (pool, sizeof (*mb));

  mb->message = log_msg;
  mb->file = tmp_file;

  ctx->log_msg_func2 = get_log_message;

  ctx->log_msg_baton2 = mb;

  return SVN_NO_ERROR;
}
```

This example assumes that the log message for the commit was obtained from the user prior to set_up_log_message_callback() being called. Either the user specified a complete log message, in which case it will be in the log_msg argument, or he or she specified a file that contains the log message, in which case the filename is in tmp_file. In either event, both arguments are placed in the message_baton, and when libsvn_client needs a log message, it will call get_log_message, which will return whichever one the user specified. If neither was specified, it will return an error.

A Simple Client

Now that you've figured out how to create an svn_client_ctx_t, set up authentication, deal with notification, provide cancellation support, and give the library a log message for committing changes to the repository, you can start making use of the major functions in libsvn_client. In this section, we walk through the process of providing some of the basic functionality from the svn program, enough that you could use these examples to throw together a reasonably functional command-line client. Some of the more esoteric commands (blame, merge, and several others) have been left out, but once you go over these examples, you should be able to figure out how to use them from the Doxygen documentation in the header files.

Checkout

Before a Subversion client can do much of anything interesting, it needs to check out a working copy. As a result, the first major function in libsvn_client you need to consider is svn_client_checkout2(). Listing 8-15 shows the function prototype.

Listing 8-15. *The svn_client_checkout2() Prototype*

```
svn_error_t *
svn_client_checkout2 (svn_revnum_t *result_rev,
                      const char *URL,
                      const char *path,
                      const svn_opt_revision_t *peg_revision,
                      const svn_opt_revision_t *revision,
                      svn_boolean_t recurse,
                svn_boolean_t ignore_externals,
                      svn_client_ctx_t *ctx,
                      apr_pool_t *pool);
```

WHY IS THERE A NUMBER AFTER THE FUNCTION NAME?

The Subversion team has decided to guarantee that the API will stay compatible through all versions of SVN 1.x. This means that any external program using Subversion libraries will work with any installed version of Subversion, regardless of what functions it uses (at least until 2.0). The developer implication of this is that when the Subversion team adds arguments to the existing functions in order, the functions cannot have the same name as the existing function, or else it would break every existing user. To solve this problem, the functions are versioned by incrementing the number at the end of the function name every time new arguments are added or something is changed in a backward-incompatible way. This goes for public structures, too, and not just functions.

To use svn_client_checkout2(), you only need call it with a few arguments. The URL argument is the directory in the repository you wish to check out, the path argument is the directory where Subversion should place the resulting working copy, and the revision argument is the revision you wish to check out.

The revision argument must be svn_opt_revision_number, svn_opt_revision_date, or svn_opt_revision_head, since those are the only revision specifications that make sense when working with the repository. If any other type of svn_opt_revision_t is used, SVN_ERR_CLIENT_BAD_REVISION will be returned. Unlike the revision argument, the peg_revision argument is also allowed to be svn_opt_revision_unspecified.

If you want the checkout to be recursive (the default behavior when checking out a directory in the svn client), then the recurse argument should be TRUE; otherwise it should be FALSE.

If you want to avoid downloading the code specified in svn:externals properties, the ignore_externals argument should be set to TRUE.

The auth_baton in the ctx argument will be used to authenticate with the repository if necessary, and the notify_func2/notify_baton2 and cancel_func/cancel_baton pairs in ctx will be called periodically as the commit progresses to notify the calling application of events as they occur and check to see if the checkout has been cancelled.

When the checkout completes, a new working copy will be present at path, and if the result_rev argument isn't NULL, *result_rev will be filled in with the revision checked out from the repository.

Add and Mkdir

Once you have a working copy, the natural thing to do is to make some changes to it. Actually modifying the contents of files doesn't require you to know how to use any special libsvn_client function; but if you want to place new files or directories under Subversion's control, you need to use svn_client_add3(). Listing 8-16 shows the function prototype.

Listing 8-16. *The svn_client_add3() Prototype*

```
svn_error_t *
svn_client_add3 (const char *path,
                 svn_boolean_t recursive,
             svn_boolean_t force,
                 svn_boolean_t no_ignore,
                 svn_client_ctx_t *ctx,
                 apr_pool_t *pool);
```

svn_client_add3() is perhaps the simplest of the major functions in libsvn_client. The path argument is a path to a file or directory within a working copy, and the function will schedule that path for addition in the next commit. If the recursive argument is TRUE, the contents of the directory being added will all be scheduled for addition; otherwise svn_client_add3() only schedules the directory itself. If the force argument is TRUE, the file is added even if it is already under version control. If the no_ignore argument is FALSE, the svn:ignore properties are used to ignore files during add. During the add, ctx->notify_func2 and ctx->notify_baton2 will be used to notify the calling application of each file that's added; and ctx->cancel_func and ctx->cancel_baton will be used periodically to check whether the operation should continue.

If you're creating a new directory, you can either create it manually via whatever platform-specific means you have available, or you can use svn_client_mkdir2() to create the directory and place it under Subversion's control in one step. In addition, you can create a directory directly in the repository by passing svn_client_mkdir2() a URL instead of a path.

Let's take a look at the prototype, shown in Listing 8-17, and see how it differs from
svn_client_add3().

Listing 8-17. *The svn_client_mkdir2() Prototype*

```
svn_error_t *
svn_client_mkdir2 (svn_commit_info_t **commit_info,
                   const apr_array_header_t *paths,
                   svn_client_ctx_t *ctx,
                   apr_pool_t *pool);
```

There are two points to notice here. First, the targets are passed in an array. This might
seem kind of odd when you're thinking about passing in working copy paths, as you could
simply call svn_client_mkdir2() more than once if you want to, but it makes plenty of sense
when you're passing in URLs to a repository and you want all of the directories to be created
in a single commit. The other thing to note is the presence of the commit_info argument which
is used when working directly on the repository. The process of performing a commit (as we
discussed earlier when describing the svn_client_commit3() function) will first use the
ctx->log_msg_func2 and ctx->log_msg_baton2 to include a log message for the commit; then
it uses ctx->auth_baton to authenticate with the repository (if necessary). Once the change is
committed, some information will be placed in *commit_info so you can determine what revision was just created in the repository.

Delete

Once you can schedule items to be added to the repository, it's only natural to want to be able
to remove them, and as you've probably guessed, you do this via the svn_client_delete2()
function. Listing 8-18 reviews the prototype.

Listing 8-18. *The svn_client_delete2() Prototype*

```
svn_error_t *
svn_client_delete2 (svn_commit_info_t **commit_info,
                    const apr_array_header_t *paths,
                    svn_boolean_t force,
                    svn_client_ctx_t *ctx,
                    apr_pool_t *pool);
```

paths is an array of const char * targets that you want to delete. The targets can be either
the URLs of items in the repository, in which case the delete will be performed directly on the
repository, or working copy paths, in which case the delete will be scheduled for the next commit. If force is TRUE, the delete will be performed even if the target contains local modifications,
otherwise local modifications will cause it to fail. While the delete is occurring, ctx->notify_func2
and ctx->notify_baton2 will be called for each item deleted, and ctx->cancel_func and
ctx->cancel_baton will be periodically called to see if the operation should continue. As usual
with making changes to the repository, ctx->log_msg_func2 and ctx->log_msg_baton2 will be
used to obtain a log message for the commit; ctx->auth_baton will be used for authentication;
and *commit_info will be filled in with information about the commit.

Copy and Move

Now that you have the ability to place new files and directories under Subversion's control and remove things you no longer want, you probably want to move on to copying and renaming. This is accomplished, predictably, via svn_client_copy2() and svn_client_move3(). Both of these functions can operate either on working copy paths, in which case they schedule the change so it can be committed later, or against repository URLs, in which case they perform a commit immediately. Listing 8-19 contains the svn_client_copy2() prototype.

Listing 8-19. *The svn_client_copy2() Prototype*

```
svn_error_t *
svn_client_copy2 (svn_commit_info_t **commit_info,
                  const char *src_path,
                  const svn_opt_revision_t *src_revision,
                  const char *dst_path,
                  svn_client_ctx_t *ctx,
                  apr_pool_t *pool);
```

The src_path and src_revision arguments determine the source to copy from. The src_path argument can be either a path to a file or a directory in the working copy, or a URL to an item in the repository. dst_path determines the destination of the copy. If the dst_path argument is a local working copy path, the copy will be a scheduling operation to be committed the next time svn_client_commit3() is run; but if it's the URL of an item in the repository, the copy will be handled on the server side as an immediate commit. During the copy, ctx->notify_func2 and ctx->notify_baton2 will be used to inform the calling application of events as they occur, and ctx->cancel_func and ctx->cancel_baton will be periodically called to determine whether the operation should continue. If a commit is being performed, ctx->log_msg_func2 and ctx->log_msg_baton2 will be used to obtain a log message, and the results of the commit will be placed in *commit_info.

Next, let's consider the prototype for svn_client_move3(), as shown in Listing 8-20.

Listing 8-20. *The svn_client_move3() Prototype*

```
svn_error_t *
svn_client_move3 (svn_client_commit_info_t **commit_info,
                  const char *src_path,
                  const char *dst_path,
                  svn_boolean_t force,
                  svn_client_ctx_t *ctx,
                  apr_pool_t *pool);
```

As you can see, the svn_client_move3() prototype is almost identical to the prototype for svn_client_copy2(), with two changes: first is the removal of the src_revision argument, which makes no sense in move (you can't move a non-HEAD revision file), and the addition of the force argument. svn_client_move3() results in a copy (as if you had called svn_client_copy2() with the same arguments), followed by a delete of the file or directory you copied from. Thus, the force argument serves the same purpose as it does with svn_client_delete2(), allowing you to force the move of a modified file in a working copy. Other than this difference, svn_client_move3() is essentially the same as svn_client_copy2().

Status

Now that you've examined several of the key functions, it's time to look at something a bit different. Getting the status of your working copy requires you to make use of some custom interfaces, as opposed to the functions you've seen so far, all of which make use of largely the same types of arguments and callbacks. The first function to break from that mold is svn_client_status2(). Listing 8-21 shows the prototype.

Listing 8-21. *The svn_client_status2() Prototype*

```
svn_error_t *
svn_client_status2 (svn_revnum_t *result_rev,
                    const char *path,
                    const svn_opt_revision_t *revision,
                    svn_wc_status_func2_t status_func,
                    void *status_baton,
                    svn_boolean_t recurse,
                    svn_boolean_t get_all,
                    svn_boolean_t update,
                    svn_boolean_t no_ignore,
              svn_boolean_t ignore_externals,
                    svn_client_ctx_t *ctx,
                    apr_pool_t *pool);
```

This prototype requires a few parameters that you haven't seen yet. The path argument is what you'd expect it to be: the path to the working copy directory you want to get the status of. status_func and status_baton are a callback/baton pair invoked for each item you're getting the status of. Exactly what items the callback gets called for depends on the values you pass in for recurse, get_all, ignore_externals, and no_ignore. If recurse is TRUE, you recurse through the target; otherwise svn_client_status2() will only check the immediate descendents of path. If get_all is TRUE, the callback will be called for all the items underneath the target directory; otherwise it's only called for *interesting* items (i.e., items that have been modified). If no_ignore is TRUE, the svn:ignore property won't be respected, and the callback will be called even for items you have ignored. If the ignore_externals argument is FALSE, then svn_client_status2() will recurse into items found in the value of the svn:externals properties.

Listing 8-22 shows the declaration of the callback function.

Listing 8-22. *The svn_wc_status_func2_t Declaration*

```
typedef void (*svn_wc_status_func2_t) (void *baton,
                                       const char *path,
                                       svn_wc_status2_t *status);
```

The baton argument is just the status_baton you passed in the svn_client_status2(); the path argument is the path to the item whose status is being returned; and the status argument is a pointer to a data structure holding all the status information about the item in question. svn_wc_status2_t and the various bits and pieces associated with it are defined in svn_wc.h; so you'll want to look there when writing a status callback function. Listing 8-23 presents an example of what one looks like.

Listing 8-23. *A Status Callback*

```
void
status_callback (void *baton,
                 const char *path,
                 svn_wc_status2_t *status)
{
  char value;

  /* a real status callback would handle many more cases here */
  switch (status->text_status)
    {
      case svn_wc_status_added:
        value = 'A';
        break;

      case svn_wc_status_deleted:
        value = 'D';
        break;

      case svn_wc_status_replaced:
        value = 'R';
        break;

      case svn_wc_status_modified:
        value = 'M';
        break;

      case svn_wc_status_merged:
        value = 'G';
        break;

      case svn_wc_status_conflicted:
        value = 'C';
        break;

      default:
        value = '?';
    }

  printf ("%c %s\n", value, path);
}
```

There are three arguments to svn_client_status2() that we haven't yet discussed: update, revision, and result_rev. These are all part of the svn status --show-updates functionality, which tells Subversion to compare the local working copy with the contents of the repository so that it can inform you if anything in the working copy is out of date relative to a specific revision. Setting the update argument to TRUE indicates that Subversion should contact the repository and retrieve this information. Included in the status structures passed to the callback function is information regarding the outdated working copy as compared to the revision specified. When svn_client_status2() returns, the result_rev argument will be filled in with the revision number of the revision the comparison is performed against. For example, if you indicate that svn_client_status2() should compare the working copy with the HEAD revision in the repository by setting the revision argument to HEAD, result_rev will be filled in with the numeric value that corresponds to HEAD.

Diff

Once you've added support to your client for using svn_client_status2(), the next obvious step is for your users to want more specific information about exactly what has changed for modified files. To do that, you'll need to use svn_client_diff3(), as shown in Listing 8-24. svn_client_diff3() presents a rather odd interface, primarily because it needs to support both the internal diff code in libsvn_diff and the use of external programs such as GNU diff. This results in a number of arguments that are used only if a particular setting in the user's configuration files is set, which can be somewhat confusing at first.

Listing 8-24. *The svn_client_diff3() Prototype*

```
svn_error_t *
svn_client_diff3 (const apr_array_header_t *diff_options,
                  const char *path1,
                  const svn_opt_revision_t *revision1,
                  const char *path2,
                  const svn_opt_revision_t *revision2,
                  svn_boolean_t recurse,
                  svn_boolean_t ignore_ancestry,
                  svn_boolean_t no_diff_deleted,
                  svn_boolean_t ignore_content_type,
                  const char *header_encoding,
                  apr_file_t *outfile,
                  apr_file_t *errfile,
                  svn_client_ctx_t *ctx,
                  apr_pool_t *pool);
```

The diff is performed between two paths, which can be either local working copy paths or URLs in the repository. Each path has a revision associated with it. There are a few flags to control exactly what files get diffed and how they're treated. If the recurse argument is TRUE, svn_client_diff3() will recurse into subdirectories; otherwise, it won't. The no_diff_deleted argument determines whether diff output should be produced for deleted files. If the ignore_content_type argument is TRUE, you will include diff output for binary files. Finally, if the ignore_ancestry argument is FALSE, svn_client_diff3() will compare items to see if one is an ancestor of the other before diffing them. If the items aren't related, they'll show up in the diff as a delete of one and an add of the other, regardless of any similarities in the content of the file. On the other hand, if ignore_ancestry is TRUE, files will be diffed regardless of their ancestry. The actual diff output will be printed in unified diff form to the outfile argument, and the diff headers for that output will be encoded using the encoding type specified in the header_encoding argument.

So what are the `diff_options` and `errfile` arguments for? As we mentioned in the previous paragraph, `svn_client_diff3()` supports the use of alternate diff programs in addition to the internal unified diff code in `libsvn_diff`. To make use of this support, you should set the `diff_cmd` option in the `helpers` section of the user's configuration to the diff command you want to use. Then, pass in an array of `const char *` command-line arguments for your diff program in the `diff_options` argument. The eventual command that's executed looks like `diff_cmd options source_file dest_file`, where `options` contains the command-line arguments you passed in the options array, and `source_file` and `dest_file` are the two files being diffed. The whole process looks like Listing 8-25.

Listing 8-25. *Using svn_client_diff3() with an External Diff Program*

```
svn_error_t *
run_diff_with_external_program (const char *diff_cmd,
                                apr_array_header_t *diff_options,
                                const char *source_url,
                                const char *dest_url,
                                apr_file_t *outfile,
                                apr_file_t *errfile,
                                svn_client_ctx_t *ctx,
                                apr_pool_t *pool)
{
  svn_opt_revision_t revision;

  revision.kind = svn_opt_revision_head;

  /* this assumes that diff_cmd is something like "/path/to/my/diff_program" */
  svn_config_set (apr_hash_get (ctx->config,
                                SVN_CONFIG_CATEGORY_CONFIG,
                                APR_HASH_KEY_STRING),
                  SVN_CONFIG_SECTION_HELPERS,
                  SVN_CONFIG_OPTION_DIFF_CMD, diff_cmd);

  /* diff_options is an array of const char * options to pass to the diff
     command */
  SVN_ERR (svn_client_diff3 (diff_options,
                             source_url,
                             &revision, /* HEAD */
                             dest_url,
                             &revision, /* HEAD */
                             TRUE,
                             TRUE,
                             FALSE,
                             FALSE,
                             APR_LOCALE_CHARSET,
                             outfile,
                             errfile,
                             ctx,
                             pool));
```

```
    return SVN_NO_ERROR;
}
```

Commit

The final function from `libsvn_client` that you absolutely need for a minimalist client application is `svn_client_commit3()`, and honestly, there isn't a whole lot to say about it. Take a moment to examine the function prototype in Listing 8-26 and you'll see why.

Listing 8-26. *The svn_client_commit3() Prototype*

```
svn_error_t *
svn_client_commit3 (svn_client_commit_info_t **commit_info,
                    const apr_array_header_t *targets,
                    svn_boolean_t recursive,
                    svn_boolean_t keep_locks,
                    svn_client_ctx_t *ctx,
                    apr_pool_t *pool);
```

As you can see, this prototype uses the same conventions as the rest of the `libsvn_client` functions that can commit a change to the repository. The `targets` argument is an array of `const char *` paths to working copy files or directories that should be committed. The `recurse` argument is a flag to indicate whether the commit should recurse into subdirectories or whether only the first level of items should be committed. We will unlock paths in the repository during the commit unless the `keep_locks` argument is TRUE. `ctx->notify_func2` and `ctx->notify_baton2` will be used to notify the caller of each item committed, and `ctx->cancel_func` and `ctx->cancel_baton` will be called occasionally to determine whether the operation should continue. As usual, `ctx->log_msg_func2` and `ctx->log_msg_baton2` are used to obtain a log message for the commit, and `*commit_info` is filled in with the result of the commit once it completes.

Simple Client Conclusion

We have by no means covered all the major functions within `libsvn_client`. In fact, large groups of functions have been omitted, such as the ones associated with properties, among others. Nonetheless, we have covered enough of the details that you should be able to use the inline documentation in the header files to implement that additional functionality in your own program, and at the very least you can always refer to Subversion's own code that makes use of these functions. In general, Subversion's APIs are consistent enough that you shouldn't have trouble figuring out how to use them on your own.

Repository Access Libraries

There are times when the interface presented by `libsvn_client` is simply too high-level for what you're trying to do. Perhaps you want to write a program that makes some kind of change to a repository that just isn't possible with the existing `libsvn_client` functions. Or maybe you want access to information at a finer granularity than `libsvn_client` gives you. In this case, when you want to communicate with the repository but don't want to go through `libsvn_client`, the logical choice is to use `libsvn_ra` directly.

Before diving into this section, you should be aware that libsvn_ra is rather complex, and this will be a *very* high-level overview of some of the basics of using it. For more in-depth information on the use of libsvn_ra, consult the inline documentation in svn_ra.h and the implementation of the various functions in libsvn_client, which are largely implemented on top of libsvn_ra. With that in mind, let's take a look at some of the basics of how to use libsvn_ra.

What You Need to Provide

Before you can create a repository access (RA) session to a URL you're going to need to build an svn_ra_callbacks2_t structure, which holds some things that the RA session will need when it's performing its job.

The easiest of the items in the svn_ra_callbacks2_t to provide is the svn_auth_baton_t member, auth_baton. To do so, create the authentication baton just as you did when using libsvn_client, and libsvn_ra will make use of it.

The other member of the callback structure that you need to fill in is the open_tmp_file callback function. When the RA layer is working, it will sometimes need to write out temporary files, and it's your job to provide those files for it. The files should be opened such that they'll be deleted when they're closed, via the APR_DELONCLOSE flag to apr_file_open(). The callback should look something like Listing 8-27.

Listing 8-27. *The open_tmp_file() Callback Function*

```
svn_error_t *
open_tmp_file (apr_file_t **fp,
               void *callback_baton,
               apr_pool_t *pool)
{
  const char *tmpdir, *ignored_filename;

  SVN_ERR (svn_io_temp_dir (&tmpdir, pool));

  SVN_ERR (svn_io_open_unique_file (fp,
                                    &ignored_filename,
                                    svn_path_join (tmpdir, "tempfile", pool),
                                    ".tmp",
                                    TRUE, /* delete on close */
                                    pool));

  return SVN_NO_ERROR;
}
```

Five other callback functions are in the callback structure: get_wc_prop, set_wc_prop, push_wc_prop, notify_progress, and invalidate_wc_props. These functions are used when the RA layer needs to interact with the working copy or notify about progress of an operation, and they're beyond the scope of this section. If you leave them as NULL, the RA layer won't try to use them, which may be appropriate for server-side operations such as the ones we're covering here.

Using the RA Session

Once you have a set of callbacks created, you are going to want an RA session to perform requests against a URL. To create one, you call svn_ra_open2:

```
svn_error_t *
svn_ra_open2 (svn_ra_session_t **session,
        const char *repos_URL,
        constsvn_ra_callbacks2_t *callbacks,
        void *callback_baton,
        apr_hash_t *config,
        apr_pool_t *pool)
```

To use this function, pass the URL of the repository you want to open as the repos_URL argument. Pass the svn_ra_callbacks2_t structure you created earlier as the callbacks argument, and pass its baton as the callback_baton argument. The client's configuration hash passed as the config argument is a hash of configuration options from the client. Once you get a session back from svn_ra_open2 through the session argument, you can perform various RA functions on it. The session structure represents an active session with the server (if this RA layer includes a server) and will be passed to the other functions in the RA plugin. The session's lifetime is the same as that of the pool that's passed to svn_ra_open2.

OPAQUE POINTERS

svn_ra_session_t is an example of an opaque pointer. *Opaque pointers* are a technique used in C programming to limit access to the internals of a library by its users. The public API forward declares a structure, which is enough for users of the API to be able to declare pointers to that structure but not enough for them to be able to create instances of it or to reveal any of the internals. Inside the library, the structure is fully defined, and the library itself is free to access the structure's internals as it sees fit. The primary reason for exposing an object to the users of your API via an opaque pointer is that you can limit what the users can do with that object by only providing them with functions that manipulate the structure in the correct manner. In addition, this keeps any details about the contents of the structure from being compiled into the programs that make use of the API, because they're all contained within the library itself. This means you can feel free to change the structure any way you want, and assuming you leave the public interface the same, your users will never have to change their code, or even recompile it.

Now that you've opened a session, you can start using the rest of the RA functions to get data from the repository in a variety of different ways, commit changes to the repository, and in general do everything that the Subversion client does with the repository. The act of committing changes to the repository is rather complex, and the functions to update, switch, diff, or get a status for a working copy are quite intertwined with the details of the rest of Subversion's code; so let's just take a look at how you can use the RA layer to browse the repository.

The simplest kind of information you can retrieve from the repository is the number of the latest revision (i.e., the current HEAD revision). To do this, you just need to call the svn_ra_get_latest_revnum() function, as shown in Listing 8-28.

Listing 8-28. *Using svn_ra_get_latest_revnum() to Retrieve the Latest revnum*

```
svn_error_t *
print_head_revnum (svn_ra_plugin_t *ra_plugin,
                   const char *url,
                   apr_pool_t *pool)
{
  svn_ra_session_t *session;
  svn_ra_callbacks2_t *ra_callbacks;
  svn_revnum_t revnum;
  apr_hash_t *config;

  SVN_ERR (svn_ra_create_callbacks (&ra_callbacks, pool));
  ra_callbacks->open_tmp_file = open_tmp_file;

  SVN_ERR (svn_config_get_config (&config, NULL, pool));

  SVN_ERR (svn_ra_open2(&session, url, ra_callbacks, NULL,
                        config, pool));

  SVN_ERR (svn_ra_get_latest_revnum (session, &revnum, pool));

  printf ("HEAD is currently revision %" SVN_REVNUM_T_FMT "\n", revnum);

  return SVN_NO_ERROR;
}
```

This example shows the general procedure for using libsvn_ra. You build your svn_ra_callbacks2_t structure, set the callbacks you'll need, call the open function to get a session, and then call the RA functions using the session.

Let's consider another simple example, this time using the svn_ra_get_file() RA function to write the contents of a file in the repository to stdout (see Listing 8-29). As you might have guessed, this is pretty much what svn cat (which is implemented in the svn_client_cat() function) does under the hood.

Listing 8-29. *Retrieving File Contents via svn_ra_get_file()*

```
svn_error_t *
cat_file (const char *repos_url,
          const char *file_path,
          apr_pool_t *pool)
{
  svn_ra_session_t *session;
  apr_hash_t *config;
  svn_stream_t *stream;
  svn_ra_callbacks2_t *ra_callbacks;
```

```
SVN_ERR (svn_ra_create_callbacks (&ra_callbacks, pool));
ra_callbacks->open_tmp_file = open_tmp_file;

SVN_ERR (svn_config_get_config (&config, NULL, pool));

SVN_ERR (svn_ra_open2 (&session, repos_url, ra_callbacks, NULL,
                                      config, pool));

SVN_ERR (svn_stream_for_stdout (&stream, pool));

SVN_ERR (svn_ra_get_file (session, file_path, SVN_INVALID_REVNUM,
                                      stream, NULL, NULL, pool));

  return SVN_NO_ERROR;
}
```

Note that to make this function really useful, you'd want to manipulate a single URL for the file in the repository, using the `svn_ra_get_repos_root` function to figure out which part of that is the URL of the actual repository, and use the remainder for the path to the file, since the `file_path` argument you pass in to `svn_ra_get_file` needs to be relative to the root of the repository.

If you're interested in more examples of how to make use of `libsvn_ra`, both for the simple functions you've seen here and the more complex ones we haven't covered, the best place to look is the source code of `libsvn_client`, which is the largest consumer of `libsvn_ra` code at the moment.

Repository Library

The layer located below the RA library is `libsvn_repos`, which provides three types of functionality you might want access to in your programs. First, there are functions that allow you to work with a repository as a whole, creating them, destroying them, copying them, and so on. Next, there is the code related to dumping and loading repositories. Finally, there are several thin wrappers around various `libsvn_fs` functions that allow Subversion to do things such as call hook scripts at various points during the process of accessing the repository. When you're working directly with a repository from your own code, you almost always want to make use of these functions so that the administrator's standard hooks continue to function, just as they would when the repository is accessed from a standard Subversion server application.

Retrieving a Repository Object

Before you can do much of anything with `libsvn_repos`, you're going to need to retrieve a pointer to an `svn_repos_t` object. You have two ways to do this: you can either use `svn_repos_create()` to create a new repository or use `svn_repos_open()` to open an existing one. Let's review the `svn_repos_create()` prototype first, as shown in Listing 8-30.

Listing 8-30. *The svn_repos_create() Prototype*

```
svn_error_t *
svn_repos_create (svn_repos_t **repos_p,
                  const char *path,
                  const char *unused_1,
                  const char *unused_2,
                  apr_hash_t *config,
                  apr_hash_t *fs_config,
                  apr_pool_t *pool);
```

The arguments are a mix of the obvious and the odd. path is the path where the new repository should be created, config is a pointer to a client configuration hash (like we used in libsvn_client), and fs_config is a hash table of const char * key-value pairs holding configuration options for the underlying filesystem. Both configuration hashes can be NULL. There are also two unused const char * arguments, which must be NULL for the time being. The actual repository pointer is returned in *repos_p.

If you already have a repository on disk, you can get an svn_repos_t pointer for it via svn_repos_open(). Using svn_repos_open() is considerably simpler than using svn_repos_create(), as shown in Listing 8-31.

Listing 8-31. *The svn_repos_open() Prototype*

```
svn_error_t *
svn_repos_open (svn_repos_t **repos_p,
                const char *path,
                apr_pool_t *pool);
```

All you do is pass in the path to the repository, and svn_repos_open() will give you back a pointer to the svn_repos_t object.

Something that might be useful when working with svn_repos_open() is svn_repos_find_root_path(). Since your user will likely give you something that translates to a path within the repository, you'll want to figure out which part of that path is the path to the repository and which part is *within* the repository. You pass svn_repos_find_root_path() the full path you have, and it returns a path that refers to the root of the repository.

With both svn_repos_create() and svn_repos_open(), the svn_repos_t * returned will be valid as long as the pool passed to the function isn't cleared. To close the repository, you just have to clear the pool.

Manipulating Entire Repositories

A few functions operate on the repository that don't require you to open the underlying repository object yourself. Specifically, if you want to destroy a repository, you can use svn_repos_delete(), and if you want to copy one, you can use svn_repos_hotcopy().

Deleting a repository is simple. Just pass the path to the repository (the same one you would pass to svn_repos_open()) in to svn_repos_delete(), and it will do the rest.

Copying a repository is slightly more complex, since there are a few more options that you must keep in mind. Listing 8-32 shows the prototype for svn_repos_hotcopy().

Listing 8-32. *The svn_repos_hotcopy() Prototype*

```
svn_error_t *
svn_repos_hotcopy (const char *src_path,
                   const char *dst_path,
                   svn_boolean_t clean_logs,
                   apr_pool_t *pool);
```

The purpose of the src_path and dst_path arguments is pretty obvious—they're just the source and destination for the copy, respectively—but clean_logs deserves a little more explanation. If you are using BDB (note that BDB keeps log files on disk for each operation), and depending on what version of BDB you're using and what your repository configuration is, either those log files are automatically deleted when they're no longer needed or they stick around until you do something with them. If the clean_logs argument is TRUE, once the log files are copied into the new repository, any unused logs that are copied into the new repository are deleted from the old one, since you already have a copy of them and they're just taking up disk space. When using FSFS, the clean_logs argument does absolutely nothing. The last function in libsvn_repos that operates on the repository as a whole that you're likely to see is svn_repos_recover2(). Listing 8-33 shows the prototype.

Listing 8-33. *The svn_repos_recover2() Prototype*

```
svn_error_t *
svn_repos_recover2 (const char *path,
                    svn_boolean_t nonblocking,
                    svn_error_t *(*start_callback)(void *baton),
                    void *start_callback_baton,
                    apr_pool_t *pool);
```

All you do is give this function the path to a repository and it will obtain an exclusive lock on the repository and perform a low-level recovery, as discussed in Chapter 3. This function does nothing on an FSFS repository. If the nonblocking argument is TRUE, an error will be returned if the exclusive lock cannot be immediately obtained. If the start_callback argument is not NULL, it will be called (and passed start_callback_baton) before recovery starts but after the exclusive lock has been required.

Dumping and Loading Repositories

There are two levels of functions dealing with dumping and loading repositories in libsvn_repos. First, there are high-level functions such as svn_repos_dump_fs2() and svn_repos_load_fs2(), which allow you to dump the contents of a repository into a stream and load the contents of a dumpfile into a repository. At a lower level are functions such as svn_repos_parse_dumpstream2(), which allow you to provide your own set of callback functions to hook into libsvn_repos's own dumpfile parser, so you can operate on a dump stream without having to write a parser yourself.

Let's first take a look at svn_repos_dump_fs2() in Listing 8-34.

Listing 8-34. *The svn_repos_dump_fs2() Prototype*

```
svn_error_t *
svn_repos_dump_fs2 (svn_repos_t *repos,
                    svn_stream_t *dumpstream,
                    svn_stream_t *feedback_stream,
                    svn_revnum_t start_rev,
                    svn_revnum_t end_rev,
                    svn_boolean_t incremental,
                    svn_boolean_t use_deltas,
                    svn_cancel_func_t cancel_func,
                    void *cancel_baton,
                    apr_pool_t *pool);
```

The function arguments are reasonably intuitive. The dump contents are written out to the dumpstream argument, and additional information about what's being done is written to the feedback_stream argument. The dump will cover revisions ranging from the start_rev to the end_rev, and if the incremental argument is TRUE, the first revision dumped will be a diff against the previous revision. Otherwise, it will include the contents of all the files and directories in repos, so that the dump can be loaded into a clean repository without losing data. If the use_deltas argument is TRUE, deltas will be used to express the file differences in the dump instead of full texts (this option has no effect on how the deltas are stored when the file is loaded back into a repository; it is just to save space). While the dump is occurring, cancel_func will be periodically called with cancel_baton to determine whether the dump has been cancelled.

On the other hand is svn_repos_load_fs2(), whose prototype is shown in Listing 8-35.

Listing 8-35. *The svn_repos_load_fs2() Prototype*

```
svn_error_t *
svn_repos_load_fs2 (svn_repos_t *repos,
                    svn_stream_t *dumpstream,
                    svn_stream_t *feedback_stream,
                    enum svn_repos_load_uuid uuid_action,
                    const char *parent_dir,
                    svn_boolean_t use_pre_commit_hook,
                    svn_boolean_t use_post_commit_hook,
                    svn_cancel_func_t cancel_func,
                    void *cancel_baton,
                    apr_pool_t *pool);
```

As with svn_repos_dump_fs2(), the arguments are rather straightforward. Subversion will read the dumpfile from dumpstream, writing out feedback to feedback_stream as it goes. If parent_dir is non-NULL, the underlying parser will reparent each node in the dumpfile to parent_dir instead of the root of the repository. parent_dir must be a directory that already exists in the repository. uuid_action controls the behavior of the loader with regard to the UUID found in the dump. If it's set to svn_repos_load_uuid_force, or if the repository is empty and it isn't set to svn_repos_load_uuid_ignore, the UUID in the repository will be updated; otherwise, it will be ignored. If either of the commit hook arguments are set, the repositories' pre/post commit hooks will be run during the loading of the dumpfile. As usual, cancel_func and cancel_baton will periodically be used to determine whether the load should continue.

To interact with the dumpfile parsing code at a lower level, you simply need to create an svn_repos_parse_fns2_t structure and fill it in with various different callback functions. Then, you pass the svn_repos_parse_fns2_t pointer in to svn_repos_parse_dumpstream2(), along with a pointer to a parse baton, which will be passed to all your callbacks as the parsing progresses. In addition, you can pass an svn_cancel_func_t and a cancel baton, which will be used (as they were in libsvn_client) to determine if the parsing should continue.

The svn_repos_parse_fns2_t structure contains eleven callback functions, each of which you need to implement to use the parser. Table 8-1 shows them in the order they're generally called in and the reasons they are called.

■**Note** Two of these functions (new_revision_record and uuid_record) also receive a pointer to the parse_baton passed in with the svn_repos_parse_fns2_t and an apr_pool_t to be used for allocations.

Table 8-1. *Callback Functions Contained in the svn_repos_parse_fns2_t Structure*

Callback Function	Implementation
new_revision_record()	Called at the beginning of each new revision. It receives a hash of const char * key-value pairs that correspond to any headers that go along with this revision. It's expected to allocate a structure that will be passed to the callbacks responsible for creating and destroying nodes within this revision and set *revision_baton to point to that structure.
uuid_record()	Called when the record corresponding to the repository's UUID is found. Its only nonstandard argument is the UUID, which is passed in as a const char *.
new_node_record()	Called at the beginning of each node and passed a pointer to the revision_baton and a hash table filled with the headers associated with the node. It's expected to allocate a data structure associated with the node and set *node_baton to a pointer to it, so it can be passed to the callbacks associated with this node.
set_revision_property()	Called for each revision property associated with a revision and passed a pointer to the revision_baton, the name of the property, and an svn_string_t * that points to the value of the property.
set_node_property()	Called for each property that is set on a node and passed the name and contents of the property, just like set_revision_property().
delete_node_property()	Called for each property that is deleted from a node and passed the name of the property.
remove_node_props()	Called to remove all properties associated with a node and passed only a pointer to the node_baton.
set_fulltext()	Called once for the fulltext of each node that represents a file and expected to return in *stream a pointer to an svn_stream_t that the parser will write the contents of the file to. If NULL is returned in *stream, the parser won't attempt to write the fulltext.

Continued

Table 8-1. *Continued*

Callback Function	Implementation
`apply_textdelta()`	Called to apply a text delta to the previous node's content and expected to return in *handler a pointer to a window handler that can apply a delta to the node's previous contents. The function may also set *handler_baton to a baton that will be passed to the window handler.
`close_node()`	Called when the node is completed and passed only a pointer to the node_baton. The node_baton is no longer needed at this point, and the memory associated with it can be freed.
`close_revision()`	Called when the revision is complete. It receives a pointer to the revision_baton, which is now no longer needed and can be freed.

Listing 8-36 presents a simple example of a dumpfile parser that counts the number of times a given file is modified in the dumpfile.

Listing 8-36. *A Dumpfile Parser*

```
/* A baton to hold the path we're looking for and the current count. */
struct count_baton {
  const char *path;
  int count;
};


/* callback to be called at the start of each revision */
svn_error_t *
new_revision_record (void **revision_baton,
                     apr_hash_t *headers,
                     void *parse_baton,
                     apr_pool_t *pool)
{
  /* the only state we need to keep is in the parse_baton, so we'll treat the
     revision baton and the parse baton as the same thing. */
  *revision_baton = parse_baton;

  return SVN_NO_ERROR;
}


/* callback to be called for each new node */
svn_error_t *
new_node_record (void **node_baton,
                 apr_hash_t *headers,
                 void *revision_baton,
                 apr_pool_t *pool)
{
  struct count_baton *cb = revision_baton;
```

```
  /* grab the filename out of the headers */
  const char *filename = apr_hash_get (headers, SVN_REPOS_DUMPFILE_NODE_PATH,
                                       APR_HASH_KEY_STRING);

  /* if it matches the path we're looking for, increment our count */
  if (filename && strcmp (filename, cb->path) == 0)
    {
      cb->count++;
    }

  return SVN_NO_ERROR;
}


/* callback to be called when we get to the fulltext of each file */
svn_error_t *
set_fulltext (svn_stream_t **stream,
              void *node_baton)
{
  /* we don't care about the content of the file, so we return a NULL stream */
  *stream = NULL;

  return SVN_NO_ERROR;
}


/* count the number of times a particular file is modified in a dumpfile */
svn_error_t *
count_times_modified (const char *path,
                      svn_stream_t *dumpfile,
                      apr_pool_t *pool)
{
  struct count_baton cb;
  struct svn_repos_parse_fns2_t parser_fns;

  /* initialize our count baton */
  cb.path = path;
  cb.count = 0;

  /* fill in the parser function callbacks.
   *
   * Note:  The empty functions used for uninteresting callbacks have not been
   * included to save space.  Just assume all they do is return SVN_NO_ERROR.
   */
  parser_fns.new_revision_record = new_revision_record;
  parser_fns.uuid_record = empty_uuid_record_function;
  parser_fns.new_node_record = new_node_record;
  parser_fns.set_revision_property = empty_set_revision_property_function;
  parser_fns.set_node_property = empty_set_node_property_function;
```

```
    parser_fns.delete_node_property = empty_delete_node_property.
    parser_fns.remove_node_props = empty_remove_node_props;
    parser_fns.set_fulltext = set_fulltext;
    parser_fns.apply_textdelta = NULL;
    parser_fns.close_node = empty_close_node_function;
    parser_fns.close_revision = empty_close_revision_function;

    /* parse the dumpstream using our callback functions and count baton */
    SVN_ERR (svn_repos_parse_dumpstream2 (dumpfile, &parser_fns, &cb,
                                          NULL, NULL, pool));

    printf ("%s changed %d times in the dumpfile\n", cb.path, cb.count);

    return SVN_NO_ERROR;
}
```

This example looks at the Node-path header for each node in the dumpfile and checks to see if it's equal to the path that is being searched for. If it is the same, the count is incremented, because that indicates the file changed in that revision. Only three callbacks are at all significant: new_revision_node(), because it needs to pass the parse_baton down as the revision_baton so that new_node_record() can see it; new_node_record(), which just does the actual comparison; and set_fulltext, which tells the parser that you aren't interested in the contents of the file and thus avoids the overhead of writing it out to a stream. Every other callback is just an empty function that returns SVN_NO_ERROR.

Wrappers Around libsvn_fs Functions

The final set of functions in libsvn_repos that you're likely to interact with are the wrappers around underlying libsvn_fs functionality. These wrappers are where features such as Subversion's system of hook scripts are implemented. The wrapper functionality provided by libsvn_repos isn't part of the underlying filesystem, so it doesn't belong in libsvn_fs. Instead, it exists as a thin wrapper over the underlying libsvn_fs functionality. The APIs for these functions are very similar to those of their underlying libsvn_fs counterparts, with the primary difference being that they use svn_repos_t objects in the place of svn_fs_ts.

Unless you have a good reason not to do so, whenever you find yourself creating a new transaction, you should use svn_repos_fs_begin_txn_for_commit() or svn_repos_fs_begin_txn_for_update() instead of svn_fs_begin_txn2(), because of the ability to execute authorization and hook scripts correctly. Likewise, when you're committing a transaction, you should use svn_repos_fs_commit_txn() instead of svn_fs_commit_txn(). When you're changing revision properties, you should use svn_repos_fs_change_rev_prop2() instead of svn_fs_change_rev_prop(). When you're changing node properties, you should call the function svn_repos_fs_change_node_prop() instead of svn_fs_change_node_prop(). And when you're changing transaction properties, you should use svn_repos_fs_change_txn_prop() instead of svn_fs_change_txn_prop(). These functions are virtually identical to the underlying libsvn_fs functions, so refer to that section of the documentation for more details.

Filesystem Library

The Subversion filesystem is perhaps the most important part of the entire system, at least from the point of view of understanding its possibilities and limitations. Essentially, it's the limitations of the filesystem that determine the capabilities of the rest of the system, and for that reason alone it's worth learning about how `libsvn_fs` works. In addition, it turns out that working with `libsvn_fs` directly gives you a ridiculous amount of power and flexibility, so learning how it works is more than just an academic exercise—you can actually do things at this level that the rest of the system occasionally obscures. In this section, we'll cover the basics of how to make use of `libsvn_fs` in your own programs.

Important Data Structures and Vocabulary

Before you can make use of `libsvn_fs` directly, you're going to need to understand some of its fundamental concepts. Each of these concepts maps to a data structure that you're going to need to make use of later when manipulating the filesystem, so we'll go over both the concepts and the data structures at the same time.

The first data structure you're going to need to interact with is the filesystem object itself, which is represented as an opaque pointer to an `svn_fs_t`. You can obtain a pointer to the `svn_fs_t` within an `svn_repos_t` object by calling the `svn_repos_fs()` function; or if you're avoiding `libsvn_repos` for some reason, you can create it via `svn_fs_create()` and then connect it with an underlying filesystem via `svn_fs_open()`. That said, you should probably be working through `libsvn_repos` unless you *really* know what you're doing, so just do that for now.

The Subversion filesystem at its most basic level is made up of nodes. A *node* is roughly equivalent to an inode in a Unix filesystem, if you've ever delved into the internals of one of those. It can represent either a file or a directory, and its contents are thus made up of either the file's contents or the list of other nodes contained in the directory. There are a few significant differences between inodes and nodes in a Subversion filesystem, the most significant being that nodes are versioned. You can change a node's contents and it's still the same node underneath; you've just created a new revision of it. Nodes never go away. When you delete something in a Subversion filesystem, all you're doing is removing the reference to that node from a new version of the directory node that holds it. The underlying node (and all its revisions) is still there. When you interact with a node in the filesystem, you generally interact with a specific revision of that node, which is called a *node revision*. The data structure that corresponds to a node in the filesystem is `svn_fs_id_t`.

The next fundamental concept in the Subversion filesystem is a *transaction*. You can create a transaction, modify it in any number of different ways, and until you actually commit the transaction, the changes you've made are invisible to the rest of the world. Once you do commit the change, the transaction becomes a new revision in the filesystem, just like any other one, and your changes are atomically visible to the rest of the world.

This means that there are two kinds of transactions. There's the initial transaction that's created as a copy of an existing revision while a commit is in progress, which you can make changes to because it's made up of nodes that are *mutable*. Then there's the postcommit form of a transaction, a *revision* in the filesystem, which you can't modify because it's made of *immutable* nodes. This concept of mutable vs. immutable nodes in the filesystem is fundamental, and much of the way Subversion works is based on it. Once a transaction is committed, it can't be changed. The only way to make a change to the filesystem is to create a new transaction, make changes to it, and eventually commit it, so it turns into an immutable revision.

It's also worth pointing out that because of their status as "revisions in the making," transactions actually exist inside the filesystem. They have names, and you can create a transaction, modify it, close the filesystem, come back later, open it, and continue right where you left off. In fact, ra_dav and mod_dav_svn rely on exactly this behavior to allow them to use HTTP, a stateless protocol that can involve many different connections between the client and the server, to function as one of Subversion's network protocols.

The data structure that represents a Subversion transaction at the C level is svn_fs_txn_t, and you can create it using svn_fs_begin_txn2(), commit transactions via svn_fs_commit_txn() (if you're using the libsvn_repos wrappers that allow hook scripts to function, you should use svn_repos_fs_commit_txn()),and abort an in-progress transaction via svn_fs_abort_txn().

The final data structure you'll need to work with libsvn_fs is called svn_fs_root_t, which corresponds to the root directory of a particular revision or transaction in the filesystem. When you're referring to a file or a directory in the filesystem, you start at an svn_fs_root_t (the root of the revision or transaction you're referring to) and then give a relative path to the actual file. You can get an svn_fs_root_t for a particular revision in the filesystem by calling svn_fs_revision_root() or for a particular transaction by calling svn_fs_txn_root().

Making Changes to the Filesystem via libsvn_fs

The general procedure for making a change to the filesystem goes like this. First, you create a transaction by making a copy of the current HEAD revision of the repository with svn_fs_create_txn(). Next, you call svn_fs_txn_root() to retrieve an svn_fs_root_t that corresponds to the root of that directory tree. Then, you make whatever changes you want by calling a function such as svn_fs_copy(), svn_fs_revision_link(), svn_fs_make_dir(), svn_fs_apply_textdelta(), svn_fs_apply_text(), or svn_fs_make_file(). Finally, you commit the transaction by calling svn_fs_commit_txn().

At any point after creating the transaction, you can back out of making your change by calling svn_fs_abort_txn(). In fact, you really should do that, since if you don't abort the transaction it will just sit there until someone comes along and cleans it up with svn_fs_purge_txn().

Consider the simple example in Listing 8-37 of how to use libsvn_fs to make some changes to a repository.

Listing 8-37. *Making Changes with libsvn_fs*

```
svn_error_t *
create_readme_file_impl (svn_fs_txn_t *txn,
                         svn_repos_t *repos,
                         const char *contents,
                         apr_pool_t *pool)
{
  svn_revnum_t new_rev;
  svn_fs_root_t *root;
  svn_stream_t *stream;
  apr_size_t len = strlen (contents);


  /* grab the root of the txn */
  SVN_ERR (svn_fs_txn_root (&root, txn, pool));
```

```
    /* create a file named README in the top level of the txn */
    SVN_ERR (svn_fs_make_file (root, "README", pool));

    /* grab a writable stream for README, then write the contents to it */
    SVN_ERR (svn_fs_apply_text (&stream, root, "README",
                                NULL, /* we're not bothering with a checksum */
                                pool));

    SVN_ERR (svn_stream_write (stream, contents, &len));

    SVN_ERR (svn_stream_close (stream));

    /* try to commit our change */
    SVN_ERR (svn_repos_fs_commit_txn (NULL,
                                      repos,
                                      &new_rev,
                                      txn,
                                      pool));
    return SVN_NO_ERROR;
}

svn_error_t *
create_readme_file (svn_repos_t *repos, const char *contents, apr_pool_t *pool)
{
    svn_fs_txn_t *txn;
    svn_revnum_t rev;

    /* figure out what the current HEAD is, so we can start by copying it. */
    SVN_ERR (svn_fs_youngest_rev (&rev, svn_repos_fs (repos), pool));

    /* start our transaction */
    SVN_ERR (svn_repos_fs_begin_txn_for_commit (&txn, repos, rev, "example",
                                                "creating a readme file", pool));

    /* if anything else fails, we need to abort the transaction, so the guts
     * of the code is in a helper function, and if that returns an error, we
     * abort the transaction before throwing the error back upstream.
     */
    svn_error_t *err = create_readme_file_impl (txn, repos, contents, pool);

    if (err)
      {
        SVN_ERR (svn_fs_abort_txn (txn, pool));

        return err;
      }
    else
```

```
    return SVN_NO_ERROR;
}
```

Of course, you don't always want to make a change to the repository. Sometimes all you need to do is read some data that's already there. This involves using several of the functions that are used when making changes to the filesystem. The primary difference is that you get your svn_fs_root_t by calling svn_fs_revision_root() instead of svn_fs_txn_root(). Then you call functions such as svn_fs_file_contents() to pull out the contents of a file, and svn_fs_dir_entries() to retrieve the contents of a directory. File contents are returned via a generic svn_stream_t, and directory contents are returned in an apr_hash_t (which maps entry names to svn_fs_dirent_t objects).

Listing 8-38 shows an example of how to list the nodes in a particular directory.

Listing 8-38. *Listing Directory Contents in the Filesystem*

```
svn_error_t *
list_directory_contents (svn_repos_t *repos,
                         const char *path,
                         apr_pool_t *pool)
{
  svn_fs_root_t *root;
  svn_revnum_t rev;
  apr_hash_t *ents;
  /* figure out what the current HEAD is, so we can start by copying it. */
  SVN_ERR (svn_fs_youngest_rev (&rev, svn_repos_fs (repos), pool));

  SVN_ERR (svn_fs_revision_root (&root, svn_repos_fs (repos), rev, pool));

  SVN_ERR (svn_fs_dir_entries (&ents, root, path, pool));

  {
    apr_pool_t *subpool = svn_pool_create (pool);
    apr_hash_index_t *idx;
    const void *key;
    void *val;

    for (idx = apr_hash_first (pool, ents); idx; idx = apr_hash_next (idx))
      {
        svn_string_t *unparsed;
        svn_fs_dirent_t *dent;

        svn_pool_clear (subpool);

        apr_hash_this (idx, &key, NULL, &val);

        dent = val;

        unparsed = svn_fs_unparse_id (dent->id, subpool);
```

```
        printf ("%s %s\n", dent->name, unparsed->data);
      }

   svn_pool_destroy (subpool);
 }

 /* you don't really have to do this, the pool cleanup will take care of
  * it for you, but hey, it doesn't hurt to speed up the process. */
 svn_fs_close_root (root);

 return SVN_NO_ERROR;
}
```

As you can see, you can retrieve an svn_fs_root_t from a revision, and then you can poke around in that revision to your heart's content.

If you're poking around in the filesystem, it stands to reason that you're probably interested in more than grabbing directory listings and file contents. Since Subversion uses a versioned filesystem, you probably want to take advantage of that by looking at the history of a given node. To do that, you use the svn_fs_history_t object, the svn_fs_node_history() function, and the svn_fs_history_prev() function. Recall that the filesystem internally tracks previous versions of a node, so you can follow that history back all the way to the node's creation. The process of listing out all those revisions looks like Listing 8-39.

Listing 8-39. *Printing Node History with libsvn_fs*

```
svn_error_t *
print_node_history (svn_fs_t *fs,
                    svn_fs_root_t *root,
                    const char *path,
                    apr_pool_t *pool)
{
  apr_pool_t *newpool = svn_pool_create (pool);
  apr_pool_t *oldpool = svn_pool_create (pool);

  svn_fs_history_t *history;
  const char *history_path;
  svn_revnum_t history_rev;

  SVN_ERR (svn_fs_node_history (&history, root, path, pool));

  do
    {
      /* use two pools here, allocating out of one of them each time through
       * the loop.  the history object needs to persist until the next
       * iteration, so we can call svn_fs_history_prev on it.  then, once
       * we're done with that history, we clear the pool it was allocated from.
       */
```

```
      SVN_ERR (svn_fs_history_location (&history_path, &history_rev,
                                        history, newpool));

      printf ("%s %" SVN_REVNUM_T_FMT "\n", history_path, history_rev);

      SVN_ERR (svn_fs_history_prev (&history, history, TRUE, newpool));

      svn_pool_clear (oldpool);

      {
        apr_pool_t *tmppool = oldpool;
        oldpool = newpool;
        newpool = tmppool;
      }
    }
  while (history);
  return SVN_NO_ERROR;
}
```

The only tricky part here is the pool handling. You need to avoid allocating everything within one pool because there's a potentially unbounded loop; but you can't just create one pool and clear it each time through, because you need the revision from one iteration to get the next one. The solution is to use two pools and alternate between clearing and using them each time through the loop.

Filesystem Library Conclusion

This section has only scratched the surface of what you can do with libsvn_fs. We haven't even looked at its ability to compute text deltas between nodes, or the concept of merging changes between trees, both of which are central to Subversion's use of the filesystem. That said, we hope you have been given enough insight to get started with libsvn_fs, and that you are set on the path to doing new and interesting things with it in the future.

Using Subversion from Perl

One of the main reasons the Subversion libraries were implemented in C is the ease with which you can make use of C libraries from other programming languages. As a result of this, several people have worked to make the Subversion API available from various different scripting languages, and out of all of them, the language that likely presents the most full-featured API is Perl. By using a combination of automatically generated SWIG code (SWIG is a tool for automatically generating bindings between C or C++ code and scripting languages; see http://www.swig.org/ for more information) and handwritten XS wrappers,[1] virtually all of the Subversion API has been made available to Perl programmers, masking much of the complexity that comes from using the C-level APIs without losing much of the versatility.

---

1. XS (eXternal Subroutine) wrappers are Perl's way of interfacing C and other language extensions into Perl.

Perhaps the best part about the Perl bindings for Subversion is the fact that they're rather well-documented. Most of the major Perl modules in the package have been filled with embedded Plain Old Documentation (POD) that the perldoc command can transform into rather nice man page-type docs. For any of the modules we discuss here, you can find more detailed documentation and even examples by passing perldoc the module's name. For example, to read the documentation for the SVN::Core module, you can just run perldoc SVN::Core.

Even when the bindings aren't accompanied by adequate documentation (and there are always going to be parts that aren't adequately documented), they have the next best thing: tests. If you're looking for details on how to do something with the Subversion Perl bindings and you can't figure it out from this book or from the embedded POD, as a last resort you can always look at the tests for the bindings themselves, which you can find in the subversion/bindings/swig/perl/native/t directory in the Subversion distribution.

This section presents an introduction to the use of the Subversion Perl bindings. It explains how to install the bindings and then how to make use of them in your own Perl scripts.

The Installation Process

Installing the Subversion Perl bindings is more complicated than building Subversion alone; and it's different from building your standard Perl module from CPAN. The main differences are because Subversion uses the SWIG program to provide a bridge between C code and Perl code; so to install them, you'll have to have a version of SWIG with Perl support installed.

We're not going to step through what you need to do to install SWIG or the Subversion Perl bindings, since the details would stand a very good chance of being out of date by the time you read this. Consult the SWIG documentation for details on installing SWIG, and the subversion/bindings/swig/INSTALL document for the Subversion-specific steps. Both are kept quite up to date, and if you follow the instructions, you will be up and running with the Subversion Perl bindings in no time.

SVN::Core

The SVN::Core module contains a number of different utilities that are used throughout the rest of the Perl bindings. In order to use the remainder of the bindings, you need to know how to use four primary elements of SVN::Core: its wrapper for APR pools; its wrapper for svn_error_ts; its code for handling svn_stream_ts from Perl; and the module for handling authentication. In addition, SVN::Core handles the calls to apr_initialize and apr_terminate that you need to do manually when using the C API.

The SVN::Pool module (which you get automatically when you use SVN::Core) provides a more idiomatic Perl wrapper around apr_pool_ts. Primarily, this means that while you can explicitly pass SVN::Pool objects into the various functions that require a pool for memory allocation, you don't have to. Instead, there's a default pool that will be used if you don't specify what pool a function should use, and there are a number of functions in the SVN::Pool namespace for managing the default pool. Using SVN::Pool to manage your pool usage looks like Listing 8-40.

Listing 8-40. *SVN::Pool Usage*

```
sub do_something {
  my $pool = SVN::Pool->new_default; # create a new default pool

  for (@_) {
    my $subpool = SVN::Pool->new_default_sub;

    # do something here that makes use of the default pool for allocation

    # now $subpool gets destroyed because it went out of scope, and the
    # former default pool is reinstated
  }

  # now $pool is the default pool, so it will be used for any function that
  # needs a pool.
}
```

The Perl bindings also provide a Perl-like wrapper around the C API's error handling. By default, there is a handler function installed that calls croak() whenever one of the underlying C functions returns an svn_error_t. Obviously, this might not be what you want to happen in your program, so to override it you simply need to set the SVN::Error::handler variable to a reference to a subroutine that should be called when an error is returned. The subroutine will be passed an svn_error_t object, and its return value will be ignored. Listing 8-41 shows an example of how to set up your own error handler.

Listing 8-41. *Setting a New SVN::Error::handler*

```
sub i_want_a_new_error_handler {
  SVN::Error::handler = sub {
    my $err = shift;

    if (SVN::Error::is_error ($err) {
      my $mess = $err->strerror ();

      while ($err) {
        $mess .= " : " . $err->message ();
        $err = $err->child ();
      }

      die $mess;
    } else {
      return undef;
    }
  }
}
```

If you don't want an error handler to be called when something goes wrong, you can set SVN::Error::handler to undef. This will cause every function to return an svn_error_t object as its first return value in the case of a failure. If the function is called in scalar context instead of array context, the error will be lost.

Another Perlish wrapper around a low-level Subversion data structure is provided for svn_stream_t. The Perl bindings allow svn_stream_ts and native Perl I/O handles to be used interchangeably. This means that when you get a stream back from the apply_text() function attached to an svn_fs_root_t's Perl representation, you can simply use print() to write data to it and close() to close it when you're done. Conversely, you can pass references to *STDOUT in to SVN::Client's cat() function to write a file in the repository to standard out.

Finally, there are the Perl wrappers for the various svn_auth functions. To use this code, you can use SVN::Core::auth_open() to turn an array of authentication providers into an authentication baton object, which you can then pass to any other function that requires authentication support. The authentication providers themselves can be built via various builder functions in SVN::Client. Listing 8-42 shows the process.

Listing 8-42. *Using Authentication in Perl*

```perl
sub build_auth_provider {
  # create an authentication baton with providers for svn.simple and
  # svn.username
  my $auth_baton = SVN::Core::auth_open ([
    SVN::Client::get_simple_provider (),
    SVN::Client::get_simple_prompt_provider (\&simple_prompt, 2),
    SVN::Client::get_username_provider ()
  ]);

  return $auth_baton;
}

sub simple_prompt {
  my ($cred, $realm, $def_username, $may_save, $pool) = @_;

  # show the user the realm and prompt for his username
  print "Realm = $realm\n";
  print "Username : ";

  # read in the username
  my $username = <>;
  chomp $username;

  # set the username in the credentials
  $cred->username($username);

  # prompt for the username
  print "Password : ";

  # read the password
  my $password = <>;
  chomp $password;
```

```
    # set the password in the credentials
    $cred->password($password);
}
```

SVN::Client

libsvn_client has been transformed into an object-oriented interface in the form of SVN::Client.
Instead of passing an svn_client_ctx_t in to each function, you create an instance of the
SVN::Client object that wraps around the client context, and you call the various libsvn_client
functions as methods on the object.

The transition from the C API to the Perl API is quite simple. You remove the client context
argument, turn anything that's an out parameter (i.e., a pointer to a pointer that will be allocated by the function) into a return value, change const char *s into scalars, and allow target
arrays to be passed in as either an array reference or a single scalar. The authentication baton,
cancellation callback, configuration hash, log message callback, and notification callback are
all passed in to the SVN::Client object's constructor.

Since the Perl API maps so closely to the C API, and the functions are well-documented in
the POD, we don't cover all of the functions here. Instead, we'll just leave you with an example
(see Listing 8-43) of how some of them are called.

Listing 8-43. *Using SVN::Client Functions*

```
sub add_file {
  my $target = shift;

  # first we create a client object
  my $client = SVN::Client->new (
    # specify a notification callback
    notify => sub {
      my ($path, $action, $nodetype, $mime, $state, $rev) = @_;

      # since all we're doing is adding, just print out something for
      # the add case
      if ($action == $SVN::Wc::Notify::Action::add) {
        print "added $path\n";
      }
    }
  );

  # recursive add target using the default pool
  $client->add ($target, 1);
}
```

SVN::Ra

libsvn_ra makes its appearance in the Perl world via the SVN::Ra module. The module is primarily
composed of an object-oriented wrapper around the functions in the RA layer. In addition to the

SVN::Ra object itself, there are also classes that wrap svn_ra_reporter_t (SVN::Ra::Reporter) and svn_ra_callback_t (SVN::Ra::Callbacks), both of which you can subclass to provide customized behavior.

The SVN::Ra object is created via the new() function, which accepts as its argument either a URL or a hash that contains the URL (accessed with the url key), an authentication baton (auth), a default pool to use (pool), a configuration hash (config), and an instance of SVN::Ra::Callbacks (callback). Each of these (other than the URL) is, of course, optional and has sensible defaults if you do not fill it in.

SVN::Ra's methods correspond directly to the member functions in the RA layer. Listing 8-44 shows a short example of how SVN::Ra can be used.

Listing 8-44. *Printing Logs Using SVN::Ra*

```
use SVN::Core;
use SVN::Ra;

sub print_log {
  my $url = shift;

  # open the RA library
  my $ra = SVN::Ra->new (url => $url);

  # call get_log over revisions from 0 to HEAD, passing it a callback that
  # simply prints out the revision, date, author, and message
  $ra->get_log ([''], 0, "HEAD", 1, 0, sub {
    my ($paths, $rev, $author, $date, $msg, $pool) = @_;

    print <<END;
$rev : $date : $author

$msg
END
  });
}
```

SVN::Repos

SVN::Repos provides a convenient wrapper around libsvn_repos, primarily through the SVN::Repos object, a wrapper around svn_repos_t. You can open an existing repository via SVN::Repos::open() and create one via SVN::Repos::create(), both of which will return instances of SVN::Repos. Then you can access most of the libsvn_repos functions as methods of that object. Any function within svn_repos.h that takes an svn_repos_t as its first argument is provided as a member function. You also have access to the underlying SVN::Fs object via the fs() method.

Listing 8-45 presents an example of how to retrieve the same log listing you saw in the previous example via SVN::Repos.

Listing 8-45. *Getting Log Data with SVN::Repos*

```
use SVN::Core;
use SVN::Repos;

sub get_logs {
  my ($repos, $path) = @_;

  # open the repository
  my $r = SVN::Repos::open ($repos);

  # call get_logs, just like the RA layer example
  $r->get_logs($path, 0, "HEAD", 1, 0, sub {
    my ($paths, $rev, $author, $date, $msg, $pool) = @_;

    print <<END;
$rev : $date : $author

$msg
END
  });
}
```

SVN::Fs

Finally, you can access the underlying filesystem using SVN::Fs, which provides access to the svn_fs_t object by way of the SVN::Fs class. There are objects to wrap the svn_fs_root_t and svn_fs_txn_t structures, and the functions in svn_fs.h map quite naturally into method calls. Listing 8-46 shows an example that lists the transactions in a repository.

Listing 8-46. *Listing the Transactions in a Repository*

```
use SVN::Core;
use SVN::Repos;
use SVN::Fs;

sub list_txns {
  my $path = shift;

  # open the repository
  my $repos = SVN::Repos::open ($path);

  # grab the underlying filesystem object
  my $fs = $repos->fs;

  # list all the transactions
  my $txns = $fs->list_transactions;
```

```
  # and print them out
  for my $txn @{$txns} {
    print "$txn\n";
  }
}
```

Using Subversion from Python

Since a number of the Subversion developers are fans of the Python programming language, it's only natural that Subversion would come with bindings that enable you to call into the various Subversion libraries from Python. And sure enough, those bindings do exist, and they have already been used by numerous applications, most notably ViewVC, the web-based repository viewer, and mailer.py, one of the hook scripts commonly used to generate commit e-mails.

Despite the incompleteness of the Python bindings, they're still quite capable of being used to write useful applications, as long as you are aware of their drawbacks and are willing to work around them. The primary issue is that while some of the modules have been transformed from the raw SWIG-processed Python code into something a Python programmer would be comfortable using (particularly svn.fs, which has seen a lot of use due primarily to ViewVC), most of the rest are rather thin wrappers around the underlying C code, and you need to understand a lot about the C API to make effective use of them. With that in mind, here are a few examples, with some commentary, of how to make use of the Python bindings to perform some common tasks.

As with the Subversion Perl bindings, the Subversion Python bindings depend on SWIG; and once you have SWIG installed there are a few specific steps you'll need to take beyond the standard Subversion installation process to get the bindings up and running. You can consult the SWIG documentation at http://www.swig.org/ for details on installing a version of SWIG with Python support, and the subversion/bindings/swig/INSTALL document in the Subversion source tree for the steps needed to install the Subversion Python bindings.

Once you have the bindings installed, you should be able to run a simple example program like the one shown in Listing 8-47, which iterates over a list of working copy files and directories given on the command line and prints out their repository URL.

Listing 8-47. *A Basic Python Example*

```
import os
import sys

import svn.core
import svn.wc

def main_func(pool, files):
  for f in files:
    # the paths passed in to subversion must be canonical,
    # which in this case, is an absolute path
    dirpath = fullpath = os.path.abspath(f)
```

```
    if not os.path.isdir(dirpath):
      dirpath = os.path.dirname(dirpath)
    adm_baton = svn.wc.svn_wc_adm_open(None, dirpath, 1, 1, pool)

    try:
      entry = svn.wc.svn_wc_entry(fullpath, adm_baton, 0, pool)
      print entry.url
    finally:
      svn.wc.svn_wc_adm_close(adm_baton)

if __name__ == '__main__':
  main_func(svn.core.svn_pool_create(), sys.argv[1:])
```

One thing to take note of is that the functions within the svn.wc module are used almost exactly the way the equivalent C APIs would be. This even goes as far as the naming conventions of the functions, many of which retain their svn_wc_ prefixes, which are largely unneeded in a language such as Python that has support for a real namespace hierarchy.

Next, let's look at an example (see Listing 8-48) that makes use of one of the more complete modules in the Python bindings: svn.fs.

Listing 8-48. *Reading a File's Contents via svn.fs*

```
import sys

import svn.core
import svn.fs

def main_func(pool, path, filename, rev=None):
  fsobj = fs.open(path, None, pool)

  if rev is None:
    rev = fs.youngest_rev(fsobj, pool)

  root = fs.revision_root(fsobj, rev, pool)
  filestream = fsobj.file_contents(root, filename, pool)
  while 1:
    data = core.svn_stream_read(file, 1024)
    if not data:
      break
    sys.stdout.write(data)

  fs.close(fsobj)

if __name__ == '__main__':
  main_func(svn.core.pool_create(), sys.argv[1], sys.argv[2])
```

Here you can see that the `svn.fs` module has made it a bit easier to work with the bindings by at least renaming its functions to remove the redundant `svn_fs_` from the beginning of the function names; but despite this the API is still closer to a C-style interface than a Python one. You must remember to explicitly pass the variable that holds the filesystem object (equivalent to the `svn_fs_t *`) or root object (equivalent to the `svn_fs_root_t *`) in to the `svn.fs` functions explicitly, rather than calling the functions as methods on the object, as you might expect in an object-oriented language such as Python.

If you're looking for more information on how to use the Python bindings, numerous examples are available to you. In the Subversion distribution itself, you can find the `mailer.py` script in the `tools/hook-scripts/mailer` directory, as well as a number of small example programs in the `tools/examples` directory. Other significant consumers of the bindings include ViewVC (http://viewvc.tigris.org/) and SubWiki (http://subwiki.tigris.org/).

As you can see, the Python bindings are certainly capable of being used to produce useful applications, but to do so, you need to become aware of the intricacies of the C-level API, which may not be quite what your Python programmers have in mind. We expect this will be corrected in the future and a more Pythonic API will be provided.

For those of you who like other languages, such as Ruby or Java, do not despair. Subversion provides SWIG-generated bindings for Ruby and a set of non-SWIG bindings for Java.

Summary

In this chapter, you learned enough to make use of the Subversion libraries in your own code. You examined the basics of APR and of the foundation libraries Subversion is built on top of. Using those, you discovered how to make use of each of the major Subversion libraries, from the high-level `libsvn_client` to the low-level `libsvn_fs`. Finally, you learned to access the Subversion libraries from other languages such as Perl and Python.

APPENDIX A

■ ■ ■

Subversion Command Glossary

This appendix contains a glossary of the various subcommands for the main Subversion executables. For each subcommand, there is a description, an example of common command lines, and a table summarizing the command's options. For svnserve, which has no subcommands, a description and table of options is included.

svn Subcommands

The primary means of interacting with Subversion is via the svn program. The following subcommands are contained in the svn executable.

add

The add command schedules files or directories for addition to the repository, placing the file under version control. The files are not placed into the repository until the next commit occurs. The following code is an example of how to run the add command to add PATH to the repository:

```
$ svn add PATH [PATH ...]
```

Table A-1 shows the options for the add command.

Table A-1. *add Options*

Option	Abbreviation	Description
--targets [argument]	None	Passes contents of the file named by argument as additional arguments.
--non-recursive	-N	Operates on a single directory as opposed to an entire directory tree.
--quiet	-q	Outputs as little as possible.
--config-dir [argument]	None	Uses the configuration files in the directory specified as the argument instead of the default configuration directory.
--no-ignore	None	Disregards default ignores and ignores that are contained in svn:ignore.
--force	None	Forces the add operation to run.
--auto-props	None	Enables automatic properties.
--no-auto-props	None	Disables automatic properties.

blame

The blame command will print the content of the specified files or URLs with revision and author information next to each line in the file. The aliases for the blame command are praise, annotate, and ann. The following code is an example of how to run the blame command and would print out blame information for TARGET:

```
$ svn blame TARGET [TARGET ...]
```

Table A-2 shows the options for the blame command.

Table A-2. *blame Options*

Option	Abbreviation	Description
--revision [argument]	-r	Interprets argument as the range of revisions to annotate with blame information.
--username [argument]	None	Uses argument as the username when accessing the repository.
--password [argument]	None	Uses argument as the password when accessing the repository.
--no-auth-cache	None	Doesn't cache the user's username and password in his or her configuration directory.
--non-interactive	None	Doesn't prompt the user for input.
--xml	None	Outputs in XML.
--verbose	-v	Prints extra information about each item.
--incremental	None	Outputs in a format that can be concatenated.
--config-dir [argument]	None	Uses the configuration files in the directory specified as the argument instead of the default configuration directory.

cat

The cat command will print the contents of the file or URL specified to standard output:

```
$ svn cat TARGET [TARGET ...]
```

Table A-3 shows the options for the cat command.

Table A-3. *cat Options*

Option	Abbreviation	Description
--revision [argument]	-r	Interprets argument as the revision to print.
--username [argument]	None	Uses argument as the username when accessing the repository.
--password [argument]	None	Uses argument as the password when accessing the repository.
--no-auth-cache	None	Doesn't cache the user's username and password in his or her configuration directory.
--non-interactive	None	Doesn't prompt the user for input.
--config-dir [argument]	None	Uses the configuration files in the directory specified as the argument instead of the default configuration directory.

checkout

The checkout command creates a working copy from the URL specified. If a path is specified in addition to a URL, the directory specified by the path will be used to hold the working copy. If multiple URLs are specified, the final component of each URL will be used as the name of the working copy, within either the path specified or the current working directory if there is no path specified. The only alias for the checkout command is co.

The following code is an example of how to run the checkout command, and would check out the repository located at URL to a local directory named PATH:

```
$ svn checkout URL [PATH]
```

Table A-4 shows the options for the checkout command.

Table A-4. *checkout Options*

Option	Abbreviation	Description
--revision [argument]	-r	Interprets argument as the revision to check out.
--quiet	-q	Outputs as little as possible.
--non-recursive	-N	Only checks out the top-level directory specified.
--username [argument]	None	Uses argument as the username when accessing the repository.
--password [argument]	None	Uses argument as the password when accessing the repository.
--no-auth-cache	None	Doesn't cache the user's username and password in his or her configuration directory.
--non-interactive	None	Doesn't prompt the user for input.
--ignore-externals	None	Ignores svn:externals when checking out.
--config-dir [argument]	None	Uses the configuration files in the directory specified as the argument instead of the default configuration directory.

cleanup

The cleanup command recursively cleans up a working copy by finishing incomplete operations and removing locks, as well as other related cleanup tasks:

```
$ svn cleanup [PATH ...]
```

Table A-5 shows the options for the cleanup command.

Table A-5. *cleanup Options*

Option	Abbreviation	Description
--diff3-cmd [argument]	None	Uses the executable specified by argument instead of Subversion's internal merge code.
--config-dir [argument]	None	Uses the configuration files in the directory specified as the argument instead of the default configuration directory.

commit

The commit command commits changes from your working copy into the repository. If paths to items in the working copy are specified as arguments to the commit command they, or any changes within them, will be committed. Otherwise, if no arguments are given, any changes within the current working directory will be committed. The alias for the commit command is ci.

The following code is an example of how to run the commit command, and would commit all changed files located in the current directory and its subdirectories:

```
$ svn commit [PATH ...]
```

Table A-6 shows the options for the commit command.

Table A-6. *commit Options*

Option	Abbreviation	Description
--message [argument]	-m	Uses argument as the log message for the commit.
--file [argument]	-F	Uses the contents of the file specified by argument as the log message for the commit.
--quiet	-q	Produces as little output as possible.
--non-recursive	-N	Operates only on a single directory, not on any subdirectories.
--targets [argument]	None	Uses the contents of the file specified by argument as additional arguments.
--force-log	None	Forces Subversion to accept the validity of the log message specified.
--username [argument]	None	Uses argument as the username when accessing the repository.
--password [argument]	None	Uses argument as the password when accessing the repository.
--no-auth-cache	None	Doesn't cache the user's username and password in his or her configuration directory.
--non-interactive	None	Doesn't prompt the user for input.
--editor-cmd [argument]	None	Uses the specified command as the editor when composing the log message for the commit.
--encoding [argument]	None	Uses argument as the encoding for the log message.
--no-unlock	None	Doesn't unlock the targets.
--config-dir [argument]	None	Uses the configuration files in the directory specified as the argument instead of the default configuration directory.

copy

The copy command is used to make a copy of a file or directory. The source and destination arguments to the copy command can be either working copy paths or repository URLs. If the destination is a working copy path, the copy will be created within the working copy and scheduled for addition at the next commit. If the destination is a repository URL, the commit occurs immediately. The alias for the copy command is cp.

The following code is an example of how to run the copy command, and would copy the location named by SOURCE to the location named by DESTINATION:

```
$ svn copy SOURCE DESTINATION
```

Table A-7 shows the options for the copy command.

Table A-7. *copy Options*

Option	Abbreviation	Description
--message [argument]	-m	Uses argument as the log message for the commit.
--file [argument]	-F	Uses the contents of the file specified by argument as the log message for the commit.
--revision [argument]	-r	Interprets argument as the revision to copy.
--quiet	-q	Produces as little output as possible.
--force-log	None	Forces Subversion to accept the validity of the log message specified.
--username [argument]	None	Uses argument as the username when accessing the repository.
--password [argument]	None	Uses argument as the password when accessing the repository.
--no-auth-cache	None	Doesn't cache the user's username and password in his or her configuration directory.
--non-interactive	None	Doesn't prompt the user for input.
--editor-cmd [argument]	None	Uses the specified command as the text editor for composing log messages.
--encoding [argument]	None	Uses argument as the encoding for the log message.
--config-dir [argument]	None	Uses the configuration files in the directory specified as the argument instead of the default configuration directory.

delete

The delete command is used to delete targets within either the working copy or the repository. If the targets are within the working copy, this schedules the delete for the next commit; otherwise it occurs immediately. The aliases of the delete command are del, remove, and rm.

The following code is an example of how to run the delete command, and would delete the location named by TARGET.

```
$ svn delete TARGET [TARGET ...]
```

Table A-8 shows the options for the delete command.

Table A-8. *delete Options*

Option	Abbreviation	Description
--force	None	Forces delete to run.
--force-log	None	Forces Subversion to accept the validity of the log message specified.
--message [argument]	-m	Uses argument as the log message for the commit.
--file [argument]	-F	Uses the contents of the file specified by argument as the log message for the commit.
--quiet	-q	Produces as little output as possible.
--targets [argument]	None	Passes contents of the file named by argument as additional arguments.
--username [argument]	None	Uses argument as the username when accessing the repository.
--password [argument]	None	Uses argument as the password when accessing the repository.
--no-auth-cache	None	Doesn't cache the user's username and password in his or her configuration directory.
--non-interactive	None	Doesn't prompt the user for input.
--editor-cmd [argument]	None	Uses the specified command as the text editor for composing log messages.
--encoding [argument]	None	Uses argument as the encoding for the log message.
--config-dir [argument]	None	Uses the configuration files in the directory specified as the argument instead of the default configuration directory.

diff

The diff command shows the difference between two versioned resources and has three possible uses. The first use involves just running svn diff in a working copy (possibly with several targets, which are files or directories within that working copy) and simply shows the difference between the current version of each target (or the entire working copy if there is no target) in the working copy and the base of the working copy. In effect, this shows you the changes you made since you last checked out or updated your working copy.

The second use compares two arbitrary trees. Each target is a URL referring to a path in the repository, optionally with a revision number (which defaults to HEAD if no revision is specified). This is used to compare items on different branches in the repository.

The third use is simply a shorthand version of the second, where the two URLs are the same, and the only difference is in the revision numbers of the two items being compared. This is used to show what changed on a branch between two revisions. The alias for the diff command is di.

The following shows the three uses of the diff command:

```
$ svn diff [PATH ...]
$ svn diff --new=TARGET[@REV] --old=TARGET[@REV]
$ svn diff -r REV1:REV2 URL
```

Table A-9 shows the options for the `diff` command.

Table A-9. *diff Options*

Option	Abbreviation	Description
`--revision [argument]`	`-r`	Uses argument as the revision to export from the repository.
`--old [argument]`	None	Uses argument as the older target.
`--new [argument]`	None	Uses argument as the newer target.
`--extensions [arguments]`	`-x`	Uses arguments when running external `diff` command.
`--non-recursive`	`-N`	Operates on a single directory only; doesn't recurse into subdirectories.
`--diff-cmd [argument]`	None	Runs argument to produce `diff` output instead of Subversion's internal `diff` library.
`--no-diff-deleted`	None	Doesn't print `diff` output for deleted files.
`--notice-ancestry`	None	Pays attention to ancestry in the repository when comparing files. This means that if you compare two files that aren't related (one is not a newer version of the other), it will show up as a diff that removes the first file and replaces it with the second, regardless of any internal differences or similarities the file contents might have.
`--username [argument]`	None	Uses argument as the username when accessing the repository.
`--password [argument]`	None	Uses argument as the password when accessing the repository.
`--no-auth-cache`	None	Doesn't cache the user's username and password in his or her configuration directory.
`--non-interactive`	None	Doesn't prompt the user for input.
`--force`	None	Forces `diff` to run.
`--config-dir [argument]`	None	Uses the configuration files in the directory specified as the argument instead of the default configuration directory.

export

The `export` command produces a clean directory tree from either the repository or a working copy. The following is an example of how to run the `export` command, producing a clean tree from the location named by TARGET into the path named DESTINATION:

```
$ svn export TARGET DESTINATION
```

Table A-10 shows the options for the export command.

Table A-10. *export Options*

Option	Abbreviation	Description
--revision [argument]	-r	Uses argument as the revision to export from the repository.
--quiet	-q	Produces as little output as possible.
--force	None	Forces export to run, even if it would overwrite an existing directory.
--username [argument]	None	Uses argument as the username when accessing the repository.
--password [argument]	None	Uses argument as the password when accessing the repository.
--no-auth-cache	None	Doesn't cache the user's username and password in his or her configuration directory.
--native-eol [argument]	None	Forces the end-of-line marker to be different from what is normally used when the svn:eol-style property is set to native. Valid options are CR, LF, and CRLF.
--non-interactive	None	Doesn't prompt the user for input.
--non-recursive	-N	Operates only on a single directory, not on any subdirectories.
--ignore-externals	None	Ignores svn:externals when checking out.
--config-dir [argument]	None	Uses the configuration files in the directory specified as the argument instead of the default configuration directory.

help

The help command prints a generic help message or, if subcommands are specified as arguments, prints the help message for each one:

```
$ svn help [COMMAND ...]
```

Table A-11 shows the option for the help command.

Table A-11. *help Option*

Option	Abbreviation	Description
--version	None	Prints version information about program.

import

The import command recursively commits a copy of PATH (which defaults to the current working directory if no path is specified) to the repository at the location URL. Parent directories are created as necessary in the repository:

```
$ svn import [PATH] URL
```

Table A-12 shows the options for the import command.

Table A-12. *import Options*

Option	Abbreviation	Description
--message [argument]	-m	Uses argument as the log message for the commit.
--file [argument]	-F	Uses the contents of the file specified by argument as the log message for the commit.
--quiet	-q	Produces as little output as possible.
--non-recursive	-N	Operates only on a single directory, not on any subdirectories.
--username [argument]	None	Uses argument as the username when accessing the repository.
--password [argument]	None	Uses argument as the password when accessing the repository.
--no-auth-cache	None	Doesn't cache the user's username and password in his or her configuration directory.
--non-interactive	None	Doesn't prompt the user for input.
--force-log	None	Forces Subversion to accept the validity of the log message specified.
--editor-cmd [argument]	None	Uses the specified command as the text editor when composing log messages.
--encoding [argument]	None	Uses argument as the encoding for the log message.
--config-dir [argument]	None	Uses the configuration files in the directory specified as the argument instead of the default configuration directory.
--no-ignore	None	Disregards default and svn:ignore property ignores.
--auto-props	None	Enables automatic setting of properties.
--no-auto-props	None	Disables automatic setting of properties.

info

The info command prints information about the given working copy path or URL. If given a URL, the revision argument is which revision of the URL to use:

```
$ svn info [TARGET]
```

Table A-13 shows the options for the info command.

Table A-13. *info Options*

Option	Abbreviation	Description
--revision [argument]	-r	Interprets argument as the revision to print.
--targets [argument]	None	Uses the contents of the file specified as argument as arguments.
--recursive	-R	Recurses through target directories.
--username [argument]	None	Uses argument as the username when accessing the repository.
--password [argument]	None	Uses argument as the password when accessing the repository.
--no-auth-cache	None	Doesn't cache the user's username and password in his or her configuration directory.
--non-interactive	None	Doesn't prompt the user for input.
--xml	None	Outputs in XML.
--incremental	None	Outputs in a format that can be concatenated.
--config-dir [argument]	None	Uses the configuration files in the directory specified as the argument instead of the default configuration directory.

list

The list command lists each target and any items within each target directory. Targets can be either working copy paths or repository URLs. If the verbose option is used, it includes the revision number of the last commit, the author of the last commit, the size of the file (in bytes), whether the file is locked, and the date and time of the last commit for each item listed. The alias for the list command is ls.

The following is an example of how to run the list command, and would list all items in the location named by TARGET:

```
$ svn list TARGET [TARGET ...]
```

Table A-14 shows the options for the list command.

Table A-14. *list Options*

Option	Abbreviation	Description
--revision [argument]	-r	Interprets argument as the revision to print.
--verbose	-v	Prints extra information about each item.
--xml	None	Outputs in XML.
--recursive	-R	Descends recursively into subdirectories.
--incremental	None	Outputs in a format that can be concatenated.
--username [argument]	None	Uses the username specified by argument as the username when accessing the repository.
--password [argument]	None	Uses the password specified by argument as the password when accessing the repository.

Continued

Table A-14. *Continued*

Option	Abbreviation	Description
--no-auth-cache	None	Doesn't cache the user's username and password in his or her configuration directory.
--non-interactive	None	Doesn't prompt the user for input.
--config-dir [argument]	None	Uses the configuration files in the directory specified as the argument instead of the default configuration directory.

lock

The lock command locks working copy paths or URLs, preventing other users from committing changes to them:

```
$ svn lock TARGET [TARGET ...]
```

Table A-15 shows the options for the lock command.

Table A-15. *lock Options*

Option	Abbreviation	Description
--message [argument]	-m	Uses argument as the log message for the lock.
--targets [argument]	None	Uses the contents of the file specified by argument as additional targets.
--file [argument]	-F	Uses the contents of the file specified by argument as the log message for the lock.
--username [argument]	None	Uses argument as the username when accessing the repository.
--password [argument]	None	Uses argument as the password when accessing the repository.
--no-auth-cache	None	Doesn't cache the user's username and password in his or her configuration directory.
--non-interactive	None	Doesn't prompt the user for input.
--encoding [argument]	None	Uses argument as the encoding for the log message.
--force-log	None	Forces Subversion to accept the validity of the log message specified.
--force	None	Forces the operation to run.
--config-dir [argument]	None	Uses the configuration files in the directory specified as the argument instead of the default configuration directory.

log

The log command prints the log messages associated with the targets (which default to the current working directory if no targets are given) over a range of revisions (which defaults to starting at HEAD and ending at 1 if no revisions are specified):

```
$ svn log [TARGET ...]
```

Table A-16 shows the options for the `log` command.

Table A-16. *log Options*

Option	Abbreviation	Description
`--revision [argument]`	`-r`	Interprets argument as the revision(s) to print logs for.
`--quiet`	`-q`	Prints as little as possible.
`--verbose`	`-v`	Prints extra information.
`--targets [argument]`	None	Uses the contents of the file specified by argument as additional targets.
`--stop-on-copy`	None	Doesn't cross copies when traversing the target's history in the repository. This is useful for only printing log information for changes that occur on the current branch.
`--incremental`	None	Prints output suitable for concatenation.
`--xml`	None	Outputs the log messages in XML form.
`--username [argument]`	None	Uses argument as the username when accessing the repository.
`--password [argument]`	None	Uses argument as the password when accessing the repository.
`--no-auth-cache`	None	Doesn't cache the user's username and password in his or her configuration directory.
`--non-interactive`	None	Doesn't prompt the user for input.
`--limit [argument]`	None	Uses argument as the maximum number of log entries to print.
`--config-dir [argument]`	None	Uses the configuration files in the directory specified as the argument instead of the default configuration directory.

merge

The `merge` command applies the difference between two trees in the repository to a local working copy. The first line in the following code example applies the difference between two URLs in the repository to a local working copy path. The second example does the same thing, but with two local working copy paths as the source of the diff. Finally, the third example is a shortcut for the case where the two source URLs are the same, such as when you're merging a specific range of changes made on one branch to another branch:

```
$ svn merge URL[@REV] URL[@REV] [PATH]
$ svn merge PATH@REV PATH@REV [PATH]
$ svn merge -r REV1:REV2 SOURCE[@REV] [PATH]
```

In all cases, if no local working copy path is specified, the current working directory will be used, unless both sources have an identical base name and that base name matches the name of a file in the current working directory, in which case the difference will be applied to that file.

Table A-17 shows the options for the merge command.

Table A-17. *merge Options*

Option	Abbreviation	Description
--revision [argument]	-r	Interprets argument as the revision(s) to merge.
--non-recursive	-N	Operates on a single directory instead of recursing into subdirectories.
--quiet	-q	Prints as little as possible.
--force	None	Forces the operation to run.
--dry-run	None	Tries the operation but doesn't actually apply any changes to the working copy.
--diff3-cmd [argument]	None	Uses the program specified as the command for merging changes into the working copy instead of Subversion's internal diff library.
--ignore-ancestry	None	Ignores ancestry when determining changes to merge.
--username [argument]	None	Uses argument as the username when accessing the repository.
--password [argument]	None	Uses argument as the password when accessing the repository.
--no-auth-cache	None	Doesn't cache the user's username and password in his or her configuration directory.
--non-interactive	None	Doesn't prompt the user for input.
--config-dir [argument]	None	Uses the configuration files in the directory specified as the argument instead of the default configuration directory.

mkdir

The mkdir command creates directories, either in the repository (in which case the targets are repository URLs) or in the working copy (in which case the targets are working copy paths):

```
$ svn mkdir TARGET [TARGET ...]
```

Table A-18 shows the options for the mkdir command.

Table A-18. *mkdir Options*

Option	Abbreviation	Description
--message [argument]	-m	Uses argument as the log message for the commit.
--file [argument]	-F	Uses the contents of the file specified by argument as the log message for the commit.
--quiet	-q	Produces as little output as possible.
--username [argument]	None	Uses argument as the username when accessing the repository.
--password [argument]	None	Uses argument as the password when accessing the repository.
--no-auth-cache	None	Doesn't cache the user's username and password in his or her configuration directory.
--non-interactive	None	Doesn't prompt the user for input.
--editor-cmd [argument]	None	Uses the specified command as the text editor when composing a log message.
--encoding [argument]	None	Uses argument as the encoding for the log message.
--force-log	None	Forces Subversion to accept the validity of the log message specified.
--config-dir [argument]	None	Uses the configuration files in the directory specified as the argument instead of the default configuration directory.

move

The move command moves a file or directory, either in the repository (in which case both source and destination must be URLs in the repository) or in the working copy (in which case both source and destination must be working copy paths). The aliases for the move command are mv, rename, and ren.

The following is an example of how to run the move command:

```
$ svn move SOURCE DESTINATION
```

Table A-19 shows the options for the move command.

Table A-19. *move Options*

Option	Abbreviation	Description
--message [argument]	-m	Uses argument as the log message for the commit.
--file [argument]	-F	Uses the contents of the file specified by argument as the log message for the commit.
--revision [argument]	-r	Uses argument as the revision for the source of the move.
--quiet	-q	Produces as little output as possible.
--force	None	Forces the operation to run.
--username [argument]	None	Uses argument as the username when accessing the repository.

Continued

Table A-19. *Continued*

Option	Abbreviation	Description
--password [argument]	None	Uses argument as the password when accessing the repository.
--no-auth-cache	None	Doesn't cache the user's username and password in his or her configuration directory.
--non-interactive	None	Doesn't prompt the user for input.
--editor-cmd [argument]	None	Uses the specified command as the text editor when composing log messages.
--encoding [argument]	None	Uses argument as the encoding for the log message.
--force-log	None	Forces Subversion to accept the validity of the log message specified.
--config-dir [argument]	None	Uses the configuration files in the directory specified as the argument instead of the default configuration directory.

propdel

The propdel command deletes a property or revision property. The aliases for the propdel command are pdel and pd.

The first line in the following example shows how to run the propdel command to delete a versioned property. The second line is an example of how to run the propdel command to delete a revision property:

```
$ svn propdel PROPNAME PATH [TARGET ...]
$ svn propdel --revprop -r REV [URL]
```

Table A-20 shows the options for the propdel command.

Table A-20. *propdel Options*

Option	Abbreviation	Description
--quiet	-q	Produces as little output as possible.
--recursive	-R	Descends recursively into subdirectories.
--revision [argument]	-r	Uses argument as the revision for the source of the move.
--revprop	None	Operates on a revision property. If --revprop is given, a --revision must also be given.
--username [argument]	None	Uses argument as the username when accessing the repository.
--password [argument]	None	Uses argument as the password when accessing the repository.
--no-auth-cache	None	Doesn't cache the user's username and password in his or her configuration directory.
--non-interactive	None	Doesn't prompt the user for input.
--config-dir [argument]	None	Uses the configuration files in the directory specified as the argument instead of the default configuration directory.

propedit

The propedit command edits the contents of a property or revision property in an editor. The aliases for the propedit command are pedit and pe.

The first line in the following code is an example of how to run the propedit command to edit a versioned property. The second line shows how to run the propedit command to edit a revision property:

```
$ svn propedit PROPNAME PATH [TARGET ...]
$ svn propedit --revprop -r REV [URL]
```

Table A-21 shows the options for the propedit command.

Table A-21. *propedit Options*

Option	Abbreviation	Description
--revision [argument]	-r	Uses argument as the revision for the source of the move.
--revprop	None	Operates on a revision property.
--username [argument]	None	Uses argument as the username when accessing the repository.
--password [argument]	None	Uses argument as the password when accessing the repository.
--no-auth-cache	None	Doesn't cache the user's username and password in his or her configuration directory.
--non-interactive	None	Doesn't prompt the user for input.
--encoding [argument]	None	Treats the value as being in the encoding specified.
--editor-cmd [argument]	None	Uses the specified editor to edit the property.
--force	None	Forces the operation to take place.
--config-dir [argument]	None	Uses the configuration files in the directory specified as the argument instead of the default configuration directory.

propget

The propget command prints out the value of the specified property or revision property. The aliases for the propget command are pget and pg.

The first line in the following code is an example of how to run the propget command to print the value of a versioned property. The second line shows how to run the propget command to print out a revision property:

```
$ svn propget PROPNAME TARGET [TARGET ...]
$ svn propget --revprop -r REV [URL]
```

Table A-22 shows the options for the propget command.

Table A-22. *propget Options*

Option	Abbreviation	Description
--recursive	-R	Operates recursively through subdirectories.
--revision [argument]	-r	Uses argument as the revision for the source of the move.
--revprop	None	Operates on a revision property.
--strict	None	Doesn't add extra newlines at the end of the property value.
--username [argument]	None	Uses argument as the username when accessing the repository.
--password [argument]	None	Uses argument as the password when accessing the repository.
--no-auth-cache	None	Doesn't cache the user's username and password in his or her configuration directory.
--non-interactive	None	Doesn't prompt the user for input.
--config-dir [argument]	None	Uses the configuration files in the directory specified as the argument instead of the default configuration directory.

proplist

The proplist command lists the properties associated with a file or directory, or the revision properties associated with a revision. The aliases for the proplist command are plist and pl.

The first line in the following code is an example of how to run the proplist command to list the properties of a location named TARGET. The second line shows an example of how to run the proplist command to get the revision properties associated with revision REV:

```
$ svn proplist TARGET [TARGET ...]
$ svn proplist --revprop -r REV [URL]
```

Table A-23 shows the options for the proplist command.

Table A-23. *proplist Options*

Option	Abbreviation	Description
--verbose	-v	Prints as much information as possible.
--recursive	-R	Operates recursively through subdirectories.
--revision [argument]	-r	Uses argument as the revision for the source of the move.
--quiet	-q	Prints as little as possible.
--revprop	None	Operates on a revision property.
--username [argument]	None	Uses argument as the username when accessing the repository.
--password [argument]	None	Uses argument as the password when accessing the repository.

Option	Abbreviation	Description
--no-auth-cache	None	Doesn't cache the user's username and password in his or her configuration directory.
--non-interactive	None	Doesn't prompt the user for input.
--config-dir [argument]	None	Uses the configuration files in the directory specified as the argument instead of the default configuration directory.

propset

The propset command is used to set a property on a specified file or directory, or a revision property on a revision in the repository. The aliases for the propset command are pset and ps.

The first line in the following code is an example of how to run the propset command to set the value of a versioned property. The second line shows how to run the propset command to set a revision property:

```
$ svn propset PROPNAME [PROPVAL | -F VALFILE] PATH [PATH ...]
$ svn propset PROPNAME --revprop -r REV [PROPVAL | -F VALFILE] [URL]
```

Table A-24 shows the options for the propset command.

Table A-24. *propset Options*

Option	Abbreviation	Description
--file [argument]	-F	Reads data from the file specified.
--quiet	-q	Prints as little as possible.
--revision [argument]	-r	Uses argument as the revision for the source of the move.
--targets [argument]	None	Uses contents of the file specified as additional arguments.
--recursive	-R	Operates recursively through subdirectories.
--revprop	None	Operates on a revision property.
--username [argument]	None	Uses argument as the username when accessing the repository.
--password [argument]	None	Uses argument as the password when accessing the repository.
--no-auth-cache	None	Doesn't cache the user's username and password in his or her configuration directory.
--non-interactive	None	Doesn't prompt the user for input.
--encoding [argument]	None	Treats the value as being in the character set specified.
--force	None	Forces the operation to run.
--config-dir [argument]	None	Uses the configuration files in the directory specified as the argument instead of the default configuration directory.

resolved

The resolved command removes the conflicted state from working copy files that contain conflicts as a result of a merge or an update. Note that this doesn't actually go into the file's contents and resolve the differences; it's just the way you indicate to Subversion that you've resolved the differences yourself, thus allowing you to commit the changes to the files:

```
$ svn resolved PATH [PATH ...]
```

Table A-25 shows the options for the resolved command.

Table A-25. *resolved Options*

Option	Abbreviation	Description
--targets [argument]	None	Passes contents of the file named by argument as additional arguments.
--recursive	-R	Operates recursively through any subdirectories within the target directories.
--quiet	-q	Outputs as little as possible.
--config-dir [argument]	None	Uses the configuration files in the directory specified as the argument instead of the default configuration directory.

revert

The revert command reverts any local changes to the target files or directories. Additionally, this will resolve the conflicted state of any files or directories that are in conflict before they are reverted:

```
$ svn revert PATH [PATH ...]
```

Table A-26 shows the options for the revert command.

Table A-26. *revert Options*

Option	Abbreviation	Description
--targets [argument]	None	Passes contents of the file named by argument as additional arguments.
--recursive	-R	Operates recursively through any subdirectories within the target directories.
--quiet	-q	Outputs as little as possible.
--config-dir [argument]	None	Uses the configuration files in the directory specified as the argument instead of the default configuration directory.

status

The status command prints the status of a working copy. Each column of the output contains a different kind of information. The aliases for the status command are stat and st.

The following code is an example of how to run the `status` command to print out status for the location named by `PATH`:

```
$ svn status PATH [PATH ...]
```

Table A-27 shows the status of the item's textual content, which is located in column 1 of the output.

Table A-27. *Column 1 of Status Output: Text Status*

Character Printed	Description
`(blank)`	The item has no modifications.
A	The item has been added.
C	The item is conflicted.
D	The item has been deleted.
I	The item is ignored.
M	The item is locally modified.
R	The item has been replaced.
X	The item is unversioned but is used by an external definition.
?	The item isn't under version control.
!	The item is missing or incomplete.
~	The item is versioned, but there's an item of a different type in its place.

Table A-28 shows the status of the item's properties.

Table A-28. *Column 2 of Status Output: Property Status*

Character Printed	Description
`(blank)`	The item has no property modifications.
C	The item's properties are conflicted.
M	The item's properties have been modified.

Table A-29 shows the lock status of the item.

Table A-29. *Column 3 of Status Output: Lock Status*

Character Printed	Description
`(blank)`	The item isn't locked.
L	The item is locked.

Table A-30 shows whether the item has been added with history, such as with a copy operation.

Table A-30. *Column 4 of Status Output: Addition History Status*

Character Printed	Description
(blank)	The item has no addition history.
+	The item is scheduled for addition with history.

Table A-31 shows an indication of whether the item has been switched.

Table A-31. *Column 5 of Status Output: Switch Status*

Character Printed	Description
(blank)	The item isn't switched.
S	The item is switched.

Table A-32 shows an indication of whether the item has been locked.

Table A-32. *Column 6 of Status Output: Lock Status*

Character Printed	Description
(blank)	There is no lock token.
K	The lock token is present (when the -u option is passed, it means the item is locked in the repository).
O	The lock token is in some other working copy (this character is only shown when the -u option is used).
T	The lock token is present but is stolen (this character is only shown when the -u option is used).
B	The lock token is present but is broken (this character is only shown when the -u option is used).

Table A-33 indicates whether a newer version of the item exists in the repository. This is only printed if the --show-updates flag is used.

Table A-33. *Column 8 of Status Output: Repository Status*

Character Printed	Description
(blank)	The item in the working copy is up to date.
*	A newer version of this item exists in the repository.

The remaining fields are space-delimited and contain either the base revision of the item and the filename, or the base revision, the last modified revision, the author of the previous change, and the filename, if the --verbose flag is used.

For examples of svn status output, you can refer to Chapter 2.

Table A-34 lists the options for the `status` command.

Table A-34. *status Options*

Option	Abbreviation	Description
--show-updates	-u	Contacts the repository and shows information about newer revisions that may have occurred.
--verbose	-v	Prints extra information.
--non-recursive	-N	Operates on a single directory instead of recursing into subdirectories.
--quiet	-q	Outputs as little as possible.
--no-ignore	None	Prints items even if they're ignored via the svn:ignore properties.
--username [argument]	None	Uses argument as the username when accessing the repository.
--password [argument]	None	Uses argument as the password when accessing the repository.
--no-auth-cache	None	Doesn't cache the user's username and password in his or her configuration directory.
--non-interactive	None	Doesn't prompt the user for input.
--xml	None	Outputs in XML.
--incremental	None	Outputs in a format that can be concatenated.
--ignore-externals	None	Ignores svn:externals when checking out.
--config-dir [argument]	None	Uses the configuration files in the directory specified as the argument instead of the default configuration directory.

switch

The `switch` command alters a working copy directory so that it refers to a new location in the repository. This is similar to an `svn update`, but in addition to moving in time (changing the revision the working copy corresponds to), you can also move in space (changing the directory in the repository it refers to). Alternatively, if the `--relocate` flag is used, simply update the working copy to refer to a new URL that references the same underlying repository. This is useful if the repository moves or if you need to access it via a different repository access layer. The alias for the `switch` command is `sw`.

The following code example shows how to run the `switch` command:

```
$ svn switch URL [PATH]
$ svn switch --relocate FROM TO [PATH ...]
```

Table A-35 shows the switch command's options.

Table A-35. *switch Options*

Option	Abbreviation	Description
--revision [argument]	-r	Uses argument as the revision to switch to.
--non-recursive	-N	Operates on a single directory instead of recursing into subdirectories.
--quiet	-q	Outputs as little as possible.
--diff3-cmd [argument]	None	Uses the specified program to merge changes into the working copy instead of using Subversion's internal diff library.
--relocate	None	Relocates the working copy by rewriting URLs.
--username [argument]	None	Uses argument as the username when accessing the repository.
--password [argument]	None	Uses argument as the password when accessing the repository.
--no-auth-cache	None	Doesn't cache the user's username and password in his or her configuration directory.
--non-interactive	None	Doesn't prompt the user for input.
--config-dir [argument]	None	Uses the configuration files in the directory specified as the argument instead of the default configuration directory.

unlock

The unlock command unlocks working copy paths or URLs:

```
$ svn lock TARGET [TARGET ...]
```

Table A-36 shows the unlock command's options.

Table A-36. *unlock Options*

Option	Abbreviation	Description
--targets [argument]	None	Uses the contents of the file argument as additional targets.
--username [argument]	None	Uses argument as the username when accessing the repository.
--password [argument]	None	Uses argument as the password when accessing the repository.
--no-auth-cache	None	Doesn't cache the user's username and password in his or her configuration directory.
--non-interactive	None	Doesn't prompt the user for input.
--force	None	Forces the operation to run
--config-dir [argument]	None	Uses the configuration files in the directory specified as the argument instead of the default configuration directory.

update

The update command updates the target working copy (or the current working directory if no targets are given) to either the HEAD revision or whatever revision is specified.

For each item updated, a line will be printed out containing an indicator of what happened and the path to the item. The indicators are A for added items, D for deleted items, U for items that aren't modified locally and have changes applied to them, C for items that are conflicted after a failed merge attempt, and G for items that have local modifications and changes merged into them. The alias for the update command is up.

The following code example shows how to run the update command:

```
$ svn update [PATH ...]
```

Table A-37 shows the update command's options.

Table A-37. *update Options*

Option	Abbreviation	Description
--revision [argument]	-r	Uses argument as the revision to switch to.
--non-recursive	-N	Operates on a single directory instead of recursing into subdirectories.
--quiet	-q	Outputs as little as possible.
--diff3-cmd [argument]	None	Uses the specified program to merge changes into the working copy instead of using Subversion's internal diff library.
--username [argument]	None	Uses argument as the username when accessing the repository.
--password [argument]	None	Uses argument as the password when accessing the repository.
--no-auth-cache	None	Doesn't cache the user's username and password in his or her configuration directory.
--non-interactive	None	Doesn't prompt the user for input.
--ignore-externals	None	Ignores svn:externals when checking out.
--config-dir [argument]	None	Uses the configuration files in the directory specified as the argument instead of the default configuration directory.

svnadmin Subcommands

svnadmin is a tool for performing various maintenance-type actions on a Subversion repository. Each of svnadmin's subcommands (other than help) takes as its first argument the path to the repository on disk.

create

The create command creates a new repository:

```
$ svnadmin create REPOS
```

Table A-38 shows the create command's options.

Table A-38. *create Options*

Option	Abbreviation	Description
--bdb-txn-nosync	None	Disables the use of fsync at transaction commit time at the BDB level.
--bdb-log-keep	None	Disables automatic log file removal at the BDB level.
--config-dir [argument]	None	Reads the user configuration files from the directory specified by argument.

dump

The dump command prints the contents of the repository to standard output in a dumpfile format, which can be reloaded into a repository via svnadmin load. If revisions are specified, only the revision or range of revisions is dumped.

The following code example shows how to run the dump command:

```
$ svnadmin dump REPOS
```

Table A-39 shows the dump command's options.

Table A-39. *dump Options*

Option	Abbreviation	Description
--revision [argument]	-r	Uses argument as the revision or revision range to operate over.
--incremental	None	Makes the first revision dumped hold only the difference between it and the previous version, rather than the normal fulltext.
--deltas	None	Uses deltas in the dumpfile.
--quiet	-q	Only prints errors; it is not an indicator of progress.

help

The help command prints a generic help message, or if subcommands are specified as arguments, prints the help message for each one:

```
$ svnadmin help [COMMAND]
```

Table A-40 shows the help command's option.

Table A-40. *help Option*

Option	Abbreviation	Description
--version	None	Prints version information about a program.

hotcopy

The hotcopy command copies a Subversion repository, placing the new copy in a location specified as the second argument:

```
$ svnadmin hotcopy SOURCE DESTINATION
```

Table A-41 shows the hotcopy command's option.

Table A-41. *hotcopy Option*

Option	Abbreviation	Description
--clean-logs	None	Deletes any unused BDB log files remaining in the source repository after they've been copied into the destination repository.

list-dblogs

The list-dblogs command lists all BDB log files for a repository. Note that modifying or deleting these log files while they're in use will damage your repository.

The following code example shows how to run the list-dblogs command:

```
$ svnadmin list-dblogs REPOS
```

list-unused-dblogs

The list-unused-dblogs command lists all BDB log files in the repository that are no longer in use and thus can be safely removed:

```
$ svnadmin list-dblogs REPOS
```

load

The load command loads a dumpfile-formatted stream from standard input into the repository:

```
$ svnadmin load REPOS
```

Table A-42 shows the load command's options.

Table A-42. *load Options*

Option	Abbreviation	Description
--quiet	-q	Only outputs information about errors, not about progress.
--ignore-uuid	None	Ignores any UUID records found in the stream being loaded.
--force-uuid	None	Sets the repository's UUID to the one found in the stream (if there is one).
--use-pre-commit-hook	None	Runs the precommit hook before each commit.
--use-post-commit-hook	None	Runs the post-commit hook after each commit.
--parent-dir [argument]	None	Loads the contents of the stream into the specified directory in the repository.

lslocks

The lslocks command prints the names of any existing locks in a repository:

```
$ svnadmin lslocks REPOS
```

lstxns

The lstxns command prints the names of any uncommitted transactions in a repository:

```
$ svnadmin lstxns REPOS
```

recover

The recover command performs BDB recovery procedures on a repository:

```
$ svnadmin recover REPOS
```

Table A-43 shows the recover command's option.

Table A-43. *recover Option*

Option	Abbreviation	Description
--wait	None	Waits instead of exiting if the repository is in use.

rmlocks

The rmlocks command deletes the specified lock:

```
$ svnadmin rmlocks REPOS LOCK_PATH
```

rmtxns

The rmtxns command deletes the specified transaction or transactions:

```
$ svnadmin rmtxns REPOS TRANSACTION
```

Table A-44 shows the rmtxns command's option.

Table A-44. *rmtxns Option*

Option	Abbreviation	Description
--quiet	-q	Only outputs information about errors, not about progress.

setlog

The setlog command sets the log message on the specified revision to the contents of the specified file. Note that because revision properties aren't versioned, this command will permanently destroy the revision's old log message.

The following code example shows how to run the setlog command:

```
$ svnadmin setlog REPOS -r REVISION FILE
```

Table A-45 shows the setlog command's options.

Table A-45. *setlog Options*

Option	Abbreviation	Description
--revision [argument]	-r	Uses argument as the target revision.
--bypass-hooks	None	Bypasses the repository's hook system.

verify

The verify command verifies the integrity of the data stored in each revision of the repository and prints an error if any inconsistencies are found:

```
$ svnadmin verify REPOS
```

svnlook Subcommands

svnlook allows you to retrieve information about the contents of a repository revision or transaction. In addition to the other arguments mentioned, all of svnlook's subcommands (other than help) take as their first argument the path to the repository's location on disk.

author

The author command prints out the author of the revision or transaction in question:

```
$ svnlook author REPOS
```

Table A-46 shows the author command's options.

Table A-46. *author Options*

Option	Abbreviation	Description
--revision [argument]	-r	Uses argument as the revision to target.
--transaction [argument]	-t	Uses argument as the transaction to target.

cat

The cat command prints out the contents of a specified file within a revision or transaction:

```
$ svnlook cat REPOS FILE
```

Table A-47 shows the cat command's options.

Table A-47. *cat Options*

Option	Abbreviation	Description
--revision [argument]	-r	Uses argument as the revision to target.
--transaction [argument]	-t	Uses argument as the transaction to target.

changed

The changed command prints out the paths that were changed within a revision or a transaction:

```
$ svnlook changed REPOS
```

Table A-48 shows the changed command's options.

Table A-48. *changed Options*

Option	Abbreviation	Description
--revision [argument]	-r	Uses argument as the revision to target.
--transaction [argument]	-t	Uses argument as the transaction to target.
--copy-info	None	Shows more details about copies.

date

The date command prints the time-stamp for a revision or transaction:

```
$ svnlook date REPOS
```

Table A-49 shows the date command's options.

Table A-49. *date Options*

Option	Abbreviation	Description
--revision [argument]	-r	Uses argument as the revision to target.
--transaction [argument]	-t	Uses argument as the transaction to target.

diff

The diff command prints a unified diff for all changed files and properties for a revision or a transaction:

```
$ svnlook diff REPOS
```

Table A-50 shows the `diff` command's options.

Table A-50. *diff Options*

Option	Abbreviation	Description
`--revision [argument]`	`-r`	Uses argument as the revision to target.
`--transaction [argument]`	`-t`	Uses argument as the transaction to target.
`--no-diff-deleted`	None	Doesn't print the differences for files that are deleted.
`--no-diff-added`	None	Doesn't print the differences for files that are added.
`--diff-copy-from`	None	Uses the copy source as the diff base.

dirs-changed

The `dirs-changed` command prints the directories that are changed in a given revision or transaction. A directory is considered to have changed if its properties are modified or any files it contains are modified.

The following code example shows how to run the `dirs-changed` command:

```
$ svnlook dirs-changed REPOS
```

Table A-51 shows the `dirs-changed` command's options.

Table A-51. *dirs-changed Options*

Option	Abbreviation	Description
`--revision [argument]`	`-r`	Uses argument as the revision to target.
`--transaction [argument]`	`-t`	Uses argument as the transaction to target.

help

The `help` command prints a help message for the program, or if a subcommand is specified as an argument, prints a help message for the subcommand:

```
$ svnlook help [COMMAND]
```

history

The `history` command prints information about the history of a path in the repository or about the root of the repository if no path is given.

```
$ svnlook history REPOS [PATH]
```

Table A-52 shows the options for the `history` command.

Table A-52. *history Options*

Option	Abbreviation	Description
`--revision [argument]`	`-r`	Uses argument as the revision to target.
`--show-ids`	None	Prints node revision IDs for each path.

info

The `info` command prints the author, time-stamp, log message size, and log message associated with a given transaction or revision:

```
$ svnlook info REPOS
```

Table A-53 shows the options for the `info` command.

Table A-53. *info Options*

Option	Abbreviation	Description
`--revision [argument]`	`-r`	Uses argument as the revision to target.
`--transaction [argument]`	`-t`	Uses argument as the transaction to target.

lock

The `lock` command prints the information about a lock in the repository:

```
$ svnlook lock REPOS PATH
```

log

The `log` command prints the log message associated with a specified revision or transaction:

```
$ svnlook log REPOS
```

Table A-54 shows the options for the `log` command.

Table A-54. *log Options*

Option	Abbreviation	Description
`--revision [argument]`	`-r`	Uses argument as the revision to target.
`--transaction [argument]`	`-t`	Uses argument as the transaction to target.

propget

The `propget` command prints the value of a specified property on a specified path in the repository. The aliases are `pget` and `pg`.

The following code is an example of how to run the `propget` command against a repository located at `REPOS`, printing the value of the property named `PROPNAME` for the path in the repository named `PATH`:

```
$ svnlook propget REPOS PROPNAME PATH
```

Table A-55 shows the options for the propget command.

Table A-55. *propget Options*

Option	Abbreviation	Description
--revision [argument]	-r	Uses argument as the revision to target.
--revprop	None	Operates on a revision property. If --revprop is given, a --revision must also be given.
--transaction [argument]	-t	Uses argument as the transaction to target.

proplist

The proplist command prints the properties associated with a path in the repository. If the verbose option is used, it prints the property values along with the names. The aliases for the proplist command are plist and pl.

The following code is an example of how to run the proplist command against a repository located at REPOS, printing the list of properties for the path in the repository named PATH:

```
$ svnlook proplist REPOS PATH
```

Table A-56 shows options for the proplist command.

Table A-56. *proplist Options*

Option	Abbreviation	Description
--revision [argument]	-r	Uses argument as the revision to target.
--revprop	None	Operates on a revision property. If --revprop is given, a --revision must also be given.
--transaction [argument]	-t	Uses argument as the transaction to target.
--verbose	-v	Prints the property values as well as their names.

tree

The tree command prints the directory tree for a transaction or a revision, starting at the path specified as an argument (if there is one), otherwise starting at the root of the repository:

```
svnlook tree REPOS [PATH]
```

Table A-57 shows the options for the tree command.

Table A-57. *tree Options*

Option	Abbreviation	Description
--revision [argument]	-r	Uses argument as the revision to target.
--transaction [argument]	-t	Uses argument as the transaction to target.
--full-paths	None	Shows full paths rather than using indentation to display the tree.
--show-ids	None	Prints the node revision IDs for each path.

uuid

The uuid command prints the repository's UUID:

$ svnlook uuid REPOS

youngest

The youngest command prints the youngest (i.e., the highest, if you're thinking numerically) revision number for the repository:

$ svnlook youngest REPOS

svnserve Options

svnserve is the network server side of Subversion's custom network protocol, handling the svn:// and svn+ssh:// URL schemes. Table A-58 shows the options for the svnserve command.

Table A-58. *Options for the svnserve Command*

Option	Abbreviation	Description
--daemon	-d	Runs svnserve as a daemon process detached from the terminal it's started from.
--listen-port [argument]	None	Uses argument as the port on which to listen for incoming connections. If this isn't used, the server will default to listening on port 3690, the official IANA-assigned port for the Subversion protocol.
--listen-host [argument]	None	Uses argument as the hostname or IP address to bind to. If this argument isn't provided, svnserve will bind to any available network connection.
--foreground	None	Runs the server in the foreground (mainly useful for debugging).
--help	-h	Displays a help message.
--inetd	-i	Uses standard input and output as the network connection, suitable for running out of inetd.
--read-only	-R	Forces read-only, overriding the repository config file.
--root [argument]	-r	Uses argument as the root directory to search for repositories.
--tunnel	-t	Runs in tunnel mode, suitable for use with an svn+ssh:// connection.
--tunnel-user [argument]	None	Uses argument as the username for the tunnel.
--threads	-T	Uses threads to handle multiple simultaneous client connections.
--listen-once	-X	Handles only one connection (useful mainly for debugging).

■ ■ ■

Subversion Compared to Other Version Control Systems

The process of learning a new tool is never easy, but the chance to compare it with a tool you know how to use can simplify the process. That's just as true with regard to version control systems as it is with anything else. With that in mind, this appendix provides comparisons of Subversion and several other version control systems, both in terms of conceptual differences and in terms of command equivalents.

Subversion Compared to CVS

Subversion and CVS are quite similar, at least from the point of view of a casual user. The general workflow and commands in Subversion are close enough to those of CVS that most CVS users can learn to use Subversion quickly. That said, there are a number of differences, most of which are places where Subversion has improved on CVS's behavior.

First off, as we've already mentioned, the workflows of Subversion and CVS are similar, as are many of the concepts. Both use a central repository and are primarily nonlocking, with manual intervention required only when conflicting changes are detected. The general "check out, modify, update, commit" strategy of making changes is unchanged between the two systems.

While both CVS and Subversion make use of a central repository, the actual server processes and the network protocols used are quite different. Subversion makes use of either a custom TCP protocol or WebDAV, and in both cases it goes to great lengths to ensure that diffs, instead of entire files, are sent over the network whenever possible. CVS often has to send the entire file from the client to the server, which can result in considerably more bandwidth being used. CVS also lacks a consistent repository access API, meaning that adding support for new network protocols is much more complicated than in Subversion, and that new features often need to be reimplemented for each protocol CVS supports.

The internals of the repositories used by CVS and Subversion are perhaps where the most differences lie. CVS makes use of RCS files to store its revision history. This means that tagging and branching in CVS are slower than in Subversion. In addition to the tagging and branching issue, CVS's repository lacks support for atomic changes, so it's possible for a commit to be interrupted halfway through, resulting in an inconsistent repository, or for someone to update while a large change is occurring, with similar results.

While CVS does have numerous third-party tools that interoperate with it, writing such a tool is considerably more difficult than with Subversion. CVS doesn't provide an API to allow third-party programs access to its functionality, so they're stuck having to either call out to the CVS binary manually or implement the functionality themselves.

CVS doesn't version directory structures, so working with directories can be problematic. Similarly, it doesn't have support for tracking renames and copies of files, so to make such changes, you have to either lose revision history or manually modify the repository by copying the RCS files by hand.

The primary user interface differences between CVS and Subversion result from the way tags and branches are handled. In CVS, tags and branches live in a different namespace than the directory tree, while in Subversion, tags and branches are simply copies of directory trees. Subversion also uses a separate `svn merge` command to handle merging changes between branches, while CVS makes use of the `-j` option to `cvs checkout`. Almost all the same functionality provided by CVS with regard to branches and tags exists in Subversion, except the ability to list all the tags or branches that contain a given file, which isn't something you often need to do. Subversion uses a slightly different—and more intuitive—user interface than CVS.

For the convenience of users making the transition from CVS to Subversion, Table B-1 lists corresponding Subversion commands for common CVS commands.

Table B-1. *CVS to Subversion Command Equivalents*

CVS Command	Subversion Command
`cvs add`	`svn add`
`cvs admin`	`svnadmin`
`cvs annotate`	`svn blame`
`cvs checkout`	`svn checkout`
`cvs checkout -j`	`svn merge`
`cvs commit`	`svn commit`
`cvs diff`	`svn diff`
`cvs edit`	No equivalent
`cvs editors`	No equivalent
`cvs export`	`svn export`
`cvs history`	`svn log`
`cvs import`	`svn import`
`cvs init`	`svnadmin create`
`cvs log`	`svn log`
`cvs login`	No equivalent (svn commands prompt for login)
`cvs logout`	No equivalent
`cvs rdiff`	`svn diff`

CVS Command	Subversion Command
cvs release	No equivalent
cvs remove	svn delete
cvs rtag	svn copy
cvs status	svn status --show-updates
cvs tag	svn copy
cvs unedit	No equivalent
cvs update	svn update
cvs watch	No equivalent
cvs watchers	No equivalent

Subversion Compared to Perforce

Perforce is a commercial version control system sold by Perforce Software Inc. (http://www.perforce.com/).

First, we'll cover the similarities between Subversion and Perforce. Both systems are designed around a central server process with users accessing the repository (or *depot* in Perforce terminology) via a client application over the network. Both use "cheap copies" as their means of providing branch support, with branches existing in the same namespace as regular files.

Perforce is based on a single central server and maintains a great deal of information about client views (which are sort of analogous to the Subversion working copy) on the server. This speeds up some operations but tethers the client to the server. Without network support, Perforce is largely crippled.

Perforce's workflow is both similar to and different from Subversion's. There's support for locking of files, but most work is done in a nonlocking manner with merging of nonconflicting changes into the client view when the user runs p4 sync. The primary difference stems from the fact that so much data is kept on the server side. When you want to make a change to a file, you need to inform the server first by running p4 edit. To enforce this behavior, files in the client view start out as read-only and are made writable only after you explicitly tell the server you want to edit them. This is a significant departure from the Subversion model, in which you can edit any file in your working copy at any time without involving the server at all.

Perforce doesn't support tracking file history across copies or renames, although you can simulate it via use of the p4 integrate command. Directory structures are also not versioned.

Perforce truly shines when it comes to its merge support. It's able to track merges between branches and has largely solved the "repeated merge" problem that still plagues Subversion.

The primary downside of Perforce (other than its reliance on the network for virtually all operations) is that its license fees are charged on a per-user basis, and for large numbers of developers this can get expensive.

To simplify the process of transitioning from Perforce to Subversion, Table B-2 contains corresponding Subversion commands for the most common Perforce commands.

Table B-2. *Perforce to Subversion Command Equivalents*

Perforce Command	Subversion Command
p4 add	svn add
p4 annotate	svn blame
p4 client + p4 sync	svn checkout
p4 submit	svn commit
p4 integrate	svn copy, svn merge, svn move
p4 delete	svn delete
p4 diff, p4 diff2	svn diff
p4 filelog	svn log
p4 lock	svn lock
p4 unlock	svn unlock
p4 resolve	svn resolved
p4 revert	svn revert
p4 opened	svn status
p4 sync	svn update

Subversion Compared to RCS

RCS is an older version control system that was the precursor to CVS. It lacks much of the functionality of newer systems such as Subversion, but it does provide many of the same basic concepts.

RCS and Subversion differ in three main ways. First, RCS doesn't provide support for accessing the repository (well, the RCS files anyway, since there's no real concept of a repository in RCS) over a network. Second, RCS uses a locking scheme to control access to each file. Before you can modify a file, you must obtain the lock, as opposed to Subversion's more liberal nonlocking scheme. Finally, RCS works on a per-file basis, meaning all the commands work on individual files, rather than on directory trees as in Subversion.

Despite these differences, there are still reasonable mappings between the RCS command set and Subversion's commands, as shown in Table B-3, and once an RCS user gets used to the idea of working with directory trees instead of individual files and using a nonlocking style of development, the transition to Subversion shouldn't be too difficult.

Table B-3. *RCS to Subversion Command Equivalents*

RCS Command	Subversion Command
ci	svn add, svn commit
co	svn checkout
rcsdiff	svn diff
rcsmerge	svn merge
rlog	svn log

Subversion Compared to BitKeeper

BitKeeper is a commercial version control system produced by BitMover (http://www.bitkeeper.com/). It's best known these days as the version control system that was used to manage the Linux kernel source tree for a few years. The Linux kernel source tree has since changed to use GIT, another version control system.

Unlike the other version control systems we've discussed, BitKeeper doesn't use a central repository to store revision history. Instead, each developer has his own personal repository, and changesets are pushed back and forth between them. It's a system that operates along the same lines as the Linux development process itself, thus it's uniquely suited to serve as the version control system of choice for Linux. When to use distributed (i.e., no central server) version control systems such as BitKeeper, and when to use centralized version control systems such as Subversion is a matter of intellectual debate, as both centralized and decentralized models have their advantages and disadvantages (which things are advantages and which are disadvantages is also a matter of great debate).

In summary, BitKeeper is an impressive system in and of itself. It provides much the same functionality of Subversion and a number of capabilities above and beyond what Subversion gives you today. That said, BitKeeper is radically different from Subversion, and any direct comparison between the two is largely unfair. They simply target different problem domains, and as such have evolved in different directions.

For the convenience of BitKeeper users who wish to make use of Subversion, Table B-4 shows some roughly equivalent commands for various common tasks.

Table B-4. *BitKeeper to Subversion Command Equivalents*

BitKeeper Command	Subversion Command
bk get	svn export
bk edit	svn checkout
bk pull	svn update
bk new	svn add
bk commit, bk ci, bk push	svn commit
bk rm, bk rmdir	svn delete
bk mv, bk mvdir	svn move
bk diffs	svn diff
bk import	svn import
bk prs, bk changes	svn log
bk status	svn status

If you're looking for a system that allows you to have a personal local repository as BitKeeper does, yet interoperates with Subversion nicely, you might want to check out SVK, which implements such a system on top of the Subversion filesystem and RA layers. SVK is available at http://svk.elixus.org/.

Subversion Compared to Visual SourceSafe

Visual SourceSafe is a commercial version control system produced by Microsoft and commonly used by developers on Windows systems. Its best feature is its excellent integration with Microsoft's development tools.

The primary difference between Visual SourceSafe and Subversion is that Visual SourceSafe makes use of a "lock, modify, check in" style of development, in contrast to Subversion's more flexible nonlocking approach. This does allow easy handling of files that can't be merged, but in all other situations it tends to be a drawback. This difference will most likely be the largest stumbling block for Visual SourceSafe users who are trying to migrate to Subversion.

Another of Visual SourceSafe's drawbacks is its lack of support for platforms other than Windows. While there are third-party tools to allow various Unix platforms to access a Visual SourceSafe repository, they're available on a limited number of platforms, as compared to open source projects such as Subversion.

Finally, Visual SourceSafe is a closed source commercial product and carries with it all the issues inherent in such products.

For the convenience of developers trying to convert from Visual SourceSafe to Subversion, Table B-5 presents a list of various Visual SourceSafe commands (using the ss command-line tool) and their Subversion equivalents.

Table B-5. *Visual SourceSafe to Subversion Command Equivalents*

Visual SourceSafe Command	Subversion Command
ss Add	svn add
ss Branch	svn copy
ss Checkin	svn commit
ss Checkout, ss Get	svn checkout
ss Delete	svn delete
ss Difference	svn diff
ss Directory	svn list
ss FileType	svn info
ss Help	svn help
ss History	svn log
ss Label	svn copy
ss Merge	svn merge
ss Move	svn move
ss Recover	svn merge
ss Rename	svn move
ss Rollback	svn merge
ss Status	svn status
ss View	svn cat

Index

forums.apress.com

JOIN THE APRESS FORUMS AND BE PART OF OUR COMMUNITY. You'll find discussions that cover topics of interest to IT professionals, programmers, and enthusiasts just like you. If you post a query to one of our forums, you can expect that some of the best minds in the business—especially Apress authors, who all write with *The Expert's Voice*™—will chime in to help you. Why not aim to become one of our most valuable participants (MVPs) and win cool stuff? Here's a sampling of what you'll find:

DATABASES
Data drives everything.

Share information, exchange ideas, and discuss any database programming or administration issues.

PROGRAMMING/BUSINESS
Unfortunately, it is.

Talk about the Apress line of books that cover software methodology, best practices, and how programmers interact with the "suits."

INTERNET TECHNOLOGIES AND NETWORKING
Try living without plumbing (and eventually IPv6).

Talk about networking topics including protocols, design, administration, wireless, wired, storage, backup, certifications, trends, and new technologies.

WEB DEVELOPMENT/DESIGN
Ugly doesn't cut it anymore, and CGI is absurd.

Help is in sight for your site. Find design solutions for your projects and get ideas for building an interactive Web site.

JAVA
We've come a long way from the old Oak tree.

Hang out and discuss Java in whatever flavor you choose: J2SE, J2EE, J2ME, Jakarta, and so on.

SECURITY
Lots of bad guys out there—the good guys need help.

Discuss computer and network security issues here. Just don't let anyone else know the answers!

MAC OS X
All about the Zen of OS X.

OS X is both the present and the future for Mac apps. Make suggestions, offer up ideas, or boast about your new hardware.

TECHNOLOGY IN ACTION
Cool things. Fun things.

It's after hours. It's time to play. Whether you're into LEGO® MINDSTORMS™ or turning an old PC into a DVR, this is where technology turns into fun.

OPEN SOURCE
Source code is good; understanding (open) source is better.

Discuss open source technologies and related topics such as PHP, MySQL, Linux, Perl, Apache, Python, and more.

WINDOWS
No defenestration here.

Ask questions about all aspects of Windows programming, get help on Microsoft technologies covered in Apress books, or provide feedback on any Apress Windows book.

HOW TO PARTICIPATE:

Go to the Apress Forums site at **http://forums.apress.com/**.

Click the New User link.